S0-BPI-314

L. RONALD SCHEMAN

GREATER AMERICA

*A New Partnership for the Americas
in the Twenty-First Century*

F
1418
.S375
2003
West

New York University Press • *New York and London*

NEW YORK UNIVERSITY PRESS
New York and London
www.nyupress.org

© 2003 by New York University
All rights reserved

The opinions expressed in this book are those of the author. They do not necessarily represent those of the Organization of American States and its member states.

Library of Congress Cataloging-in-Publication Data
Scheman, L. Ronald.
Greater America : a new partnership for the Americas in the twenty-first century
/ L. Ronald Scheman
p. cm.
Includes bibliographical references and index.
ISBN 0–8147–9834–9 (cloth : alk. paper)
1. Latin America—Relations—United States.   2. United States—Relations—
Latin America.   3. United States—Foreign relations—21st century.   I. Title.
F1418.S375 2003
303.48'27308—dc21   2003010369

New York University Press books are printed on acid-free paper,
and their binding materials are chosen for strength and durability.

Manufactured in the United States of America

10   9   8   7   6   5   4   3   2   1

To Lucy
Boundless love and unwavering support

We are no longer who we were.
We are not yet who we will be.
> —On the wall of the Greater Maya
> Temple in Tikal, Guatemala

Statesmen stand or fall on their perceptions of trends.
> —Henry Kissinger

Contents

Acknowledgments

Acknowledging the help of the often wise and generous people who influence the writing of a book of this scope is a prodigious task. I am indebted to so many people whose ideas and perceptions have stimulated my thinking and opened my eyes to the realities of the Americas. I must admit that most of them knew not what they were doing as we spoke. Their influence, however, was profound and is deserving of acknowledgment. In particular I would cite Enrique Iglesias, President of the Inter-American Development Bank and many of my colleagues on the Board of the Bank, including Humberto Petrie, Moises Pineda, Andrés Solimano and Antonio Claudio Sochachewski. Other officials of the Bank include Nancy Birdsall, Ricardo Hausmann, Robert Devlin, Miguel Martínez, Ciro de Falco, Ricardo Santiago, Carlos Ferdinand, and Jacques Rogozinski.

I especially want to thank my wife, Lucy Duncan-Scheman for her profound insights into the culture and dynamics of the region. Her suggestions on reading the manuscript were invaluable. In particular, I want to acknowledge her patience for many months at the farm on bright sunny week-ends while I was huddled over the computer instead of enjoying her company. I am also grateful to César Gaviria, Luigi Einaudi, Mack McLarty, Alex Watson, Shahid Javed Burki, Richard Bernal, Sam Santos, Jeff Davidow, Leon Fuerth, Henry Raymont, Peter Romero, Georges Fauriol, Mark Falcoff, Luis Lauredo, Norman Bailey, Susan Kaufman Purcell, Miguel D'arcy de Olivera, Richard Feinberg, Sidney Weintraub, Moises Naim, Jorge Dominguez, Nicolas Ardito Barletta, Miguel Angel Rodriguez, Jaime Daremblum, Eduardo Ferrero, Esteban Tomic, Rodolfo Gil, Ellsworth John, Dennis Antoine, Lisa Shoman, Peter Boehm, Alfonso Quiñonez, Alejandro Orfila, Ed Marasciulo, Francisco Aguirre Baca, and Frank Gómez, all of whom helped my understanding of the realities and the potential of the region.

Nor would the book have been possible without the patience and tireless effort of my assistant of many years, Cece MacVaugh, who has the unique talent of being able to read my handwriting. I hasten to add Carmen Saghy and Maria Eugenia Peredo-Cohen. A special thanks is due to Despina Papazoglou Gimbel, Margaret Barrows Yamashita, and Nicholas Taylor of the editorial staff of NYU Press and to Kristin Au-Clair, who labored with the manuscript. My appreciation to Despina's entire team is unbounded for saving me hours of work and transforming my manuscript into a far more professional product than I ever could have achieved on my own.

Introduction

THE IDEA FOR THIS BOOK first came to me a few years ago after speaking at a college in Nebraska. One of the students asked me to explain why Latin America was important to the United States. It was one of those innocent questions often asked by good students that go right to the heart of the issue, and it forced me to go back to basics.

I had long believed that the trends in markets and economics in Latin America and the Caribbean held great promise for the United States, that the potential synergy of markets, technology, and resources could be competitive in the global economy. I was convinced that the indirect implications of poverty in Latin America were like a time bomb for stability and would plague the region as well as U.S. domestic politics until prosperity began to permeate the region. I also knew that the growth of the U.S. Hispanic population, which we often forget populated North America long before the Pilgrims landed on Plymouth Rock, could have a great influence on the culture and politics of the United States.

The most compelling reason for me to write this book, however, rested in the desire of the people of Latin America and the Caribbean for democracy. Democracy is under siege in this world, as the events of September 11, 2001, vividly brought home to us. Most developing countries either ignore it or practice democracy cynically as part of a power game. But its consolidation and expansion are important to the United States, and Latin America and the Caribbean are the next major areas of the developing world that have the ability to embrace real democracy.

Thus, this book is dedicated to several closely related purposes. The first is to describe why Latin America and the Caribbean are important to the United States and vice versa; the second is to call for a thoughtful reformulation of U.S. foreign policy priorities as they relate to the Americas; and the third is to look to the future for a concept of a potentially great community of nations, including Canada, that I call Greater America.

In the coming century, as global competition extends from the battlefield to the boardroom, the Americas hold the greatest promise as partners for the United States. The rate of these nations' economic growth and their ability to deliver on the promise of democracy, however, are directly and intimately related to their access to investment and markets. It is both common sense and important to future generations of Americans that we address these issues in the Americas more coherently, consistently, and with greater foresight.

Focusing the interest of the United States on this hemisphere is not easy. Historian Arthur Schlesinger noted that the United States' interest in Latin America peaks periodically in what he saw as thirty-year cycles. His theory is well grounded in the history of the recent century. When President Bill Clinton called a summit meeting of the democratically elected presidents of the American nations in Miami in 1994, it was the first time in thirty years that an American president had met with his counterparts. The previous major effort was during President John F. Kennedy's Alliance for Progress in 1961. Preceding that was President Franklin Delano Roosevelt's Good Neighbor Policy announced in his inaugural address in 1933. The interim periods were punctuated with neglect. Earlier in the century, in 1903, FDR's cousin President Theodore Roosevelt turned an eager eye to Latin America. His "Big Stick" diplomacy was capped by the construction of the Panama Canal in which the United States was deeply involved in intrigue to induce Colombia's province of Panama to secede. Indeed, Roosevelt's policies touched off a flurry of U.S. military interventions in the Caribbean that lasted through and beyond World War I until FDR ended them in the 1930s.

If the cycle holds true, our interest should be about to wane once again. I hope, however, that a new pattern will begin with President George W. Bush's declaration that the Americas are one of the top U.S. foreign policy priorities. No U.S. president ever has made such a statement with such forcefulness as a defining criterion at the beginning of his administration. It is a good omen for the future and especially for the monumental task of joining all the Americas in a giant free-trade area by 2005. The powerful impact that NAFTA has had on Mexico— economically, socially, and politically—hints at what this could mean for the other countries of the hemisphere. There is no question but that NAFTA has been the most powerful driving force for the opening and modernization of Mexico, as we will discuss later.

In the past decade, the countries of the Americas have begun to embrace democracy, the protection of human rights, and open markets. In the twenty-first century they have the potential to become some of our most important allies, together with western Europe, to advance respect for human rights, the rule of law, and the well-being of all people in our global economy. The process, however, is volatile and will be achieved only as a result of determined policy. The failure of the economic policies of the 1990s to deliver a better life or to make inroads on the pervasive, degrading poverty of the region have led to skepticism and a search for alternative approaches to development. The ongoing and profound changes in global economic relations make the road ahead even more precarious.

It is time for a comprehensive review of our relations with the other nations of the Americas. The last such study of the United States' interests in the Americas was made by the Kissinger Commission in 1984 at the request of President Ronald Reagan to help galvanize public opinion for the United States' role in the Central American civil wars. Accordingly, the commission's focus was exclusively on Central America and the Caribbean. The major countries of the hemisphere—Brazil, Argentina, Chile, and the other nations of South America—were outside its scope. Given the vast changes taking place in the nations of the Americas and the increasing impact of regional issues on our domestic economic and social concerns, we should reassess the premises for those relationships. The growing role of the Hispanic and Caribbean communities in the United States as our largest minority group makes it even more imperative to reconsider the fundamental interests of the United States in the Americas in the twenty-first century.

I am not arguing that the Americas should be central to our foreign policy. No region is central; rather, issues are central. But given the issues that most concern the United States, Latin America and the Caribbean are important. After physical security, the principal issues for the United States rest on four pillars: economic (open markets and transparency in commercial dealings), political (democracy and the rule of law), social (the abolishment of ignorance and poverty), and moral (respect for human rights). These are increasingly related to international activities that know no borders. Drugs, disease (HIV/AIDS), arms traffic, international crime, and migration are obvious examples. I believe that the more we reflect on the factors that will influence global power in the future, the more important that the evolution of the Americas into thriving, productive democracies will become.

As we are taught in this age of computers, we always need to try to simplify complexity. I will try to do that in this book. But I warn the reader that my goal is not to present a balanced analysis. This is a book of advocacy. There has been enough negative writing about Latin America and the Caribbean. My goal is to present a vision of the future that builds on the positive and constructive achievements of the hemisphere, addresses the problem areas, and presents the case for change in our foreign policy priorities to place greater emphasis on the Americas.

I will focus not on transitory current political issues but on the evolution of the region and the longer-term trends. I will take the reader on a journey through the factors influencing U.S. foreign policy and the history of U.S. relations with the Americas. Then I will discuss current trends toward the consolidation of democracy, the policies that have brought the Americas to the point that we are today, and the emerging powers and attitudes in the Americas. I will address the problems of democracy related to poverty and corruption in juxtaposition to the markets and resources that will enable the region to create productive employment and compete in the global economy. Last, I will discuss the future potential of the Americas and offer my recommendations for a constructive policy.

The events in Latin America in the early years of the twenty-first century have been disturbing. Economic growth in the region slowed dramatically in 2002, confronting solid economies, such as those of Uruguay and Brazil, with the prospect of deep recession and weaker ones with a crisis of confidence and backlash over the free-market reforms of the 1990s. Argentina's economic meltdown, increasing guerrilla warfare in Colombia, anarchic populism in Venezuela, and the precarious balance of many democracies do not detract from but, in my view, rather, prove my point. Despite the region's underlying commitment to democracy, the leadership is lacking. The events of the 1990s prove that the yearnings for democracy and an open society may never be realized without the strong commitment of the United States. The United States accounts for more than 80 percent of the hemisphere's economy. The nations of the Americas depend on outside investment, and investors are influenced by confidence in the future that the commitment of the United States provides. After the 1994 Presidential Summit of the Americas, when the United States paid attention to the Americas, confidence in the future soared among the people and investors alike. In the competitive global economy of the twenty-first century, the needed investment will not come in the quantity and quality required without far larger markets to serve. Thus, open access to the markets of the United States—and of Europe—are vital to the region's economic growth.

The events of September 11, 2001, deeply affected people everywhere and reshaped the United States' priorities to fight terrorism. In this, Latin America is not a novice. Random violence in Colombia kills thousands of people annually. The people of Peru suffered a similar trauma for years with the terrorist Sendero Luminoso group. Kidnappings and murders followed by repression and "disappeared" people afflicted the countries of the Southern Cone for almost twenty years in the 1970s and 1980s. The civil wars of Central America in the 1980s caused hardship and dislocation for innocent civilian populations. And the drug trade continues its destructive path through Latin America and the Caribbean. Thus the United States and Latin America share an interest in eradicating terrorism of all kinds.

The principal claim of democratic political movements to improve their constituencies' standard of living and provide for their security is related to the economy. The need for a more attentive and responsive policy in the Americas is even more important with the spread of low-cost communications. TV and the Internet stimulate people's demands while at the same time they facilitate international crime. Threats to personal security through violence, kidnappings, and organized crime have become one of the greatest risks to democracy in Latin America.

In the Americas, the ability of the governments to "deliver" a better standard of living goes to the heart of the new democracies' electoral politics. The economic reforms promoted by the developed nations, the International Monetary Fund, and the U.S. Treasury Department have fallen far short, after ten years, of delivering results. (Note that I did not say State Department. Having worked with both Treasury and State for years, I can confirm that the U.S. Treasury Department plays a far more critical role in our policies affecting the hemisphere, which are predominantly economic, with little coordination between these two departments.) The little progress that had been made in improving the standard of living falls far short of what is required for sustained democratic development or to make inroads on the extreme poverty.

The United States is also now championing a free-trade area which will be an unprecedented amalgam of the most developed with some of the least developed economies of the world. Converting the closed, protectionist, state-controlled economies of the Americas into open-market global competitors will take time. Building the educational systems, skills, transparency in governance, a civil service that serves rather than obstructs, and infrastructure to make the region attractive to investment will not be easy. Bloated, centralized government structures must be trimmed to realistic and sustainable sizes that the tax base can support, a process that will leave considerable economic and social dislocations in its wake.

The key is opening the markets of the United States and the world to Latin America so that these countries can produce value-added goods and sell them. The consumer base of Latin America is far too small to generate the number of jobs needed for the growing populations. Without jobs, neither viable democracies nor respect for the rule of law nor open markets can follow. Without jobs, education can become counterproductive and lead to even more alienation that undermines democracy. And without open markets, it is almost impossible to attract the level of investment needed to create those jobs. In a global economy, investment and global security are connected. It will therefore require far more sensitivity to the interaction of domestic political dynamics and the impact of the global economy on the underlying social issues than the United States has shown to date.

Fortunately for the forces for change (although unfortunately for the people who have suffered through it), the traumas suffered by Latin America in the form of hyperinflation, economic depression, and military dictatorships during the 1980s produced a small measure of patience. That gives democracy time, but not much. As an Argentine worker told me during the difficult economic situation after the Mexican financial crisis in 1995, "Yes, it is difficult. But you cannot imagine how difficult it is to get your salary on Friday and have to buy everything you can that night because you do not know how much it will be worth the next morning." In 2002 Argentina demonstrated that people can endure an inept, corrupt government for just so long.

The response to the social and economic problems of the Americas cannot be half measures. Rather, credible, sustained, long-term measures are required to create more prosperous nations in the Americas. The attitudes and policies of the United States loom large, simply because without access to larger markets the countries will be unable to overcome their deep-seated social problems in the time the modern world allots. Whereas foreign policy will always be dominated by immediate threats to peace and security, the most cost-effective, long-term policy to combat global and domestic criminal activity is the growth of viable, responsible, responsive democracies. Is the United States capable of implementing this type of policy? What options does it have? What kind of future do we face in a global economy in which most of the growing market demand will be outside our borders?

I believe that the United States can make a major difference in the Americas, that it is in the United States' interest to do so, and that by doing so we will reinforce our global strategic position in the twenty-first century. To achieve that, I argue for an American alliance that encourages democracy, human rights, and human dignity. Such an alliance could become a major player in the global economy and offer an important swing vote for our common values in global politics. Conversely, indifference or neglect by the United States could tip the scales to regressive populism and a reversion to wishing for strong men to save the day.

I strongly believe that the United States and the other nations of the Americas have a common destiny. To realize this destiny, much of the responsibility rests, first, with the countries of the Americas to open their societies to greater transparency and accountability in government, to respect the rule of law, and to address their problems of poverty. The more we ponder the future of democracy in the region, the more we will see the need to redefine the institutional framework by which the nations relate to one another. Equally important is our recognition that we cannot do it alone. We need to change the quality of our relations with one another. If we join with the other countries of the Americas to develop new relationships, I am confident that within a few decades all the Americas will be transformed into a major economic and political force.

I have seen Latin America and the Caribbean from the inside and the outside, and I can confirm that all the elements to make it happen are there. I call this the emergence of Greater America. The concept embodies no imperial pretensions but, rather, foresees an association of democracies, which includes Canada. In time we will see it evolve into a Great American Common Market. It is important to give the American people a comprehensive perspective on the potential of the Americas because, in the final analysis, it is they who will decide whether the vision of Greater America can come true.

PART I

STORMY RELATIONSHIPS, NEW DYNAMICS

1

Global Wallflower

Overlooking the Americas in U.S. Foreign Relations

> For this world which seems to us a thing of stone and flower and blood
> is not a thing at all but is a tale. And all in it is a tale and each tale the
> sum of lesser tales and yet these also are the selfsame tale and contain
> as well all else within them. So everything is necessary. Every least
> thing. This is the hard lesson. Nothing can be dispensed with. Nothing
> despised. Because the seams are hid from us. The joinery. The way in
> which the world is made. We have no way to know what could be
> taken away. What omitted. We have no way to tell what might stand
> and what might fall. And those seams that are hid from us are of
> course in the tale itself.　　　　　—Cormac McCarthy, *The Crossing*

CORMAC MCCARTHY'S PERCEPTION of the workings of our universe may seem unusual to introduce a book about United States' relations with its neighbors in the Americas. To me, however, it is fitting. Latin America and the Caribbean have long been the orphans of U.S. foreign policy. While they are our major trading partners and one of our largest future markets, they are virtually ignored in the conduct of our global affairs.

This is rapidly changing. The growing presence of people of Hispanic and Caribbean origin in the United States and the role of the American nations in some of our more intractable domestic issues makes their policies an indispensable part of "the way in which our world is made." Anyone who cares about the implications of the changing demographics of the United States needs to understand this. The 2000 census showed that the descendants of the nations south of us have now become the largest single minority group in the United States. If we fail to grasp the significance of this change for our economic growth, our trading patterns, and the well-being of our society, we will be disregarding what will become one of the most influential factors in the future politics of the United States.

In addition to the impact of the Hispanic and Caribbean populations on our national culture, the changes in our societies have affected every aspect of global relations. Experts argue about the importance of nations that have nuclear weapons or those that control important resources, those whose economies are presently dominant, or those whose animosities threaten to engulf innocent civilians. But equally important are those nations that control the resources for the future and those that have the potential to strengthen the community of nations committed to democracy and the peaceful settlement of disputes. In this context, the nations of the Americas will increasingly come to the forefront. While their role in global history until now has been marginal, they will be neither small nor irrelevant in the world evolving in the twenty-first century. As national borders fade in the mix of technology, information, and capital flows, the Americas will be swept into the swirl of U.S. concerns in ways that are just becoming clear. No solutions to the issues that will affect the growth and prosperity of the United States in the twenty-first century can work without taking into account the politics and prosperity of the nations of our hemisphere. They are an integral part of the joinery.

THE "AFTERTHOUGHT"

One of President George W. Bush's first foreign policy pronouncements was that Latin America has too long been "an afterthought in American foreign policy."[1] The reasons for that are, for the most part, valid. First, none of the countries of the region, except Cuba's venture into a nuclear alliance with the former Soviet Union, has ever posed any tangible security threat to the United States. Indeed, the absence of such a threat is said to have caused Henry Kissinger to describe Latin America's strategic importance as "a giant dagger pointed at the heart of Antarctica." Nothing about the region conveyed a sense of urgency. The economies were too small, the population too sparse, and communications too primitive for the countries to engage in military competition like that marking the history of Europe. In the violent physical struggles of the twentieth century, Kissinger's working premise was valid.

Second, our nation has been preoccupied for almost all of the twentieth century with challenges to our physical security emanating from overseas. Latin America was remote and relatively benign compared with other violence-prone regions of the world. Nowhere in the Americas were found the ruthless competition, belligerence, and violence that were prevalent in Europe. With few exceptions,[2] the hemisphere's international relations in the twentieth century were marked by bickering among contending local political factions, not by issues threatening global security. Imagine, however, what our policies might have been if a person like Hitler had gained power in Brazil or Argentina and tried to dominate South America, as Germany did in Europe. Or if Mexico built a nuclear arsenal? We paid attention to Russia, with an economy half the size and a population smaller than Brazil, because it placed a priority on militarization and belligerence. But in large part we ignored Latin America because it did not.

Third, Latin America lost the battle of public opinion in the United States because the region was generally perceived as indifferent to the needs of its own society and hostile to democratic values. Instead of dealing with its domestic problems, the region practiced what some pundits called the "politics of evasion." No society that tolerated chaotic economic policies, turned its back on widespread poverty, and indulged in corruption while ignoring basic government services such as education and health care could be taken seriously as a democracy, regardless of its leaders' rhetoric. In the United States, James Reston of the *New York Times* wrote that Americans would do anything for Latin America but read about it.

Several years ago, two newspaper articles highlighted the contradictions of these attitudes. One sharply criticized President Bill Clinton for failing to stem the flow of drugs coming into the United States through the Caribbean nations. The other claimed that the president's efforts to bolster economic development in the Caribbean through more open trade would harm our economy. It seemed as though the author of each article was oblivious to the issues the other was addressing. One does not have to be an international relations expert to understand the "joinery" between these issues.

The reality that Cormac McCarthy described is as relevant to relations among nations as it is to relations among people. Policymakers can no more recommend strong measures to stop drugs and at the same time be indifferent as their countries remain mired in poverty than they can build a power plant and disregard the transmission lines. Poor young men who have no hope for gainful employment because they have had no education—and do not even know why education is important—may still have an entrepreneurial spirit. That is, drug peddling is an expression of their own brand of enterprise. Why are we surprised when some young people choose violence or drugs? The real surprise is that more do not follow this path.

In sum, as the dramatic events of recent years have shown, Latin America's relevance to U.S. interests is growing. No other group of countries affects U.S. domestic issues more than the nations of the Caribbean Basin and Latin America. We are linked to them for economic, social, and demographic reasons. This was made clear in the civil wars in Central America in the 1980s, which were one of the main causes of the highest inflow of illegal immigrants our nation has ever seen. In the 1990s, economic reform in the region helped U.S. exports boom. In Colombia, incessant pressure from the drug industry led to the largest mobilization of U.S. aid since the Vietnam War. Natural disasters such as El Niño and hurricanes devastated the infrastructure of South and Central America, setting back development efforts by decades and prompting major international relief efforts. In addition, in many areas, poor people seeking a better life are devastating rain forests and destroying the environment.

In 1998, a succession of events stemming from financial crises outside the region touched off widespread recession and unemployment that caused U.S. exports to the region to plunge. Collapsing commodity prices from the Asian financial crisis undermined economic reforms. Brazil's currency first wavered and then plummeted despite repeated efforts by the Brazilian government and the international community to protect it against the Asian crisis. Then in 2001, the reverberations from the Brazilian measures to correct its currency imbalance triggered the collapse of the Argentine currency, which could no longer sustain its idealistic but rigid policy of fixing its currency at parity to the dollar. The response to the sharp cutbacks in budgets and social services was a loss of confidence in the ability of open markets to address the region's social problems. Interest rates throughout the region spiked sharply upward, and stock markets tumbled as investors withdrew their money. The cost of money to both business and government soared, causing businesses to default on loans, banks to fail, and unemployment to reach record heights. Millions of people who had risen to the middle class on the wave of prosperity that accompanied the conversion to a sound currency suddenly lost their balance. Cynicism about the ability of democracy and open markets to deliver on their promise of a better life spread rapidly. Compounding the disillusionment was the conspicuous self-enrichment of some political leaders that stood in sharp relief against the burgeoning social problems and humiliation of the middle class.

The response by Latin America and the Caribbean to the financial crisis of the late 1990s ironically demonstrates the promise for the future. This time no countries backtracked on their commitments to democracy and open economies. Instead, most governments tightened their economies and maintained their reforms toward open markets and fiscal responsibility adopted during the 1990s. The Inter-American Development Bank and the World Bank provided massive loans specifically to maintain social services in the face of pressure to cut government budgets. Unlike the policies of the 1980s, which raised tariffs, took control of the currency, and instituted a wide range of protectionist measures, these were never on the table in the 1990s as possible alternatives. The result was that the economies quickly rebounded and 1999 did not become a replay of the 1982 collapse when the Mexican government defaulted on its foreign debt and sparked a decade-long recession throughout Latin America.

The Mexican financial crisis of 1982 is an important case study, as it shows how closely Latin American affairs and the United States are tied. At that time, the major exposure of U.S. banks was in Latin America. Pressed in the 1970s by the U.S. government to recycle "petrodollars" from the money that flooded into the Middle East and the international financial system from the higher oil prices, U.S. banks offered long-term loans to Latin America against short-term deposits from the Middle East nations that were flush with cash but had no way to place it into the global economy. In several prominent cases, the total amount of the loans from individual U.S. banks to the region exceeded their capital base. This meant that if the banks had to write off their long-term Latin American loans, they would be legally insolvent. The resulting contraction of liquidity would have deeply affected the U.S. economy and led to a global recession almost immediately. It would have forced banks to reduce their lending to their U.S. customers for reasons beyond the dynamics of the internal U.S. market. No U.S. government could allow that to happen. The Latin American governments were immediately forced to guarantee all loans, even those from the private sector, in order to give some semblance of eventual repayment. The result saddled Latin American taxpayers with unmanageable debt and a situation that appeared hopeless for at least a generation.

The repercussions in Latin America were widespread. No new loans were forthcoming. Income plummeted, unemployment soared, and millions of middle-class families were plunged into poverty. As financial reserves dwindled, the values of Latin American currencies began a precipitous decline, which made it impossible for businesses, even with good domestic markets, to repay their dollar loans. U.S. foreign policy experts were paralyzed. Regardless of the pundits advocating emergency measures to help, the predicament of the U.S. banks had created a trap. The responsibilities of the U.S. Treasury Department and the Federal Reserve were different from those of the State Department. The Fed's primary concerns about the integrity of the U.S. banking industry forced it to forbid U.S. banks to take any more risks in Latin America. Moreover, its rules reducing their exposure forced many banks to refuse to renew even those loans that were being properly serviced. Bankruptcies erupted throughout the region as bank liquidity disappeared and neither business nor individuals could roll over their loans.

Within two years, U.S. trade with Latin America fell by more than 50 percent. No one could afford imports. More than 2 million jobs were lost in the United States, and as a result, for a decade the unemployment rate was unable to fall below 7 percent despite the growing economy here. Bewildered Latin Americans, who had been showered with loans from U.S. banks during the previous decade (which was how their debt rose to $400 billion) suddenly found themselves completely adrift.

Contrast this with 1995, when a similar sequence loomed on the horizon and the Clinton administration daringly put together a $40 billion rescue package for Mexico. The banks regained confidence that their debts would be repaid and thus rolled over their loans, albeit with greater prudence and more regulatory guidelines. The Mexican government accepted the larger obligations, and business rebounded in record time.

The lessons of the 1980s go far deeper. At that time, the Latin American governments pretended to find a way out of their insolvency by printing money. The result for those workers lucky enough to keep their jobs was that real wages tumbled as inflation exploded. Indeed, two decades later, the per capita income in the Americas is only now reaching the levels of the 1970s. The lessons do not stop there. When legitimate trade and investment came to a halt, the drug trade soared. Drug addicts seemed to be the only people who would shell out money for a Latin American product. Within a few years the narcotics network, always a menace, flourished as never before because poor people and public officials alike found the temptation of drugs irresistible in economies submerged in depression. As inflation exceeded 5,000 percent in some Latin American countries, millions of people in the growing middle class were dragged into poverty. Crime began to rise throughout the region as underpaid police forces were cut. Within the next decade almost 10 million legal and unknown numbers of illegal immigrants poured into the United States, generating a backlash by the U.S. public to stem the flow of immigrants.

For the United States the consequences of these dislocations were predictable. From the Caribbean Basin, from where transportation to the United States is easy and inexpensive, motivated refugees took the risk of leaving desolation behind and striking out anew. The civil wars of Central America accelerated the flow when thousands of refugees illegally crossed the U.S. border, at great risk to their lives. The tragedy of a nonproductive Cuba, where there was no means to earn a living except through the state, motivated almost thirty thousand people to abandon their country each year, not including the hundred thousand who fled in the Mariel boat lift during President Jimmy Carter's term in office. The continuing flow of refugees from Haiti accelerated when anarchy took over in the early 1990s. In all these situations, people were willing to risk their lives through lands they did not know or at sea in makeshift rafts, in order to escape stagnation and a life without hope.

In the United States, Miami was first to feel the brunt of the 1980s collapse. Newly flourishing businesses built on trade with Latin America crashed. Real estate, in contrast, began to boom as wealthy people poured in from Central and South America. In that period, those who had money in Latin America moved it out as quickly as they could in order to maintain its value in the face of erratic government policies that resorted to the printing presses to stave off bankruptcy. The flood of refugees overwhelmed welfare systems from Florida to Texas to California, exhausting social services and causing state budgets to go into deficit.

In short, the repercussions from the Mexican economic collapse in 1982 illustrate why Latin America has become an increasingly important part of the "joinery" underpinning the U.S. economy. In a world highly leveraged—in trade, in finance, in our treatment of our environment, in every country—"no thing can be dispensed with." In human behavior, everything is sensitive and mobile. The slightest glitches can unravel delicate and complex interrelationships. Domestic turmoil in a region with which we share a porous two-thousand-mile border is not a trivial issue for the United States.

THE SCENARIO CHANGES

Few people remember that in the 1960s and 1970s, Latin America was the fastest-growing region in the world, outpacing even the Asian countries. As a result of the attention showered on the region by President John F. Kennedy's Alliance for Progress and the contrasting turmoil in Asia during the Vietnam War, the Americas was the darling of the investment community. In the 1970s, as I noted, Latin America was awash with money. The resulting debt, partially caused by the major banks' extravagant and irresponsible lending policies, far exceeded the region's capacity to repay it and so made it one of the world's highest borrowers in relation to its tax base. This unsustainable scenario quickly collapsed and immersed the region in one of the most severe depressions in its history. Pundits were concerned that these hard-pressed people would soon react, follow the calls of Fidel Castro, and explode in social chaos and revolution, but they did not. To the contrary, the painful lessons the region learned became the crucible for a new Latin America.

More recent history demonstrates the pace at which changes are occurring in the region. Ten years ago, widespread depression ruled Latin America following the intractable debt crisis. But since then the following has come to pass:

1989–91: Commercial banks restructure all Latin American debt.
1993: NAFTA (North American Free Trade Association) is established.
1995:. The United States rescues Mexico from financial crisis with $40 billion in credits.

1996: Recovering, the region accelerates its economic adjustments and banking reforms.

1997: Asia's financial crisis begins, but Latin America seems to be insulated.

1998: Russia's financial default severely affects emerging markets, but again, Latin America holds the line.

1999: The United States leads with $41 billion of credits from the International Monetary Fund (IMF) to bolster Brazil's economy. Brazil's currency falls, but the availability of the credits spurs recovery within a year.

2002: Argentina, reeling from the dislocations in its own economy resulting from Brazil's decision to float its currency, can no longer maintain its rigid economic policies. Its inept handling of the transition to float its currency causes a collapse of the economy. Unlike previous financial crises, the failure of the United States and the IMF to agree to buttress its economic system triggers a downward spiral in Argentina's economic and political institutions.

Both perspective and potential throughout Latin America and the Caribbean were affected by the debt crisis and economic depression of the 1980s. The seemingly slow pace of economic growth in the last two decades has greatly changed social, political, and economic forces—in urbanization, in civil society, and in attitudes. The global economy has also created a broad array of new forces. During the last few years the people of the Americas have tried to sustain their democracies and adjust their economies to cope with a global economy in which they were minor players and in which the prices for their primary products were beyond their control.

The measures taken in the 1990s show what enlightened, realistic policies, external support of the reformers, and hope can accomplish. Open markets, economic deregulation, and increasing foreign and internal investment have led to economic integration. The reduction of tariff barriers from an average of more than 80 percent to 10 to 15 percent today has helped form an aggressive, increasingly confident private sector. While these trends have come under pressure in the early 2000s, the impact of the underlying reforms remains strong. The recent movement of some countries to follow Panama and use the dollar as their legal tender could change the entire region. Ecuador adopted the dollar as a bulwark against economic indiscipline. In El Salvador, within a few months after the move to dollarization, interest rates fell from 17 percent to 11 percent; interest rates on credit cards declined from 34 percent to 18 percent; and mortgages were extended to thirty years—all unprecedented for the region.

There is another, darker, side of the picture, however. The cold data of economic growth mask the widespread poverty throughout the Americas. Large sectors of the population profiting from the global economy are growing richer while the poor fall further behind. Income distribution in the Americas, already among the most unequal in the world, has become further skewed in a global economy in which education is paramount. Social inequality, poor income distribution, and low-quality education are the principal impediments today to consolidating democracy and economic growth in the region.

Many other problems crowd the agenda for the Americas. The institutions that form democracy and define its responsiveness to its people are weak. Civil service is rudimentary, leaving much room for mischief and corruption. Credit institutions for small and medium enterprises are scarce. And weak judicial systems undermine citizens' confidence in fairness and discourage commercial transactions.

The recession in the United States in 2001 and the failure of the economic reforms to attract investment have spread dismay and disillusionment, in contrast to the determination and promise of the region throughout the 1990s. Alongside that disappointment, though, is a new generation of Latin Americans and Caribbeans who have a more pragmatic view of these issues. They also are aware of their governments' shortcomings and are more impatient about their ability to correct them. The region has greatly changed in the last decade and, for the most part, for the better.

THE GROWING HISPANIC AND CARIBBEAN INFLUENCE

Salsa now outsells ketchup as a condiment in the United States. In California and Texas, José is now the most popular name for baby boys, and Maria is the favorite name for baby girls. Dulce de leche, a type of caramelized milk favored by Latin Americans, is now sold in Starbucks, Häagen Daz, and McDonald's. Even M&Ms have a new Latino flavor.

Ricky Martin, Gloria Estafan, and Jennifer Lopez have had an extraordinary influence on our popular culture. Sammy Sosa dominates baseball. T-shirts in Texas sport the slogan "I didn't cross the border; the border crossed me." As anyone who knows markets understands, Hispanic markets in the United States are exploding. The people who purchased La Prensa, New York's largest Spanish-language newspaper, are predominantly old-line U.S. investors. Today, the reality of our two-thousand-mile border with Mexico, our gateway to Latin America, is taking on a new dimension. Hispanic culture, the dominant culture of the Americas, is now permeating Anglo-U.S. culture with unsuspected implications for domestic and foreign policy.

President Lyndon Johnson often remarked that the roots of U.S. foreign policy reach deep into U.S. domestic policy. If so, the Hispanic culture is about to make a major difference in our policy. We are already the fourth-largest Spanish-speaking country in the world after Spain, Mexico, and the Philippines. Hispanics populated the southwest United States when it was still part of Mexico, becoming part of the United States after it annexed one-third of Mexico's territory in 1848. The Hispanic population had inhabited that land for three centuries.

Nonetheless, many Hispanics today are recent immigrants, accounting for the largest number of immigrants to this country in the last two decades. As the native U.S. Hispanic population combines with the second generation of these immigrants to assume a more active role in U.S. economics and society, this long quiescent ingredient in the American "stew" will transform the United States as profoundly as did the influx of Europeans in the last century. Since 1960, the largest group of legal immigrants has been Mexicans. Already in the 2000 census, Hispanics were our largest minority, and by 2015 it is projected that they will comprise almost 20 percent of our population. When added to the Caribbeans, they will dramatically transform the culture and politics of the United States. One does not have to be in Florida, Texas, or California, where the Hispanic names of the cities and streets proclaim their origins. Today their influence is apparent in the voting lists and in the boardrooms of our corporations. The current CEOs of Alcoa and the Bank of Boston are Brazilian; the recent CEOs of Coca-Cola and Kellogg were Hispanic; and Hispanic names continually pop up among the top executives of major corporations, especially in the technology and telecommunications industries; for example, the head of Microsoft's global sales, Orlando Ayala, is a native Colombian.

These influences go both ways. The highest attendance at any National Football League exhibition game was in Mexico City. The most pervasive music in the world is jazz, a unique blend of U.S., African, and Latin forms. And of course, U.S. brands such as Levi's and McDonalds are now as ubiquitous throughout the Americas as they are in the world.

While most first-generation Hispanics are like other immigrant groups in seeking to be "more American than the Americans," the issue for us today is how future generations will relate to their cultural heritage. The majority of lower- and middle-class Hispanic Americans have the same problems as do other lower- and middle-class citizens in the United States. They are worried about their security, health, and education and the care of their children and elderly. As those income groups most vulnerable to free trade, they strongly opposed NAFTA and fast track authority for President Clinton. A 1992 survey found that less than 12 percent of the Hispanic populations of California and Texas supported NAFTA but that more than 25 percent opposed it unconditionally. Fifteen of the seventeen members of the Hispanic Caucus in Congress voted against President Clinton's bid for fast track authority in 1997, sealing its defeat. De la Garza and DeSipio's studies indicate that Mexican immigrants "have little interest in Mexican politics and are extremely critical of the Mexican government." In polls taken in the 1990s, 85 percent of Mexican Americans said that the Mexican government's corruption and inefficiency were more to blame than U.S. policies for Mexico's economic difficulties.[3] In that regard, they fall in the grand tradition of immigrants fleeing oppression and deprivation in their native countries to seek a better life in the United States.

The election to president in 2000 of the opposition-party candidate Vicente Fox did more than break the monopoly hold of the main Mexican political party, the Institutional Revolutionary Party (better known as PRI). The election has had a profound impact, even if only symbolic, on many issues, including the Mexican law affirming Mexican citizenship as a birthright and approving the dual nationality of naturalized Mexicans living in the United States, which now qualifies them to vote in Mexican elections. Recently, two candidates for governor of the state of Zacatecas, José Olvera of the PRI and Ricardo Monreal Avila of the Partido Revolucionario Democrático (PRD), went to Los Angeles to campaign for the votes of "Zacatecanos living in the United States."

Monreal candidly noted that "this is where the action is." And indeed it may be, as an estimated 450,000 Zacatecans live in the Los Angeles area.[4]

Perhaps most important are the personal ties joining U.S. citizens of Hispanic descent with their families remaining in Latin America. Remittances from the United States have become a principal source of foreign exchange earnings for Latin America and the Caribbean, almost as great as export revenue. The total annual remittances, according to the Inter-American Development Bank exceed $20 billion a year, with Mexico receiving almost $9 billion, El Salvador and the Dominican Republic approaching $2 billion a year, and countries of the Caribbean nearly $1 billion. Ironically, in these days of slashing foreign aid budgets, Latin America and the Caribbean receive more "foreign aid" dollars from remittances than they have ever received from government programs. This "aid" goes directly to the private sector and the poor, thereby circumventing government bureaucracies and entering the local economy directly and immediately. When Jamaica decided to attract foreign deposits into its banking system, it specifically targeted Jamaicans living in the United States with their high-interest CDs. It worked well. Millions of dollars were repatriated to Jamaica, helping revive the economy in the early 1990s.

In the poorer countries of Central America and the Caribbean, emigration has relieved pressure on hard-pressed social services. When the U.S. immigration law provided for the repatriation of illegal immigrants, Central American countries pleaded that they could not afford the financial burden. Nicaragua made a special plea and, with a quick study of U.S. political techniques, succeeded in lobbying Congress to suspend the law for its country. As the United States pressed forward with the repatriation of illegal immigrants, the flip side of the issue became clear. One of the biggest problems is the few immigrants who come to the United States, never get a job, and become petty criminals. Languishing in U.S. jails with professional criminals, many return to their country as hardened experts and have now become the main operators in the drug-trafficking network. Considering the billions of dollars the United States spends annually on drug interdiction, this gratuitous reinforcement of the ranks of the lawless in the Americas is a folly. El Salvador's wave of teenaged gangs is directly traced to young people returning from the United States. Given their native countries' badly trained police forces, they have relatively easy pickings, feeding the violence and crime sweeping the region. It is a problem generated in the United States that we can ill afford to ignore.

In business, Hispanic entrepreneurs, virtually nonexistent in the 1970 census, today are owners of businesses that account for almost $200 billion in sales and employ more than a million people. The innate entrepreneurial spirit of Latin Americans and Caribbeans is demonstrated daily in urban communities, where Peruvian, Dominican, and Jamaican immigrants who had virtually no opportunity to start a business or obtain credit in their native countries become active and sometime prosperous small businessmen in the United States. Like other immigrants, many Hispanic and Caribbean businessmen also start businesses with their countries of origin, where they know the language and understand the business environment.

Hispanics throughout the United States are taking another lead from the Cuban community in Miami, which has remade that city into one of the busiest commercial centers in the country. Increasingly larger segments of the U.S. Hispanic community are beginning to perceive their native lands as good sources of business. As Hispanic businesses grow, they will find they have a competitive advantage in doing business with their former native lands, which in turn will affect our trade with the region. Already Hispanic Chambers of Commerce are growing at an unprecedented rate. The creation in Washington, D.C., of the Greater America Business Coalition is another signal that the increasingly savvy Latin Americans are beginning to contemplate how they can influence the U.S. power structure.

The increasing influence of the Hispanic community is also being felt in the U.S. government. In many western congressional districts, the growing Hispanic vote is a swing vote. The role of Hispanic descendants in Congress and government is everywhere apparent. The former secretary of energy and the ambassador to the United Nations, Bill Richardson; the former secretary of transportation, Federico Peña; the current secretary of housing and urban development, José Martinez; and Congressman Esteban Torres of California, who almost single-handedly assembled the consensus leading to the establishment of the North American Development Bank as part of the NAFTA treaty negotiations, all signal the future. The recent formation of the Hispanic Foreign Relations Council indicates the growing consciousness of their influence on international issues. The example of the Cuban American

Foundation's lock on U.S. policy toward Cuba for almost thirty years has not been lost on them. The Caribbean influence will be buttressed by the appointment of Colin Powell, of Jamaican descent, as the U.S. secretary of state.

The voices of the Hispanic and Caribbean communities are still disproportionately quiet in the political arena, however. A large percentage of the U.S. Hispanics and Caribbeans are still ineligible to vote because of their lack of citizenship, although in the last two presidential elections, they were the highest percentage of any minority group of eligible voters who voted. In coming decades, as their American children vote, their voice is certain to encourage the U.S. government to focus on Latin American issues.

The recent effort by President George W. Bush to promote closer U.S.-Mexican relations and the recognition by the U.S. labor movement that a more liberal immigration policy may be good for everyone promise to accelerate Latin American and Caribbean immigration. While the record of these communities in maintaining contact with their families is extraordinary, the real impact will not be felt until the Latin American and Caribbean countries begin to pay closer attention to their U.S. diaspora and forge political links with it, as Israel has done with the United States' Jewish community. The next step will come when the American nations begin to lure their young people to return to Latin America and the Caribbean for education and as volunteers to help build services in the social sector and for democracy, similar to the way that Israel developed the kibbutz in the 1950s and 1960s. When that happens, U.S. policies toward the region should change even more.

REGAINING PERSPECTIVE

Perhaps the most important consideration is that the nations of the Americas are the next area of the world in which democracy and human rights can flower. Apart from protecting our shores, the spread of democracy, the rule of law, and respect for human rights are the main lines of defense for the United States. All other U.S. foreign policy goals flow from a world at peace, open markets, freedom for human initiative, and broad-based prosperity among the people.

Latin America today has the beginnings of political liberty, but not real representative democracy. It has open markets but not a viable market economy. It has trade agreements, but a poor infrastructure for trade. The old statist approaches are being discarded, but the institutions enabling citizen participation are not yet ready. Latin America has tried hard to put the closed, authoritarian dictatorships and protectionist economies behind it. It is in everyone's interest that they succeed.

What interests and alliances must we pursue to make that happen? What will we need to do to maintain the dominance of the Americas in the international competition of the twenty-first century? Considering how Europe has moved quickly to absorb central and eastern Europe, I have little doubt that if Latin America and the Caribbean were on Europe's doorstep, a movement would be well under way to incorporate them into its economic sphere. Europe today supplies far more foreign aid, almost triple the amount, to Latin America than does the United States. The European Union has now concluded its own free-trade agreement with Chile and has declared its intention to conclude a free-trade agreement with the countries of the Southern Cone before a free-trade agreement of all the Americas is established.

In summary, in the twenty-first century, Latin America will play a far different role than it has in the past. Its constituency in the United States will exert more influence. The issues most affecting global security will no longer be armies and missiles crossing borders, but competition for market share. As the principal destination for U.S. exports, the expanding markets and abundant natural resources of the Americas are a major asset. A greater focus on the Americas will foster economic growth (the fastest-growing markets in the developing world are in the Americas), political growth (the next major area to embrace democracy and open markets in the developing world is the Americas), security (the issues of drugs and illegal migration are preeminently problems of cooperation with the nations of the Americas), industrial strength (with the world's largest untapped natural resource deposits, especially in energy, investment in the Americas ensures industry an uninterrupted supply in times of turmoil), and sound environmental practices (the vast rain forests of the Americas today are unquestionably the most delicate area vital to global environmental protection).

Conversely, the potential and the problems of the Americas will pose different challenges to the United States. With the changes that have taken place in the Americas in the last decade, it is plausible, for the first time, to consider the potential of a Greater America.

2

The United States and Latin America

Tackling History

IN THE TWENTY-FIRST CENTURY, a prosperous Latin America will make more difference to the United States than any other area of the world, not only because of its growing domestic influence on U.S. life, but also because of its intrinsic wealth and resources. Herbert Bolton, a historian of the early twentieth century, predicted this decades ago. Shortly after President Franklin Roosevelt declared his Good Neighbor policy in the 1930s, Bolton described the bonds between the United States and Latin America in an essay entitled "The Epic of Greater America." His vision captured the Americas' diversity of cultures, in which each part of the hemisphere influenced the others' development. He referred to a process of nations "growing side by side" and traced a history that, to him, demonstrated a "fundamental Western Hemisphere solidarity." He described an Hispanic America that was far richer and more developed than Anglo America in the early part of its history but that, because of social issues, lost out in the Industrial Revolution. He predicted that in the not too distant future, Hispanic Americans would outnumber Anglo Americans and that Latin America's "great reservoir of raw material" would fuel the world and bring it to the forefront of global politics.[1]

Bolton illuminated Latin America's long, complex relationship with our republic and reflected the European powers' competition for the riches of the Western Hemisphere. Arthur Whitaker, an expert on U.S.-Latin American relations in the mid-twentieth century, spoke of "the Western Hemisphere Idea," which describes the concept of the Americas as a region allowing the flowering of human freedom and liberty.[2] This theme has been visited and revisited by statesmen and philosophers throughout the hemisphere since the beginning of our histories. Both Bolton and Whitaker sensed the great drama that would

27

eventually unfold in a hemisphere free of enmities among peoples and with a sense of destiny.

As we measure the challenges of national interest and power in the twenty-first century, these ideas gain new relevance. When the United States begins to pay closer attention to the Americas than it has in the past, the resulting integration, confidence, and growth will strengthen the global forces of democracy, create a stronger economic base for both the United States and the Americas, alleviate the pressures on our domestic economy from drugs and migration, and provide an impetus to increase the wealth and prosperity of all the people.

There is a remarkable divergence in the public and private sectors' perception of the Americas. Most people would never guess from U.S. foreign policy experts' strategies that one of the U.S. private sector's highest priorities today is investment and market development in Latin America. The media are equally misleading. Article after article analyzes Europe, Japan, Russia, and Southeast Asia; few discuss Latin America. The Latin Americans have a saying, *"No llora, no mamma,"* which, roughly translated, means, "Without crying, Mama won't come," our variation of the squeaky-wheel theory. If the nations of the hemisphere were more threatening or were armed with nuclear weapons, the United States would surely pay attention. But Latin America was the first area of the world in which all nations agreed to a create a nuclear-free zone in the hemisphere. Although that news was never deemed worthy of note, the media did fill the front pages with accounts of human rights abuses, terrorism, and kidnappings in Colombia and Peru. Readers were inundated with war stories during the Central American civil wars in the 1980s, and we hear whenever trouble erupts in Cuba or Haiti. Violence and corruption dominate our images of the Americas. Yet, outside of drug trafficking, Latin America has never been a serious security threat to the United States. It appears that the real problem is that the United States has it too good.

It therefore is not surprising to find that the U.S. government has not made a strategic analysis of our policy goals toward Latin America since President John F. Kennedy's Alliance for Progress in the early 1960s. Despite the strong rhetoric of President George W. Bush, the United States has not formulated a well-reasoned case for our interests in the Americas and a long-term strategy of how to pursue them. The government has not defined the strengths, developed the assets, and realized the region's potential. All its several efforts to improve relations among the nations of the hemisphere during the twentieth century were reactionary, prompted not by any perception of benefits that might derive from better relations with Latin America but from security concerns.

The first effort was the imperative to protect the region from threats of penetration from the ideological conflicts in Europe, which was the motivating force behind President Franklin Roosevelt's Good Neighbor policy in the 1930s. Similarly, President John F. Kennedy's Alliance for Progress in the 1960s was fashioned largely from the United States' concern that the Soviet Union would take advantage of the social ferment in the region, especially after Fidel Castro assumed power in Cuba. Communist penetration was certainly the reason for President Ronald Reagan's Caribbean Basin Initiative (CBI) in 1982 after he involved the United States directly in the civil wars that traumatized Central America in the 1980s and then after his unilateral intervention to remove the left-leaning government of Maurice Bishop from the tiny island of Grenada. Not until Presidents George H. W. Bush and Bill Clinton began to pay attention to the region outside the terms of the cold war were U.S.–Latin American relations considered in the context of long-term mutual interests. Indeed, President George W. Bush's pronouncements early in his term hold great promise for new understanding of and new dimensions to our relationships.

SECURITY AT THE FOUNDING OF THE UNITED STATES

It has not always been that way. The first concern of the founding fathers of our country, highlighted in the U.S. Constitution and the opening arguments in the *Federalist Papers*, was security. For George Washington, security was the premise for his warning about avoiding foreign entanglements. He did not want the new nation to become embroiled in Europe's pursuit of its own interests, primarily because his main concern was defending the integrity of the republic's territory from the European powers. Hostility from far more powerful European nations posed an imminent threat to the republic's survival. The new United States had the French in the west in Louisiana, the Spanish in the south in Florida, and the British in the north in Canada and dominating the seas to the east. President George Washington's farewell address, influenced by this predicament, declared that the new nation had a large enough task to protect its borders at home and must not waste its energies and resources in ventures abroad. Security was the nation's primary interest, the main responsibility of the federal government, and one of the principal reasons for the states to join in a union.

The main area of concern for U.S. security at that time was the Caribbean, as it was for almost all of the early part of the United States' history. Most of Europe's major bases and forts were there. The sea-lanes for shipping commerce were the United States' life line, but the islands of the Caribbean were the favored harbors for the strong navies of England, France, and Spain as well as for pirates.

In the first fifty years of our history, Presidents Thomas Jefferson and James Monroe wrestled continuously with the European monarchies who blocked the United States' westward expansion. Securing the borders to the west and south was the dominant security issue for the United States until shortly before the Civil War. In a complex relationship that resulted in the United States' purchasing the Louisiana territories from France and Florida from Spain, the United States was both wooing and wary of the European powers. Later, as the United States began to settle the west and the U.S. Navy was able to dominate the waters of the Caribbean, those concerns receded.

The years between 1794 and 1800 were probably the most dangerous in U.S. history. Besides being threatened by Europeans with beachheads on the north, west, and south of the newly formed United States, the revolution in France had taken an ugly turn. The replacement of Robespierre and Danton by the Directorate changed France's position vis-à-vis the New World. Prompted by France's increasing rivalry with Great Britain, the Directorate wanted to confine the former British colonies, which they still viewed as an ally and asset of England, to a narrow band on the coast to the east of the Appalachians and take the rest of the new world for France. Pirates and raids on sea commerce were common. France entered into a secret treaty with Spain in 1800, the Treaty of Ildefonso, and took control of all of Louisiana and Florida. The French quickly began to arm Quebec, seeking to drive south, stir up the Indians in the west, and expand their Louisiana base to press the new United States from the west. They also planned to open another flank with aggressive moves from Florida in the south. France began raiding U.S. shipping, and privateers sank or plundered more than three hundred ships. The threat to be met by the new administration of John Adams was the most formidable ever faced by a U.S. government.

To complicate matters, the Republicans (now the Democrats), led by Thomas Jefferson, saw the French Revolution for human liberty in a positive light and tried to downplay the conflict. Alexander Hamilton and the Federalist Party of Washington and Adams (later the Republicans) wanted to use this conflict to solidify a new alliance with England. John Jay had already signed a treaty in London granting trading posts in the northwest to England and increasing commerce.

It was Thomas Jefferson, in a variation of Washington's concerns about the European powers' interests, who first noted the budding community of interests between the United States and Latin America. He wrote about the incipient independence movement in Mexico and Cuba: "We consider their interests and ours as the same, and that the object of both must be to exclude all European influence from the hemisphere."[3] In 1811, he commented on the prevailing sentiment of the day:

> What, in short, is the whole system of Europe toward America but an atrocious and insulting tyranny? One hemisphere of the earth, separated from the other by wide seas on both sides, having a different system of interests . . . is made subservient to all the petty interests of the other, to their laws, their regulations, their passions and wars.[4]

Jefferson had no illusions about the state of affairs in Latin America. "History . . . furnishes no example of a priest-ridden people maintaining a free civil government," he said in a letter to Alexander Von Humboldt, the famous naturalist. This was later repeated by President John Quincy Adams, who asserted that "Latin America had few points of contact with the United States and nothing in common."[5] Jefferson continued, however, to affirm that these

> priest-ridden [nations], in whatever governments they end, they will be *American* governments, no longer to be involved in the never-ceasing broils of Europe. The European nations constitute a separate division of the globe; . . . they have a set of interests of their own in which it is our business never to engage ourselves. . . . The insulated state in which nature has put the American continent should so far avail it that no spark of war kindled in the other quarters of the globe should be wafted across the wide oceans which separate us from them.[6]

These words were "the first full flowering of the Western Hemisphere idea in the America system," Whitaker noted.[7] Even if he bemoaned the "priest-ridden" nations, Jefferson emphasized that "in whatever governments they end, they will be *American* governments." This was the defining issue for him. He also pointed out the common interests of the people of the Americas, ensuring that a new system of interests and of governing developed in this hemisphere would be free from the contentious relations of the European states, which at the time were contending with the French Revolution, the Holy Alliance, and desperate efforts to preserve the monarchies.

After Napoleon's invasion of Spain in 1808 prompted independence movements throughout Latin America, the new United States was tempted to side with the Latin American patriots. In 1815, Henry Clay deplored the machinations of the Holy Alliance, speaking of the "glorious spectacle of eighteen millions of people struggling to burst their chains and be free." Within a few years, Clay was advocating meeting the menace from Europe with a new "system of which we shall be the centre and in which all South America will act with us."[8]

The appraisal by Secretary of State John Quincy Adams prevailed, however:

> That the final issue of their [Latin America's] present struggle would be their entire independence from Spain, I had never doubted. . . . I wished well to their cause; but I had seen and yet see no prospect that they would establish free or liberal institutions of government. . . . Arbitrary power, military and ecclesiastical, was stamped on their habits and upon all their institutions. Civil dissension was infused into all their seminal principles. . . . I had little expectation of any beneficial result to this country from any future connection with them, political or commercial.[9]

A critical influence on the United States' behavior in this period, little discussed today but dominant in the minds of Adams and Monroe at the time, was the growing tension with Spain over the southern border in Florida. General Andrew Jackson's assaults on Florida unsettled the Spanish, who were already under siege at home. Intense behind-the-scenes negotiations convinced the Spanish that they would fare better by relinquishing their North American claims. A treaty agreeing to buy Florida for $5 million was signed with Spain on February 22, 1819.

As long as the negotiations were continuing, the United States faced a real conflict of interest in confronting the Spanish monarchy.

It is difficult for us today to appreciate the intensity of the emotions motivating the leaders of the young United States. Threats of invasion from Europe faced them on all fronts. During President James Monroe's administration, a "holy alliance" was formed by the monarchs of Europe with the express purpose of reasserting the rights of their monarchies. Their efforts to support King Ferdinand VII of Spain only complicated matters. The United States was not about to allow the monarchies to reestablish Spanish hegemony in the newly independent countries of Latin America. But it also wanted to avoid having to take sides in the disputes among the contending European powers.

The events of the 1820s set in motion the forces that dominated U.S.-Latin American relations for the next century. With Simón Bolívar on the north and José San Martín on the south, the Latin American elites conquered all the Spanish armies in South America. The final battle of Ayacucho was fought in 1824 as the two armies joined forces to defeat the last of the Spanish armies. President Monroe encouraged the new Latin American states to become republics and recognized the new nations on March 8, 1822. Congress promptly appropriated money for "such missions to the independent nations of the American continent as the President might deem proper."[10] The emperor of Portugal, Dom Pedro of the House of Braganza, added strength to the Latin American identity when he abandoned Portugal, transferred the seat of his monarchy to Brazil, and declared the independence of Brazil in September 1822.

The Monroe Doctrine was introduced shortly afterward as the precursor of the tension among the three main currents of U.S. foreign policy: isolationism, which dominated this period; multilateral international activism, which was being proposed to the United States by the British; and unilateral international activism, which President Monroe favored. The British, whose trade with South America in 1822 surpassed their trade with the United States, became alarmed when the French armies moved into Spain in 1823 to help King Ferdinand VII defeat a liberal constitution. Fearing a French-Spanish alliance to reconquer South America, George Canning, the British foreign minister, urged the United States to warn European conspirators against any intervention in the hemisphere. On its part, the United States was concerned that the French-Spanish alliance might encourage the French to try to recover Louisiana. The prevailing opinion in America was expressed by John Calhoun, the secretary of war, who wished to join with Canning. Calhoun suspected "that the underlying motive of the European monarchs was jealousy and hatred of the United States, whose turn would come after Mexico had fallen." This was the prevailing American opinion.[11] Calhoun was joined by Henry Clay, who advocated a complete political and commercial break with Europe in favor of "a human freedom league in America [unifying] . . . all the nations from Hudson's Bay to Cape Horn."[12]

Even the skeptic, isolationist secretary of state, John Quincy Adams, began to feel more comfortable with the United States' neighbors to the south. He commented that "a political hurricane has gone over three-fourths of the civilized portion of earth . . . leaving at least the American atmosphere purified and refreshed" and that the nations of South America were "transformed into eight independent nations . . . seven of them republics like ourselves."[13] The linkage of U.S. interests in the Americas to an isolationist policy vis-à-vis Europe was beginning to take shape.

A wide range of issues influenced the Monroe administration at the time, including the determination of the Holy Alliance to support the efforts of the Russian czar in 1821 to extend Alaska as far south as Oregon. In the end, however, the issue of Cuba caused Monroe and Adams to make their own unilateral declaration. Canning proposed that neither the United States nor Great Britain seek to acquire any part of Spanish America, thereby giving credence to the rumor that Cuba might vote to join the United States. In a message to Congress on December 2, 1823, President Monroe announced in his famous Monroe Doctrine that

> the American continents . . . are not considered as subjects for future colonization by any European powers . . . [and] the political systems of the allied powers is essentially different . . . from that of America. . . . We should consider any attempt on their part to extend their system to any portion of this hemisphere as dangerous to our peace and safety.[14]

In the next forty years, the threat of the Holy Alliance faded. Pre–Civil War America found its neighbors in the Caribbean caught in the struggle among the states for the balance of power regarding the issue of slavery. To balance the number of antislavery states entering the union, the proslavery states had to find new allies. In addition to the territory acquired by the United States in the Mexican War, the southern states looked toward Cuba and Central America to become new slave-holding states.[15] Proslavery zealots tried to take advantage of the weak nations of Central America and recruit them as allies. The most famous of these, William Walker, even tried to set up his own empire in Central America in 1856. After landing in Nicaragua with an army of fifty-eight adventurers and proclaiming himself "president" of Nicaragua, he set about to conquer all of Central America. He was ultimately defeated and executed in 1860, but not before he set in motion the rapid spread of what was called "Yankeephobia," which had originated earlier that decade in Mexico.

The relationship between the United States and Mexico was particularly tense during this time. Throughout the nineteenth century, the United States chipped away at Mexican territory, annexing almost a third of it in 1848. Secretary of State (and later President) James Buchanan advocated establishing a "protectorate" over all of Mexico, giving rise to the first round of "Yankeephobia." In his memoirs, President Ulysses S. Grant termed the U.S.-Mexican war "one of most unjust wars ever waged by a stronger against a weaker nation." This strained and contentious relationship continued well into the twentieth century when the U.S. Marines landed at Vera Cruz in 1914, and General John Pershing led an expedition deep into Mexican territory searching for Pancho Villa in 1916. Mexico's reaction was to turn inward and try to insulate itself from the voracious appetites of its neighbor to the north. After World War II when the United States suggested discussing collective security, prominent Mexicans commented cynically that the only foreign intervention they feared was from the United States.

In the wave of prosperity following the U.S. Civil War, the United States began to assert its position in the hemisphere as an extension of Manifest Destiny. It also began to counter the continuing threats from the European powers, which took advantage of the United States' distraction during the Civil War to pursue their colonial interests. France reoccupied Mexico, where Napoleon III installed a puppet emperor, Maximilian. Spain moved to occupy the Dominican Republic. The implications of neither action was lost on Latin America or the United States. In 1871, the legislature of the newly reliberated Dominican Republic voted to become part of the United States, encouraged by President Grant. The effort failed by only one vote in the U.S. Senate. It is hard to imagine U.S. history if that accession had succeeded.

As commercial interests grew in the latter part of the nineteenth century, President Grover Cleveland authorized his secretary of state, James Blaine, to call a conference of all American nations. The conclave launched what became the Pan American Union. This tentative initial step received an immediate positive response led by Domingo Sarmiento, Argentina's staunchly pro–United States president. Yankeephobia was quickly transformed into Yankeephilia, an affinity for the United States. The conference led to the establishment of the American Customs Union, uniform customs regulations, trademark and copyright laws, and a common currency. Commerce, then as now, was foremost on the hemispheric agenda. In Secretary Blaine's description of the initiative, he boasted of a hemispheric trade regime as "annexation by trade," and the initial proposals were for a customs union of all American nations. Although this program never succeeded, the Pan American Union ultimately evolved into today's Organization of American States and became the world's first modern international organization.

At the time that President Cleveland held the Pan American Conference in 1889, colonialism was resurgent in Europe. Germany, England, and France were expanding their colonial empires in Africa and Asia and were looking for new worlds to conquer. Instability in South America, including the devastating War of the Pacific among Chile, Bolivia, and Peru, as well as a number of debt defaults, made the region vulnerable to still predominant European interests. South America was the source of most of Europe's investments, and by 1889, South American trade with Europe had quadrupled that with the United States. The lack of raw materials in Europe and the easy access to South America's mines and, conversely, South America's eagerness to import fine European manufactures, produced a congenial arrangement. But South America's debts were rapidly growing as investors clamored for a better infrastructure to reach remote mining areas. With Europe becoming increasingly impatient with the huge debts, the Americas welcomed Cleveland's invitation.

Before the people could absorb the idea of hemispheric cooperation, the Spanish-American War sparked a rash of nationalist fervor in the United States that frightened and alienated Latin America. President Theodore Roosevelt's decision to build the Panama Canal deeply involved the United States in the Caribbean again. At the turn of the century, Roosevelt's diplomatic efforts were capped by a successful conspiracy in which the United States actively encouraged the leaders of Panama, which was then a sleepy province of Colombia, to rebel and form a new country more to the U.S. government's liking. After the province of Panama broke away from Colombia in 1903, the United States struck a deal with the new independent government of Panama to build a canal through the isthmus.

In the next decade, as the United States proceeded to intervene unilaterally in Nicaragua and Haiti, it appeared that Roosevelt's principal contribution to global politics was his declaration, the so-called Roosevelt Corollary to the Monroe Doctrine, that the U.S. government would be responsible for guaranteeing stability in the hemisphere. The United States declared its right to intervene unilaterally anywhere in the hemisphere "to prevent others from intervening." In Roosevelt's words, "in the Western Hemisphere the adherence of the United States to the Monroe Doctrine may force the United States, however reluctantly, in flagrant cases of . . . wrongdoing or impotence, to the exercise of an international police power."[16] According to Arthur Whitaker, "Instead of abolishing intervention in the Western Hemisphere, Roosevelt explicitly sanctioned its practice and claimed for the United States a monopoly of the right to engage in it."[17]

This concept became known as Roosevelt's "big stick" diplomacy, which resulted from the dispatch of warships to Venezuela by Germany and Great Britain in 1902 to collect on the defaulted international bonds issued by the Venezuelan government. Under the guise of preserving political and financial stability, the United States had declared that it had a vital national interest in keeping the Europeans from military adventures in Latin America. Roosevelt's assertion of U.S. power in the hemisphere to ward off Europe in that period touched off several U.S. interventions after World War I.[18] Although these actions saved Latin America from other interventions by creditor nations, they won few friends for the United States.

After President Woodrow Wilson was elected in 1912, he attempted to return to Cleveland's original intention twenty years earlier by calling for a Pan American pact. The objective of his effort was to protect the republican form of government in Latin America and to guarantee territorial integrity. Its principal element was the forerunner of Wilson's later global plans. That is, the purpose of the pact was to establish a model for the judicial resolution of international disputes with mutual guarantees of territorial integrity and detailed procedures for the settlement of boundary disputes. Its call to control arms exports would in effect multilateralize the Monroe Doctrine and abolish the Roosevelt Corollary. But Wilson's proposals were aborted by World War I and were never revived, as he then turned his attention to pressing these same policies on a global basis through the League of Nations.

Later, when the executive and legislative branches of the U.S. government engaged in a monumental battle over its participation in the League, Latin America was again forgotten, with one major exception. The United States, now newly preoccupied with stability in the region, impatiently intervened in several countries of the Caribbean, the Dominican Republic, Nicaragua, and Haiti, for the ostensible purpose of straightening out their chaotic financial affairs. These "civilizing missions" as Wilson unfortunately termed the ventures, brought with them, however, a touch of the U.S. missionary zeal. Whenever the United States trained the military of a country to protect its security, almost invariably the military leaders used the training to arrogate power for themselves. The most egregious example was the long-running dictatorships of Molina Trujillo in the Dominican Republic and Anastasio Somoza in Nicaragua, both of whom had been officials of the U.S.-trained national guard.

In the 1920s, those interventions and the increasing U.S. investment in the region as European influence subsided after World War I, defined the United States' Latin American policies. This continued until 1933 when President Franklin D. Roosevelt attempted to pacify the region to forestall the spread in the hemisphere of Europe's latest turmoil. He addressed Latin America's concerns about the United States' unilateral interventions by embracing the doctrine of nonintervention and pledged that the United States would abide by the rule of law in what he called a Good Neighbor Policy.

After World War II, U.S. interests created a new role for the country in the advent of globalism. Regional issues became subordinate to the United States' new global role, with one notable exception. The United States moved to complete a defense pact first with the nations of the Western Hemisphere by signing the Rio Treaty in 1947. That event was completely overshadowed a year later by the North Atlantic Treaty Organization (NATO), the Marshall Plan, the onset of the cold war, and Western Europe's belated recognition of its dependence on the United States as the world's dominant power.

During the postwar period the Latin American economies began to languish after a short flush of prosperity spurred by the war's high demand for resources. The annual population growth of more than 3 percent overshadowed all development efforts. The continent's role in world trade rapidly stagnated as the economies remained dependent on single products for foreign exchange. In 1959, 62 percent of Brazil's export earnings came from coffee, 71 percent of Chile's from copper, 78 percent of Colombia's from coffee, 58 percent of Bolivia's from tin, and 57 percent of Honduras's from bananas.

The United States was shocked into recognizing the deteriorating conditions when Vice-President Richard Nixon was stoned during a visit to Caracas in 1958. Fidel Castro's challenge from Cuba in 1959 led President John F. Kennedy to launch a new initiative, the Alliance for Progress, in 1961. He challenged all of the Americas when he asked them to "demonstrate to the entire world that mankind's unsatisfied aspiration for economic progress and social justice can best be achieved by free men and women working within a framework of democratic institutions."[19]

The Alliance for Progress set in motion the machinery to reverse the downward trend. The effort came less than a decade after the Marshall Plan had already transformed Europe and was influenced by its idealism and success. The Alliance was meant to mobilize private and public capital in Latin America (with only 10 percent coming from the United States) in a massive effort to construct a modern, pluralistic, industrial-based society there. A good idea, but it was impeded by the contradiction of encouraging industrialization by means of protectionist policies in a world of already highly protected economies.

Although the Alliance got short shrift when the United States became distracted a few years later by Vietnam, it was the foundation for huge investments in infrastructure, electric power, transportation, communications, roads, and housing. It thus helped create the institutions that gave the middle class a chance to grow and create the diverse financial and power base necessary for a pluralistic society. Home mortgage institutions, free labor unions, universities, capital markets, foundations, and private philanthropy all took root during the 1960s.

Only today are we beginning to understand the critical role of the Alliance in opening Latin America to modern democracy and the global economy. Within a decade after the Alliance was launched, Latin

America was touted as one of the fastest-growing regions in the world. Taking advantage of the economic advances of the Alliance and the commodity boom caused by the Vietnam War, it seemed like the beginning of a new era. With prosperity everywhere, however, the region began to indulge in a nationalist fervor leading to the acceleration of statist controls in the economies. Venezuela nationalized its entire oil operation, and Chile elected a Marxist president. Activist social movements started a wave of kidnappings and terror that soon galvanized a reaction from the military. Before long, South America was immersed in one of the darkest, most repressive periods of its history. Military dictatorships took control in almost every country except Colombia and Venezuela. Central America became locked in a civil war that set back its development for decades.

Financial collapse followed in 1982. The history of modern Latin America begins with the debt-induced depression that it caused. The two main reasons for the collapse were, first, the Latin American countries' failure to adjust to the oil price shocks of 1973 and 1979 and, second, the lack of controls or accountability for the flood of dollars that suddenly inundated the region. At the time, Venezuela was the region's only oil-exporting country. By the time the second oil shock arrived in 1979, all the other nations were confronted with a new economic reality that required radical adjustments in their budgets and standards of living. But instead of cutting back and trying to dampen the inflationary pressures caused by the huge increases in energy costs, they attempted to maintain their standard of living by borrowing. For a few years they were able to continue the charade. But the end came in August 1982 when Mexico admitted that it could no longer meet its international financial obligations and defaulted on its debt payments. The walls quickly came tumbling down.

The ensuing debt debacle of the 1980s changed everything. Investments in infrastructure, social services, education, health, and housing came to a halt as revenues plummeted and governments were strangled by their inability to tap international capital markets. Governments obtain money by taxing, borrowing, or printing it. But Latin Americans did not like to pay taxes, and they could no longer borrow. So they resorted to the printing presses, but that did not work either. The resulting inflation devastated the economies and hit the poor especially hard. The number of persons living below the poverty level tripled.

One observer summarized the situation:

By the early 1980s Latin America was littered with state institutions and subsidized, protected production and living standards for which it could no longer pay and afflicted by a degree of regulation that discouraged investment, competition and production. High inflation rates had become chronic, exacting a terrible economic and social price, particularly from the disadvantaged least able to pay for it. Even the services that the state did manage were in evident decay. And, having borrowed mightily to sustain this crumbling edifice, the governments of the region were extremely vulnerable to the debt crisis precipitated by international recession, high interest rates and falling commodity prices experienced during the early 1980s.[20]

The pain to individual citizens was manifested in the deteriorating purchasing power of their wages and in the mushrooming rate of unemployment. The Mexican peso, which stood for many years at 12.5 to 1 U.S. dollar, collapsed to 25 to 1, and then shortly thereafter fell to 125 to 1, a collapse of 1,000 percent within a few years, before beginning a free fall. To understand what this meant, imagine that when the exchange rate was 12.5 pesos to 1 U.S. dollar, a business took out a loan of $1 million and needed to earn 12.5 million pesos to repay the loan. Then, suddenly, it needed to earn 125 million pesos to pay the same loan. Aside from the inflationary impact of raising prices to meet that obligation, no business was able to raise domestic prices that fast, and many went bankrupt.

The result was both capital flight and people flight. People flight, familiarly referred to as the "brain drain," was accelerated by social upheaval. Urban guerrilla forces terrorized the cities with widespread, indiscriminate violence, kidnappings, and bombings. The security forces and military reacted with brutal repression. Hoards of people—the intellectual elite and the wealthy—joined the march abroad. Many of the poor tried the same and became illegal immigrants, risking their lives to escape the turmoil that swept the region. Miami boomed with new money and new enterprising people who arrived by plane. New Mexico and California were inundated with impoverished immigrants who trekked across porous borders.

Latin America was depressed both economically and psychologically, leaving a residue of neglected investment and social dislocations from which the region is still recovering. Indeed, the impact was more severe than the Great Depression of the 1930s. The damage to the region's economic and social structures is incalculable. Not only did new investment stop, but the existing infrastructure deteriorated from the lack of funds for investment or maintenance.

The collapse led to a restructuring of wealth and political power in a way that would have pleased Vladimir Lenin. One of his principal tactics in the Russian social revolution in 1918 was to destroy the economic base of the old Russian oligarchy by inflating the economy, making their hoarded money worthless, and then issuing a new currency that placed the new proletariat on an equal footing. A variation of this, although with vastly different causes and motivations, now occurred in Latin America. For much of its history, Latin America had been in the grip of a strong oligarchic and authoritarian tradition rooted in its heritage from Spain. But the debt crisis broke that grip. The oligarchies, whose wealth was rooted in landownership, were greatly weakened when land values collapsed. In contrast, a growing class of entrepreneurs transferred their more liquid assets abroad for safekeeping and saw them appreciate. As the traditional landed oligarchies lost their hold on power, the authoritarian role of the military weakened as well. The military, which enjoyed its power when the treasuries were full, abandoned it as the treasuries emptied.

New entrepreneurs began to emerge. Inspired by the accelerating global technological and communications revolution, changes that were beginning to affect the region even before the debt crisis, pragmatic leaders turned to the United States and made obtaining access to U.S. markets and technology a high priority. They needed to attract investment to create employment. With a population of which 50 percent were under the age of seventeen, they were eager to find a viable role for the region in the global economy. By the early 1990s the region was ready for new thinking.

LATIN AMERICA VIS-À-VIS EUROPE

Historically, the issues of inter-American cooperation have always been framed by the triangular relationship with Europe. Frequent comments by North Americans about the Southern Hemisphere's links with Spain are paralleled only by Latin Americans' observations of the United States' ties to Europe, especially England. In the seventeenth and eighteenth centuries, Latin America was generally isolated from and ignored by the United States while Europe perceived it as one of the world's most exotic places. Its seemingly inexhaustible natural resources were the principal source of Europe's wealth. Gold and silver were plundered shamelessly by the Spanish monarchs and their lackeys. Today the descendants of those who did the pillaging express outrage, but at the time the plunder enabled Spain to remake itself from an insignificant country into a world power. With Latin America's wealth, Spain bought and sold much of the art and culture of Europe and enriched the church to assuage the guilt of its corrupt court life. Meanwhile, Europe's intellectuals and poets fantasized about romantic Latin America.

Despite its continuing rape of the region's wealth, Europe contended to be Latin America's motherland throughout its history. For the first three centuries after Columbus's discovery, South America was far more prosperous than the undeveloped United States, and Latin Americans were strongly linked emotionally to Europe. For most of its history, the United States was a bystander to events in Latin America, as it had virtually no commerce or interchange with these countries.

Given the difficulties of communications and transportation, South America developed essentially isolated from Europe's intellectual currents. Only the wealthy could afford the three months it required to travel back and forth to Europe, and their interests were invariably linked to Spanish business, Spanish trade, and Spanish influence. The region also lacked the ethnic and religious diversity of North America, which required democracy to balance their competing interests. The more uniform settlement and unchallenged rule of the Spanish crown and the monopoly in religion of the Catholic Church in Latin America meant that there was little practical need for democracy.

With the revolutions at the beginning of the nineteenth century, a new chapter in the relationship of Europe and Latin America began. After the brutal President Juan Rosas at the beginning of the nineteenth century, Argentina had one of the region's more enlightened presidents, Domingo Sarmiento, by the end of the century. In Mexico, the country progressed from the dictator Santa Ana to the liberal Benito Juárez. Everywhere, the region progressed from authoritarian governments in the early nineteenth century to strong liberal democratic movements by the end of the century. By the early twentieth century, most Latin American countries had embraced the open markets and democracy. These institutions were not strong enough, however, to withstand the social and economic pressures of the Great Depression of the 1930s.

The concept of the Americas as a new world of freedom came to the fore with the revolutions of the early nineteenth century, led by men like Simón Bolívar, José de San Martín, Bernardo O'Higgins, and Francisco Santander. The revolutions, however, were stillborn, since they were led by an aristocratic elite that generally took an authoritarian approach to governance. The new republican governments in Latin America meant that the oligarchy could maintain power without obeisance to the Spanish crown rather than granting liberty and a voice in government to the racially mixed citizenry.

Simón Bolívar, whose daring and imagination captured the spirit of the region, was more troubled about Latin American–U.S. relations than the turmoil in Europe at the time. He was skeptical of democracy and the future of South American–North American relations. Moreover, his view was the reverse of Jefferson's, as his attitude toward the United States reflected the oligarchical and authoritarian attitudes of the Spanish hierarchical social structure. "Do not go to the United States," he warned. "It is omnipotent and terrible, and its tale of liberty will end in a plague of miseries for us all." While Jefferson and Adams projected an uncertain future for liberty in "priest-ridden societies," many of the emerging Latin American leaders disdained liberty as a disruptive force in society. When Bolívar called an hemispheric conference in 1826 to unite both Americas, he agreed only reluctantly to invite the United States, commenting that it would be like "inviting the cat to the mice's party."

Bolívar's pessimism about the United States was matched by his cynicism about Latin American unity. Observing internal bickering, power struggles, and provincialism shattering his dream of unified South America, he pronounced Latin America "ungovernable" and added his memorable phrase that "the man who serves the revolution is plowing the sea." Octavio Paz, a Mexican philosopher-poet, took this a step further when he described the leaders heading the independence movements of that period as incapable of consolidating anything but themselves.

The ensuing events reveal the complexity of the relationship between South and North America. South and Central America, which comprised eight nations when President Monroe recognized them in 1822, split into eighteen nations within a few decades. With the threat from the Holy Alliance subsiding, the "latent anarchy of the colonial regimes," as described by one historian of the time, flourished. Alternating bouts of despotism and civil war depleted the countries' energies, and the tropical climate barred most of the region from benefiting from the Industrial Revolution. Indeed, if it were not for the invention of air conditioning, which changed the demography of the world, Latin America could well have remained an industrial backwater.

Beginning in the twentieth century, these patterns rapidly changed. As Europe sank deeper and deeper into chaos, Latin America began to experience the same wave of immigration from Europe as did the United States. Immigration was an important influence in accelerating the transformation of the region. Refugees from Hitler's Germany, Mussolini's Italy, Franco's Spain, and East Europe flocked to the region to live or as a way station until they could obtain a visa to the United States. The arrival of these educated people began to inject new life into industry. While the unrelenting heat and climate in these days BAC (Before Air Conditioning) restricted their ability to manufacture and compete, they were among the first global entrepreneurs when the economies began to expand after World War II.

The immigrants from diverse cultures, one of the driving creative forces of the culture presently emerging in the United States, never acquired the level of influence in Latin America as they did in the United States. Most of the Latin American countries reacted to the deep ethnic divisions within their indigenous communities with policies more akin to the apartheid policies of South Africa than to the exclusionary conflicts of Europe. Such policies discouraged migration, which was part of the reason that—except for those escaping from Europe in the 1930s—the countries of the Americas have not become a haven for migration as the United States has.

The convulsions that tore Europe apart in the first half of the twentieth century turned it inward and resulted in a dramatic decline of European influence in Latin America. It became abundantly clear to anyone alive at the time that Europe was no longer an example to emulate. After the war, the leaders of Europe were totally absorbed in rebuilding their devastated societies and had neither the interest nor the resources to pay attention to other parts of the world. Its colonial empires were dismantled, and Europe busied itself coping with the new management and production giants coming from the United States. Aided by the rapidly expanding reach of the new communications media and Hollywood, rock and roll replaced the European influence throughout the Americas.

3

U.S. Security

Shifting Realities

IF IMMINENT THREATS to the nation's physical security were among the foremost concerns of our founding fathers, and the almost continuous wars to frustrate authoritarian powers determined to destroy democracy dominated the twentieth century, the twenty-first century will test the United States in more dramatic ways. Today, as always, the nation's physical security is a priority, but for citizens living in the twenty-first century, the United States appears to be a world unto itself. By the 1990s, conflicts in foreign countries posed no physical threat and, in many ways, seemed peripheral to daily life. The appalling attacks of September 11, 2001, changed that. For the first time, the security of the continental United States was breached in a manner that forever changed the sense of invulnerability that dominated strategic thinking of the twentieth century. Today, we realize that globalization applies to chemical, biological, or nuclear weapons that can cross national frontiers almost as readily as can capital or technology. This new dimension of security for the United States means thwarting the use of those weapons as much as it reflects the traditional concerns of preventing hostile powers from gaining control of areas near U.S. borders or of resource bases that could threaten the survival of friendly democracies.

Accordingly, our attention has come to be dominated not only by aggressive nations but also by fanatic, anarchical terrorist groups possessing weapons of mass destruction or resources that can be planted in our midst, abusing our own open institutions. Rapidly evolving transportation and communication patterns are producing new security priorities. Routes for infiltrating instruments of mass mayhem, including biological and chemical weapons, run through neighboring countries. The stability of those countries and their ability to afford adequate, effective security forces are real concerns. Not only do conflicts in other parts of the world continue to loom as potential breeding grounds for wider conflict, but global poverty and desperation generate alienation among angry and fanatic people who feel they have little to gain from existing institutions and little to lose from venting their frustration. The objective of a foreign policy that protects long-term U.S. interests in this environment must both neutralize so-called rogue nations and influence the evolution of the world in which multitudes of disenfranchised persons, gradually awakening through mass communications, can have hope for prosperity and achievement. This is the "new world" that our policies must address.

Among the changes in the global economy during the last several decades, three are pivotal to our relations with the nations of our hemisphere. The first is the end of a century of hot and cold wars pitting major powers against each other, thereby removing the main sources of tension in the world and one of the principal sources of tension between the United States and Latin America. The end of these wars has freed economic resources needed for the development of our societies, most of which had been diverted too long by the exigencies of global warfare. In the new world, the waning influence of the defense industries has been offset by rising liquidity in international financial markets.

The second major new factor is technology. As it relates to security, the advance of global technology has put power and weapons in the hands of stateless, formerly isolated, criminal organizations. The Internet and low-cost communications and travel enable widely separated cells, whether international terrorists or domestic insurrection groups, to operate as integrated fighting units. Within the Americas, the Internet demonstrates that no place is off limits to the advance of technology. The military dictators who dominated Latin America in the 1970s learned the hard way that technology thrived best in the hands of the private sector and that they had to embrace private enterprise if their countries were to benefit from competitive technology.

The third component of this equation is the realization of viable open markets. This, together with democratization, is directly linked to achieving real benefits from human creativity and the advance of technology. Technology and research thrive only in stable societies in which creativity is rewarded and all people have an opportunity to develop their talents. The benefits of this creativity will be greatest in open markets with a global reach.

In short, whereas the old world order tried to defend against physical threats of armies crossing frontiers, the new world order seeks to protect against attacks by alienated minorities and rogue states that lack the power for sustained aggression. Whereas the old world order tried to isolate production within national borders, the new world order seeks to promote open flows of information, technology, and capital across frontiers. Whereas the old world tried to protect markets, the new world seeks to reduce the costs of production through the international division of labor. Whereas the old world order was oblivious to the global environment, the new world order recognizes that our grandchildren may have a much harder life unless we respect it.

SECURITY ISSUES FOR THE TWENTY-FIRST CENTURY

Several years ago, speaking at a Lions Club luncheon, I was engaged in a debate over the goals of U.S. foreign policy. The variety of opinions expressed were mostly motivated by traditional fears and the imperative of physical security. Predictably, the only consensus was on the priority to protect the nation's physical integrity. But many of the people attending also were committed to a perceived humanitarian obligation and thought the United States should nurture the spread of democracy as the ultimate long-term component of security.

The most vehement disagreements emerged when I asked *how* we could best protect our security. Everyone agreed that a military shield was necessary. But was it sufficient? What were the real sources of insecurity? Most recognized that long-term security depended on a more tranquil world that respected the rule of law. They concluded that ultimately such a world would result only from improving economic conditions. The United States and the world would be safe only to the extent that our foreign policy was successful in helping build confidence and tolerance among groups with historic rivalries and channeling them into more productive enterprises.

How can the United States help achieve this? Can we do it alone, or do we need to cooperate with other nations? While most of the people at the luncheon considered some form of multilateral cooperation necessary, they disagreed on how to go about it. Some considered formal cooperation through international organizations to be indispensable.

Others resisted relying on formal international institutions in which decisions could be dominated by "foreigners."

These questions are not trivial. Security issues, as I noted earlier, were the basis for the creation of the United States in the first place. They were uppermost in the minds of James Madison, Alexander Hamilton, and John Jay when they wrote the *Federalist Papers* to convince their countrymen of the merits of a union of states. They defined the rationale of unification to an eager but skeptical citizenry in 1788 by focusing on security as the most important reason for the states to unite and cooperate. This counsel was given under the adverse geopolitical circumstances they faced, a world in which their only protection against oligarchies with almost unlimited resources in arms and wealth was the isolation imposed by a wide ocean. John Quincy Adams warned against an America that would exhaust its meager resources if it ventured abroad "in search of monsters to destroy," which would, he continued, "involve the United States beyond the power of extrication in all the wars of interest and intrigue, avarice, envy and ambition" that pervade the world.

These conditions have changed dramatically. Our resources today are the most powerful in the world. The United States' military superiority, combined with the physical expanse of our territory, the vastness of our natural resources, and our demonstrated ability to dominate modern technology have helped end the squabbling among the European powers. We may remain unchallenged for the foreseeable future by governments that might decide to wage war, but as the events of September 11 reminded us, the "monsters" now have easy access to our midst. Today's frontierless societies would astound even President Adams.

THE NEW NATIONAL SECURITY: NOT BY ARMS ALONE

Given the tangible security threats facing the Western world in the twentieth century, foreign policy experts correctly considered Latin America as marginal to U.S. interests. The evolving global economy of the twenty-first century, however, is very different. Instantaneous communications and ease of transport bring new factors into play. As Alan Greenspan, chairman of the Federal Reserve, observed, "The United States cannot be an oasis of prosperity in a world of financial turmoil.

We have an enormous stake in the stable development of the rest of the world." In 1996 the Presidential Commission on America's National Interests emphasized several factors affecting the consolidation of a democratic government and a relevant foreign policy. The commission declared that the future of democracy made it a national priority to "prevent the catastrophic collapse of major global systems: trade, finance, markets, energy systems and the environment."

Only a few decades ago Henry Kissinger advocated a balance of power based on the interplay of multiple instruments ranging from psychological to physical force. But in the world of tomorrow, economic power will be decisive. In economics, the evolution of the global connection was slow in coming, but its impact is now upon us. For a country that contains 4 percent of the world's population and produces 25 percent of the world's goods, the political and economic health of foreign countries affects us in profound ways. The sustained growth of the U.S. economy in the twenty-first century and beyond will relate more to our success in selling goods of value to other nations than to the expansion of our domestic market. Conversely, poverty in other nations will impede growth and leave pockets of envy and alienation that technology will feed with new and cheaper weapons. Global production and communications mean that other parts of the world can affect the way each of us earns our living, the products we produce, the prices we pay for the products we consume, and the entertainment we enjoy. Indeed, the global network of culture, commerce, and conflict is the heart of the web of influences that touch every part of our personal and national existence. The issue will be how to make the transition from a Kissingerian traditional balance of power based primarily on military capability to effective power in which skill in the boardroom and communication with the public determine the outcome. It is in that transition that Latin America will become a strong asset for the United States.

The Americas are very relevant to the new security threats, international crime and terrorism, which were revealed to the United States on September 11. We learned that individual acts of terrorism can flaunt frontiers and reach into the core of our nation. The new dangers cannot be compared with the brutal wars of the past but may be far more devastating and debilitating to freedom and democracy. No longer do we have the luxury of dealing with a clearly defined, visible enemy. The need to contain these threats requires strong attention to routes of vulnerability and our core alliances.

The events of September 11 were foreshadowed by former U.S. Secretary of Defense William Cohen, who warned in 1999 that our vigilance against those who seek to inflict damage on the United States "will require greater international cooperation, intelligence collection abroad and information gathering by law enforcement agencies at home." He added,

> The race is on between our preparations and those of our adversaries. We are preparing for the possibility of a chemical or biological attack on American soil because we must. There is not a moment to lose. . . . The United States now faces something of a superpower paradox. Our supremacy in the conventional arena is prompting adversaries to seek unconventional, asymmetric means to strike our Achilles heel. At least 25 countries, including Iraq and North Korea, now have—or are in the process of acquiring and developing—weapons of mass destruction . . . [and] arsenals of smallpox. . . . And looming is the chance that these terror weapons will find their way into the hands of individuals and independent groups—fanatical terrorists and religious zealots. . . . This is not hyperbole. It is reality.[1]

Shortly afterward, a new book from China on modern warfare listed more than twenty different types of unconventional warfare and argued that "the more complicated the combination—for example, terrorism plus a media war plus a financial war—the better the results." If the rules of war were set by the West and "if you use those rules, then weak countries have no chance. But if you use nontraditional means to fight, like those employed by financiers to bring down financial systems, then you have a chance."[2] Future threats to security, indeed, will be very different.

In addition, the enormous amounts of money controlled by criminal elements today threaten the stability of global financial management and the banking systems, as the Chinese strategists noted. Criminality organized to avoid or thwart the rule of law is now a major threat to stability in developing democratic nations. The anarchy that has overtaken Colombia as a result of its drug wars is an example of how national authority can disintegrate and vigilante paramilitary groups can be created by fearful citizens who are determined to defend themselves in the face of lawlessness.

The challenge confronting us was outlined by Senator John Kerry in his book *The Next War*. He offers what he believes are conservative estimates that far more than $400 billion of illicit money circulates annually in the various money centers around the world. According to reports presented to the U.S. Senate, "Drugs are the single best selling product in the world today, netting by *conservative* estimates $420 billion a year or, more realistically, $1 trillion. . . . And the numbers are growing. As the market expands, the drug trade is changing from top to bottom [and] power is being consolidated at each level."[3] We now know how the radical terrorists in Afghanistan took advantage of our own financial institutions to bring violence into our midst. The drug kingpins have long exploited our rules regarding privacy and the complexity of our financial system. They secure their transportation and distribution networks by using money and violence to corrupt governments and subvert civil authority in smaller countries.

Senator Kerry points out that in many foreign jurisdictions, "the air force allows use of their landing strips; air traffic controllers protect shipments and flight plans. The police, too, are cooperative. . . . Many of their highly touted seizures of drugs were prearranged with the cartels."[4] Because governments cannot control the flow of private capital, they also cannot stop the flow of illicit goods or the laundering of money. Indeed, most of the money is laundered in the United States, where most of the illicit gains originate, and we have been unable to stop it.

Laundering money takes many forms, some even constructive. Before the Cali cartel in Colombia was dismantled, it had a record of public philanthropy that put the rest of the Colombian private sector to shame. The cartel financed health clinics and built schools and other buildings. Anyone who has admired the marvelous restoration of the colonial city of Cartagena, Colombia, or wondered how the massive building spree was financed in remote La Paz (Bolivia) or Panama in the midst of the debt crisis will recognize the work of money laundering. One of the classic ways to clean money is to buy land and pay construction workers in cash. At the end of the process, the launderer will own a legitimate multistory condominium or office complex, ready to collect legitimate rents.

Technology will be the ultimate facilitator or frustrator of international crime. In either case, the United States will be at the center as the principal exporter or victim of criminal activity. Former Attorney General Janet Reno once commented that a major concern of the Department of Justice in the future will be stopping computer hackers in Calcutta from robbing a bank in Ohio, or stopping Iraqi hackers from paralyzing a country's computer network. The United States is developing the capacity to defend itself from most of these threats. A more serious problem for global stability will be those same hackers robbing banks in Bolivia and Burundi.

The only meaningful protection against cross-border terrorism and crime will come from nations collaboration for the common purpose of defeating them. Our policymakers recognize this, and efforts are now under way among nations using Interpol. Long-term security, however, will require collaboration to foster prosperity and address the sources of poverty, the breeding ground for alienation. Achieving this globally is an important objective, and achieving it among democracies and in Latin America is a real possibility. Far more can be done to combat crime in nations committed to democracy with well-defined interests in trade and economic growth than in corrupt oligarchies with no mutual interests except money and power.

Cleaning up the breeding grounds of crime in the Americas will be far less costly and more constructive than taking direct action against organized criminal syndicates. Our record in Colombia is a good example. Congress felt compelled to approve an appropriation of $1.3 billion in 2000 to combat a drug-driven insurgency in Colombia after a misguided U.S. policy to ostracize Colombia helped weaken the Colombian government to a point of collapse in the 1990s. The unrelenting campaign by the United States to destabilize the elected Colombian government, refusing to "certify" it for three years, seriously damaged its ability to discipline its hard-pressed, underfinanced security forces. It opened the way for criminal organizations to earn enormous sums of money through kidnappings and bank robberies. Today, strengthened guerrilla groups have entered into an unholy alliance with the drug industry, providing them with resources for insurrection and crime. While I was the U.S. director of the Inter-American Development Bank, I was instructed to vote *against* a loan to combat the influence of drug cartels by providing alternative employment opportunities to poor farmers in Colombia because of our decertification law. Today, the $1.3 billion appropriated for reinforcing the Colombian government is four times more than all the development assistance we give to all of the

Americas. At that time, a more intelligent effort to strengthen the antidrug efforts would have cost a fraction of that amount. If citizens can earn a decent standard of living without drug money, their chances of resisting temptation are far greater than if they are poor.

DEMOCRACY: THE NEW NATIONAL SECURITY

Consolidating democracy in the world in the twenty-first century is an unprecedented challenge. A unique insight into the factors influencing its development may be found in an analogy to Albert Einstein's law of energy. His simple equation, $E = mc_2$, energy as the product of physical mass times the square of the velocity of light, contains elements of the same forces, but of a different kind of energy, with which democracy will have to contend. With considerable license, I would adapt the underlying premise of Einstein's law of physics equating the energy of a society to the mass of people (m) and the velocity of communications (c). If we multiply the size of the population by the velocity of the speed of their access to information and education, we will get a fair estimation of a society's potential creativity and energy. The corollary, however, is more relevant to our discussion. The larger the mass of people that have access to information without concomitant education, the more explosive the mix will be. For a society to be viable, citizens receiving education and information must have an opportunity to participate in government and a chance for social mobility. The only practical application of these factors is democracy.

First, new democracies trying to consolidate their institutions have a much different task from that which faced the founders of our republic. A vigorous civil society is vital to the integrity of a democracy today, but civil society can also make demands that a country has no means of addressing. These demands produce pressures for immediate action that are unprecedented in human history. Whether this anger is reflected in the mobilization of protesters at the World Trade Organization meeting in Seattle or the organization of *campesinos* in the coca-producing areas of Bolivia, it can be communicated more rapidly and organized more effectively than ever before in history. With the increasing fluidity of people and commerce, far broader and more self-aware constituencies and interests make participation in government essential and consensus tenuous. Considering that most nations of the world have yet to undergo the transition to democracy, the world of the future will continue to be a tinderbox.

The intellectual ferment spurred by the continuing advances in communications will penetrate every level of every society whether or not governments want it. Instability will continue to plague many areas of the world as people grapple with the information revolution and the yearning for fairness in government. In turn, political instability will nurture lawlessness, and technology will put new weapons in the hands of the discontented. Latin America has long had to live with the violence and terrorism that struck the United States on September 11. In the United States today, the vulnerability we feel for the first time is what many countries of the Americas have felt for decades in the war against drugs and the struggle for a fairer society. International commerce and the supply of natural resources will continue to be at risk of disruption, as occurred in the Middle East during the oil embargoes of the 1970s and the Gulf War of 1990.

Second is the issue of limited resources to address the enormous social demands in a participatory democracy. Competition for investment and the ease of hiding capital mean that democratic governments will continue to have difficulty raising taxes. Democratic governments must respond to the needs of their population, which means hard choices in allocating resources to attract investment, create jobs, and provide education, heath care, and social services. The cost of building a road or a port is just as expensive, maybe more so, in Colombia as in California. Security, whether internal or international, is costly.

Third is the chasm between the rich and the poor, both within countries and between developed and developing countries. Lord Acton, a geopolitical philosopher of the nineteenth century, observed that the most formidable enemy of democracy is the ignorance and superstition of poor people craving a better life. For the Americas, social problems rooted in poverty, disparities in income, and lack of education limit the ability to create productive jobs in the modern world. Poverty's real danger to democracy is its impact not on the poor but on the educated young and intellectuals. Shimon Peres, the former prime minister of Israel, explained: "Crime comes from poverty; fanaticism comes from poverty, drugs come from poverty, terrorism comes from poverty."[5] Almost all the tangible threats to our domestic economic and social fabric derive from people, especially educated people, alienated by the lack of opportunity.

Fourth is the issue of accountability. Poor, uneducated people relentlessly bombarded by information that they cannot digest are easy targets for the unscrupulous. This is one reason for the growing cynicism about democracy in the Americas. Although representatives are elected, they end up representing no one but themselves. Given the complexity of decision making in a democracy, irresponsible politicians have many opportunities for personal gain. Unaccountable leaders can disregard the cost of social repression or international conflict. When people such as Saddam Hussein decide to invest in missiles instead of food for children, *they* are starving the children, and the children have no recourse. When unaccountable politicians divert money from education for corruption, *they* are stealing from the social improvement of their people. In societies with large, uneducated populations, as we have in the twenty-first century, charismatic but disreputable political leaders have new and unprecedented temptations to defraud their people.

Fifth is international crime and narcotics traffic, which not only undermine democratic leaders but also lead to violence and personal insecurity. This, in turn, diverts resources from the social issues needed for economic growth and open markets. Such pressures are almost impossible to handle in new democracies under siege from the drug lords, especially small countries with meager tax bases. The equipment and logistical capabilities of the drug forces are generally far more sophisticated than those available to the governments that are responsible for protecting their citizens. Moreover, the drug industry is extremely wily and mobile, always seeking the weakest link. Under pressure in one locale, it moves to another. In the last decade, the base of cocaine production moved from Peru and Bolivia to Colombia and is now in the process of moving back again as pressure mounts in Colombia. In the Americas, it is clear that we will defeat the drug mafias only through concerted action. It is of a magnitude and importance for the survival of democracy to demand an effort with the same intensity and collaboration that NATO had for the cold war.

Sixth is a more subtle problem. Whether or not democracies wage hot war, they never stop waging economic war. International relations in the twenty-first century will thus be what they have always been throughout history: competition for economic advantage, but without the convenience of armies to back up a nation's claims. Like people, countries and corporations all abide by the same rules. Income must be balanced with outgo. If small countries want to buy the products of technology—whether automobile parts, aircraft, or computers—they must have hard currency to pay. This means that they must be able to sell something to earn hard currency. The corollary is equally important. If we in the United States want to export our high-tech goods to buy oil or gold, we must be certain that other countries can earn the dollars to pay for our products.

The significance of these factors is changing along with the issues generating conflict among nations. Our foreign policy officials must keep up with these changes because the spread of democracy worldwide is important to the United States. Democracy makes a substantial difference in the behavior of states in the international arena. Consensus building discourages impulsive action on any issue. "All politics is local" applies as much to Brazil and Bangladesh as it does to Massachusetts. We also know from experience that democratic values are meaningful and that open, inclusive, accountable political systems that respect minorities and reflect a plurality of interests are better global citizens. Respect for human rights derives from respect for the laws and is a product of the rule of law.

For this reason, democracy is the most important instrument to ensure security in the Americas—and everywhere else. We will both feel and be safer in a world that shares democratic values. President Bill Clinton's idea of "democracy enlarged," rooted in the policies of his predecessors, placed a high priority on bolstering democratic government throughout the world to meet new and as yet unimagined challenges. The consolidation of democracy in the Americas will ensure that the values of our society—respect for human rights, the rule of law, the machinery to effect social change without violence, economic growth, and the protection of the global environment—dominate the governance of our global economy.

In short, the paramount long-term interest of the United States is to build the bases of democracy in the world and a coherent system of commerce among nations that will encourage enterprise and economic growth. Unaccountable authoritarian regimes sooner or later breed corruption, which inevitably explodes and creates major setbacks to economic growth. Stagnant economies cannot make headway against poverty. And the battle against lawlessness, crime, drug traffic, illegal migration, and a deteriorating environment simply cannot be won in societies in which poverty and its product, corruption, prevail.

Clearly, the first line of action for the United States and the other nations of the world promoting freedom, democracy, and open markets relates to the strength of the U.S. domestic economy. This is our principal asset and the cornerstone of a viable foreign policy. President Clinton observed that

> in this new era foreign policy and domestic policy are increasingly intertwined. For us to be strong at home, we must lead the world. And for us to be able to lead the world, we must have a strong and dynamic economy at home and a society that is addressing its problems aggressively and effectively.[6]

However, as Cormac McCarthy observed, the joinery is complex. We must learn to relate economic growth in the developing world to our own interests. Security for the world increasingly depends on security for the United States. The nuances are frequently obscure. For years the United States ignored economic issues in the Americas and supported dictators because we thought it served our interests in blocking communism. By the 1960s, though, we began to realize how counterproductive that policy had been. Today, we are doing the same thing in the Middle East in the fight against terrorism. One hopes that it will not come back to haunt us, as did our support of the Somozas and the Trujillos, as the tensions resulting from the desire for a voice in government spreads throughout the world.

To protect the U.S. economy, it is equally important to protect our allies' economies. The economic fallout in the Americas of the September 11 attack were devastating. Tourism, imports, and remittances abroad from families all fell. The inevitable spread of U.S. economic distress to the other countries of the Americas destabilized their vulnerable economies, put increasing pressure on democracy, and threatened to increase the drug trade and illegal immigration. In the future, such destabilization of neighbors will also destabilize supplies of resources for our industry, market share in the global competition, stability in global capital flows, and open markets.

The next major region of the world committed to adopting democracy is Latin America. But this democracy is being challenged by the same lawless elements that attacked the United States on September 11, 2001. The countries of the Americas do not have the economic or tax base to enable their people to rise out of poverty and defeat the drug peddlers who are undermining confidence in democratic leadership. Only by working together will we meet these challenges. To the extent that democracy is consolidated in our hemisphere, we strengthen our protection of democracy and respect for the rule of law and human rights everywhere.

DEMOCRACY: LATIN AMERICA'S ELUSIVE LINK

Latin America's experience with a decade of military dictatorships beginning in the mid-1970s was one of the bleakest periods of Latin American history. The repression of dissent affected almost every level of society and every country, and thousands of people, mostly young university students, simply disappeared. By the mid-1980s, the people of almost every country in Latin America rushed to embrace democracy. The newly independent nations of the English-speaking Caribbean never had this experience of repression and never wavered from their commitment to democracy. In Latin America, however, the arrogance of the military regimes perpetrated one of the most brutal repressions of social dissent since the days of Adolf Hitler. Their grip weakened as economic conditions worsened in the debt crisis brought on largely by inept leadership. At that point, Latin America entered a new chapter of its history.

As we enter the twenty-first century, democracy in the Americas is again faltering. Open markets and economic reform have failed to deliver on the promise of a better life. Unemployment is at the highest level in history. The collapse of Argentina's economy even after adhering to the International Monetary Fund's monetary prescriptions sent shock waves through the region's intellectual community that were almost as profound as the collapse of the Soviet system. The failure of economic reforms and their insensitivity to social issues have produced cynicism and declining confidence in the capacity of democracy to manage social change.

Recent polls of Latin Americans demonstrate a growing impatience with their elected leaders' ability to address issues of security and bring economic prosperity. Only 34 percent are satisfied with the functioning of democracy, while 80 percent consider that corrupt politicians are the most serious problem for the survival of democracy. Although an overwhelming majority still consider democracy preferable to any other kind of government, the number has fallen sharply since the early 1990s. Thirty-one percent of the people now consider themselves politically right of center, compared with 24 percent only five years ago. In contrast, those who see themselves as left of center declined from 20 percent to 14 percent.[7]

One reason for this change is that the countries have embraced open markets but have failed to take seriously the need to respect the rule of law and the critical role of a viable institutional infrastructure to ensure fairness and accountability. Widespread corruption and the pursuit of self-interests by private-sector and public-sector employees alike have severely eroded confidence in democratic institutions. In addition, changing demographics, rapid urbanization, and universal access to information have touched every country. Urbanization throughout the region is one of the highest in the world: more than 70 percent. And the more ambitious of the poor migrate to the United States, legally or illegally, to the promise of jobs and freedom from government repression.

As long as the poor remained predominantly rural, as they did throughout history, their isolation and conservatism were notorious. They resisted changing their diet no less than their politics. But with the beginning of the twenty-first century, they and their children have become urban dwellers. The lack of education in an isolated rural community has produced a predominantly timid, religious, largely obsequious population. The motto was "Always smile at the man with the gun." Their demeanor and attitude, however, change rapidly in the city, especially of those born in the urban slums. The urban environment has weakened family and religious ties, and uneducated children are vulnerable to populist appeals. Disillusionment with political corruption and alienation because of the sense of unfairness make for a political tinderbox.

The disruption of democratic governance in the future will not come from the overthrow of a democratic government. It will come from the distortion of the institutions by populist leaders that use the institutions of democracy for autocratic power. It will come from "democratically elected" strong men who give lip service to democracy but tolerate corrupt and inept officials that perpetuate social inequities. Sooner or later these explode. And when they do—at least in the Americas—the United States will be among the first to feel the shock waves.

In short, Latin America is far from a democracy based on respect for the rule of law. Their laws benefit their elites and leave little for their poor. Without confidence in the fairness of its institutions and respect for the rule of law, democracy cannot be sustained. Corrupt governments cannot foster democracy. Inept governments cannot address the potential and promise of global markets. Unaccountable governments cannot create democracy. Economic growth cannot be sustained in such an environment. Market failure is inevitable wherever democracy fails.

It is now clear that the market reforms urged by the United States and the developed nations are important but inadequate for building democracy alongside economic growth. There is little question that economic reforms to create an environment for investment and productive employment are essential to provide an escape from poverty. To strengthen confidence in democracy, however, free-market reforms cannot ignore the large constituents that live outside the economic mainstream. The reforms must be implemented with great sensitivity to social realities. Although the market can produce goods, it cannot address social issues emanating from a grossly unequal distribution of income and weak basic government services for health, education, and personal security. Although investment will come to small countries only through an economic system that allows them to produce for larger markets, the stresses produced by these reforms affect primarily the poor and disadvantaged. Economic adjustments impact many protected interests and especially affect the job security of the middle class. These imbalances must be addressed, or a loss of confidence in the reforms will risk a severe backlash.

The real promise for democracy in the Americas is in stronger institutions and professionalism in the civil service, as is beginning to be achieved in some of the larger nations and throughout the Caribbean. This is reflected in the increasing self-confidence of the stronger democracies and in regional cooperation to protect democratic institutions. The Organization of American States' Inter-American Democratic Charter, signed, symbolically, on September 11, 2001, calls for the exclusion of and sanctions against any government that does not come to power by way of democratic procedures. While a wave of dismay spread among the government of the Americas when the United States appeared to renege on this commitment in the attempted coup in Venezuela in April 2002, it was significant that all the other nations of the hemisphere joined together to condemn the attempted disruption of democratic continuity, despite their misgivings at the perceived violations against democratic freedoms by the Chávez government itself.

The commitment to democracy has been reinforced in many places and many ways. Members of the Mercosur Common Market declared democracy as a unconditional requirement for membership, similar to that of the European Union. Brazil and Argentina earlier demonstrated their commitment by taking strong action against recent threats to a democratic succession in Paraguay. Similarly, democracy will benefit from a NATO-like determination and coordinated mobilization of resources to defeat the drug trade.

The real test, however, will be the negotiations for a free-trade agreement of the Americas. The economic adjustments required by institutionalizing free trade between the most developed and the least developed economies in the hemisphere will place enormous stresses on the poorer countries and their nascent democratic institutions. The Europeans were extremely sensitive to this disequilibrium in planning their European Community. They established a special fund to assist the poorer countries—Spain, Portugal, Greece, and Ireland—to enable them to compete on a more equal basis. The Americas have even greater disparities. The achievements of a free-trade agreement for the Americas will indeed be for naught if at the same time they undermine confidence in democratic institutions. It is in the interest of the United States to make certain that this does not happen.

4

The Emerging
Inter-American Partnership

THE MEXICAN PHILOSOPHER OCTAVIO PAZ described the contrasting stereotypes of the Americas. North Americans, he asserted,
view themselves as realistic and practical people and regard Latin
Americans as romantics and idealists. The Latin Americans, however,
see the reverse, considering themselves as the realists and the North
Americans as the romantics.

Paz explains the differences by pointing to the realities of their lives.
Latin Americans perceive North Americans as idealists who think all
problems can be solved, that people can do anything to which they set
their mind, and that the world can be made a good place. Latin Americans, in contrast, see human motivation and behavior very differently.
They consider human motivation and the environment to be violent
and corrupt, but they accept that and manage their lives accordingly. To
North Americans, the apparently self-centered approach of many Latin
Americans and the absence of a strong feeling of civic responsibility are
detriments to development. To Latin Americans, this is not alienation or
fatalism; it is simply realism, a recognition of the way the world works.

For years many U.S. citizens have objected to what appeared to be
hypocritical, authoritarian, inward-looking, and often corrupt Latin
American societies. The stereotypical U.S. views of Latin Americans
that they are unrealistic, romantic, authoritarian, and corrupt is an odd
variation on Thomas Jefferson's observation about a "priest-ridden
people." Latin Americans consider North Americans as hypocritical in
their moralistic attitudes toward others yet permissive in their conduct
at home. The United States assumes that the pervasive poverty and unequal income distribution in Latin America means an absence of social
responsibility, but actually Latin Americans are obsessed with fear and
anxiety over their social problems and try to alleviate poverty with government intervention and subsidies instead of an open society.

Mystics take a different but equally fatalistic view. An artist friend from Buenos Aires once asked me why anyone would try to improve things in Argentina. "Any country existing under the configuration of stars that are over Argentina," he mused, "is hopeless." Not being an expert in astrology, I was unable to evaluate his opinion. But his frustration was real. Both observations, his and those reported by Paz, reflect attitudes toward government that consider civic initiatives futile, that whatever happens is either just the way the world is or it is someone else's fault.

These views form one of the great enigmas in the United States' understanding of Latin America: the contrast between the stronghold of authority compared with what appears to be cynicism toward the underpinning of democracy: the rule of law. A Spanish friend once described the perpetual tension between the readiness of the Spanish to embrace authority contrasted with the fierce individualism of the Spanish settlers and their lack of trust in the state. Despite Spanish traditions of deference to the state, he considered that the distrust of authority permeated their being, just as it did in North America. The family had always been far more important than public institutions. Trust and loyalty were almost total within the family but were given only sparingly to anyone outside it, including institutions. In any conflict between the rule of law and the interests of the family, the family came first.

The difference in the origins of the settlers of the two continents is one explanation of the contrasts. North America was settled by people escaping oppressive governments, all of whom harbored deep suspicions of government. These settlers from different groups, though all were relatively equal in power and independence, were vastly different from the relatively homogeneous societies from which they came. In North America, for the first time, different religious and cultural elements trying to live together had to have democracy. They used their distrust of authority to raise the rule of law to a higher plane, as the only way their divergent interests could be reconciled peacefully.

Latin America, in contrast, was settled by wards of the Spanish monarchy. These settlers had no conflict with Spain. Whereas the United States was populated by people of many different religions fleeing persecution in Europe, Latin America had but one overwhelmingly dominant and authoritarian religion, Roman Catholicism, the religion of the Spanish state. There was little competition of ideas. Indeed, given the difficulties of communication, the region was relatively isolated from the revolution of ideas that were spreading in Europe in the wake of the Industrial Revolution.

Even the wars of independence in Latin America in the early nineteenth century were different from the American Revolution. These were not a broad-based revolution seeking freedom for the people, but insurrections of the local ruling elites that saw an opportunity to wrest power away from a weakened Spanish monarchy struggling on the Continent against Napoleon. These elites merely substituted their own statist oligarchies for the Spanish statist colonial government. Simón Bolívar's frustration with the inability to create a union of the various new Latin American republics was attributed to the fact that, separated by large swaths of uninhabited land, each republic had its own elitist power structure. In addition, the generally hot and humid climate slowed the development of industry. Until the advent of air conditioning it would have been impossible to establish a competitive industrial plant in the south. Air conditioning fundamentally changed not only the continent's economics but also its demographics. But even if the climate had been more hospitable, the countries earned so much from their export of raw materials, especially gold and silver in their early history, they had little incentive to develop their manufacturing capacity. Their abundant exports enabled them to import everything they needed. In other words, Latin America began as an extension of an authoritarian, statist government in league with an authoritarian religion in an environment that was flush with wealth, and it remained that way right through independence.

The sources of poverty and the disequilibrium in Latin America's social structure can be traced directly to the attitude of the Catholic Church in the region's early history. In the United States, the Native American communities were completely segregated—in every sense of the word—while a homogeneous society evolved among the white settlers. Native Americans were relocated to barren pieces of land called reservations, and their isolation was rationalized by calling them "sovereign nations" within the United States. The white settlers' need for farm labor was not considered in their policies toward the Native Americans. Where extra labor was required, the settlers preferred slaves imported from Africa.

Spain's policy toward Latin America's native indigenous communities reflected the policies of the church, whose missionary zeal embraced the indigenous people as souls to be saved. Rather than keep them outside society, the church saw them as creatures of God and tried to bring them into the church. Although the Spanish saved their souls, that was about all. They used their labor but left them uneducated and poor. Thus the natives who had been integrated into the settlements became a perpetually destabilizing element. This segment of the population, analogous to slaves in the southern United States, was a vital part of the economic structure but a marginal part of the legal structure. A permanent underclass—in many countries, a majority of the population—with neither a voice nor a vote in governance, they were a constant threat to the elites.

The Latin American elites are well aware that the society constructed by their forefathers kept much of the population from sharing the economic benefits of the state. For their part, these outsiders saw the state as the controlling force against their anger at being forced to live in poverty. Because they were not slaves, as in the United States, an authoritarian structure was the most practical means to control them. Physical power was needed and respected, but it undermined the rule of law. In short, Latin America did not have poverty because of its authoritarian government. Rather, it retained its authoritarian government because of its poverty, which it felt helpless to alleviate and preferred to ignore.

The differences between authoritarian control and individualism were apparent on every level. In the beginning of their history, the Latin Americans' acceptance of authoritarian governance for the purpose of maintaining social order contrasted with the anarchy that prevailed under the superficial state control of the economy. The colonial state maintained itself by collecting import and export duties and appropriating its portion of the share that was owed to Spain. No salaries were paid to the governors of the Spanish colonies. The crown expected them to take care of themselves by subtracting part of the remittance to the crown for their own welfare, with only a veneer of accountability. As long as the regents received their portion, they had few qualms about their subordinates and the other elites appropriating theirs. Thus while they seemed to embrace the authoritarian rule, they also only superficially deferred to the rule of law.

The Latin Americans' relationship to the Catholic Church was similar. While giving lip service to the church, most people disregarded the church's teachings, especially their application in society. This was mirrored in the national sport of avoiding taxes, disregarding the poverty surrounding them, and turning a blind eye to the arbitrariness or un-equal administration of justice. How many of the society, not only the oligarchy, preferred to bribe and buy favors rather than adhere to a transparent, fair regime? Indeed, this was authoritarian security with almost anarchical license for the elites.

The colonial governments' mercantilist roots resulted in Latin Americans generally considering the state as the principal actor in the nation's economic life. This aspect of the complex interrelationship of the individual and the state continued virtually unchanged until well into the twentieth century. New influences flooded in after World War II, especially in the 1960s, when President John F. Kennedy pressed hard for the ideas of representative democracy, social and economic partici-pation, and a voice in government in the Alliance for Progress. Just as quickly as those ideas began to permeate the society and new voices began to be heard from the young people and the poor, there was a strong reversion to even more repressive authoritarian government. The dictatorships of the 1970s were a direct result of this conflict be-tween fear of the implications of the poverty in their midst and the rec-ognized need to come to grips with the underlying social tensions. As a result, large sectors of the population opted for the perceived shelter of the authoritarian state. The combination of political fears, economic pressures, social tension, and traditional mercantilism joined to pro-duce the economic nationalism and central-planning policies that dom-inated the thinking of the post–World War II generation. This mixture created an environment in which governmental intervention spread to all aspects of economic activity. By the early 1980s the continent was dominated by dictatorships controlling almost all economic policies.

A LONG-TERM LOVE-HATE RELATIONSHIP

A Brazilian friend of mine once observed that the trouble with the United States was that "you always want to win five to zero." Why not a U.S. policy, he asked, that allows the Latin to win one or two games but the United States wins the title? It is clear that both the United States and Latin America will have to work hard to overcome the prejudices and preconceptions generated many years ago.

The roots of this resentment are well established in the historical record and are reflected in the erratic U.S. policies toward the region. As

I noted earlier, during most of its history, the United States ignored the other nations of the Americas, and when it paid attention, it was more frequently to intervene or to exert pressure on behalf of U.S. commercial interests. This attitude was reciprocated by Latin Americans who looked mainly to Europe for both commerce and culture, and most of the Caribbean countries were British, Spanish, or French colonies. Until the twentieth century, Latin America was richer than the United States and predominantly a European enclave. The influence of the United States has always been marginal, its interventions almost exclusively in the Caribbean basin. Even so, until recently the Latin American intellectual tradition had only disdain for the United States.

This attitude was reinforced by the United States' behavior during the twentieth century. Its policies swung wildly from strong interventionism to a total lack of interest in the region. After World War II, the favorite sport of Latin American intellectuals was finding ways to blame the United States for all the region's problems. Even today, anti-American resentment can be found among many sectors of the population. It can be detected in the rhetoric of President Hugo Chávez of Venezuela, the unabating harangues of Fidel Castro, and the ferment of anti-elitist guerrilla movements.

Notwithstanding the complex relationship, as a people we have always been extraordinarily comfortable with each other. U.S. citizens who go to Latin America are quickly intoxicated by the spirit and warmth of the people. In private, however, they deplore the lack of seriousness and the presence of corruption in doing business.

Latin Americans have similarly ambiguous feelings about the United States. They enjoy coming here for the material goods, comfort, and friendliness of the people, but they resent the attitude that Hispanics are second-class citizens. Most of all, they resent the perceived hypocrisy of U.S. policy, which they consider overly moralistic toward Latin culture while being strongly permissive at home.

Nonetheless, Latin Americans admire and have affection for the people of the United States. Almost every poll in Latin America shows the United States as the most admired country. Even today, the greatest ambition of many Latin Americans, rich or poor, is to go to the United States. This is the ultimate poll: people vote with their feet. The implication is that even though our relations deteriorate from time to time, they quickly rebound when U.S. policy changes. When U.S.-Latin American relations hit rock bottom after the spate of unilateral interventions in the 1920s, they quickly rebounded with Franklin D. Roosevelt's Good Neighbor policy. John F. Kennedy's Alliance for Progress was put into place shortly after the United States' "covert" intervention in Guatemala in 1954 and the stoning of Vice-President Richard Nixon in Caracas. Relations quickly surged once again despite the remonstrances of Fidel Castro. In short, the complex relationship is undergirded as much with admiration as with resentment.

THE EVOLVING INTER-AMERICAN RELATIONSHIP

On June 27, 1990, when President George H. W. Bush proposed an almost revolutionary new plan for expanding trade and investment in the Western Hemisphere, he did so with little fanfare. His plan, known as the Enterprise for the Americas initiative (EAI), was designed to meet the new global economic challenges facing the nations of the Americas and to help them emerge from the debt crisis by pursuing a growth policy. It offered a significant package of economic benefits to the nations of the Americas in return for strong measures to reform their economies and open their internal markets to foreign investment and trade. The reward for each country that undertook these reforms was to be a bilateral trade and investment agreement with the United States. The president offered to enter into trade consultations and negotiations immediately, with a view to concluding such agreements, according to a State Department official, "with our ultimate goal of a free hemispheric market."

While very little was heard in the United States about the Enterprise for the Americas Initiative, the other nations of the hemisphere took very seriously the goal of free trade with the United States. It quickly became the motivating force for opening societies to democracy and markets to private investment. Nearly every nation of Latin America and the Caribbean signed up. Within the first year after President Bush held out the carrot, seven nations—Bolivia, Chile, Colombia, Costa Rica, Ecuador, Honduras, and Mexico—had signed preliminary investment agreements. (Bolivia and Mexico signed even before the policy was formally announced.) Other countries rapidly got in line, and a new openness toward the United States began to permeate the region. Argentina's President Carlos Menem seized the moment to form close ties with the United States and even joined in sending troops and supplies to various international hot spots at the United States' request. Brazil, however, which had also maintained close ties with the United States, began to be concerned about U.S. economic influence extending further into South America, which it seemed to covet as its own market. Brazil thus rushed its plans to consolidate its role in its neighbors' markets by combining forces with Argentina, Paraguay, and Uruguay to form a South American common market, Mercosur, and even began to speak of a South American free-trade area, to counterbalance U.S. initiatives in the north.

President Bill Clinton's decision shortly after the 1992 election to press forward with the North American Free Trade Agreement (NAFTA), gave bipartisan substance to President Bush's initiative. His decision to hold a presidential summit in Miami in 1994 and to advocate a broader free trade area for all the Americas took the initiative to its next logical level: periodically holding summit meetings of the American nations' heads of state. The seeds of this initiative, as I noted earlier, were planted in the first meeting of the American nations in Washington, D.C., in 1889, when the Pan American Union was created. It was reflected in Woodrow Wilson's Pan American Pact, Roosevelt's Good Neighbor policy, Kennedy's Alliance for Progress, Ronald Reagan's Caribbean Basin Initiative, and Bush's Enterprise for the Americas Initiative. Today, President George W. Bush has enunciated his intention to give the Americas top priority in his administration.

The relationship between Latin America and the United States was strengthened in 1995 when President Clinton took one of the most daring steps in the history of U.S. relations in the Americas. After the monumental effort that went into securing NAFTA, the collapse of the Mexican economy in early 1995 aborted any further action to expand the effort. Prompted by the analysis of the then undersecretary of the treasury, Lawrence Summers, the president approved an unprecedented $40 billion financial package to rescue the Mexican economy.

On the one hand, the 1995 financial rescue of Mexico gave substance to the rhetoric about a new breakthrough in the United States' relations with the Americas. The rescue was somewhat reminiscent of the challenge confronting the Allies after World War II. After the experience of World War I that left a defeated, destitute Germany facing an impossible financial burden with reconstruction and reparations, the

Allies knew that there was no better way to court trouble from their neighbors than to leave them in poverty. The huge sums of money from the Marshall Plan that were directed to reconstruct the devastated Axis powers after the war enabled the people to rebuild their lives and promoted production, creativity, and trade that gave rise to one of the most prolonged periods of sustained prosperity the world has ever known.

The first Mexican crisis in 1982 replayed the lesson of World War I. With the United States ignoring the potential repercussions of the financial collapse, a depression engulfed all of Latin America. Then the failure of the U.S. government and commercial banks to act, as we will discuss in more detail in the next chapter, caused a downward spiral in the economies of Mexico and of all of Latin America. In contrast, the $40 billion rescue package of the Clinton administration in 1995, taken at enormous political risk, underscored the administration's understanding of the earlier experience and the importance of the region's prosperity to the United States. The bailout, however, effectively precluded any further initiatives for a hemispheric free-trade area until the results of the rescue effort were clear.

The complexities of the United States' relations with Latin America were compounded by the Democrats' loss of Congress in 1994, which touched off a battle for the future of the U.S. political machinery. With the attitude and declarations of the new Republican majority led by Newt Gingrich, this political battle placed domestic issues front and center. Winning back Congress became the *only* issue for the Democrats. In their view, no less than the entire future course of the nation was at stake, and no talk of Latin America or free trade would be allowed to interfere.

When George W. Bush was elected president in 2000, he went out of his way to make an unusually strong commitment to the hemisphere. His first state dinner at the White House was for Mexican President Vicente Fox. At the presidential summit in April 2001, Bush reaffirmed his commitment to the agreement for free trade throughout the Western Hemisphere by 2005. While the Bush administration has been diverted by the conflict of terrorism and the Middle East, the record is one of growing bipartisan support from three consecutive U.S. presidents who see our nation's prosperity and domestic problems as linked to the prosperity of the entire Western Hemisphere.

Congress's passage of trade promotion authority in 2002 offers, for the first time in a decade, the prospect of realizing a free-trade agreement for the Americas, at a propitious time. Overcoming the economic crisis in the Americas created by the recession in the United States and the reverberations of the financial collapse in Argentina are the first challenge for the United States, Latin America, and the Caribbean in the twenty-first century.

5

The Trauma of the 1980s

THE MODERN HISTORY of Latin America begins with the debt-induced depression of the 1980s. When Carlos Menem was elected president of Argentina in 1989, inflation was so far out of control that his predecessor, President Raúl Alfonsín, had given up and left office five months ahead of the end of his term. His economic team was unable to stem the hyperinflation, approaching an annual rate of 5,000 percent. Nothing worked. Municipal services were failing; streets were unclean; electricity was constantly cut off; commuter trains frequently broke down; and phone service was virtually nonexistent, with a three-year wait for a new telephone.

President Menem and his finance minister, Domingo Cavallo, did what every expert considered virtually impossible. They stopped inflation dead in its tracks. Within a year it was down to single digits, accomplished by tying the Argentine peso to a rigid plan that prohibited the government from printing money unless it was backed by hard currency reserves. Public enterprises were privatized with immediate improvements in services. Power plants were built, trains cleaned up, and telephones installed in days. Until the fallout from the Brazilian financial crisis and currency devaluation in 1998, the economy was growing at a robust rate and making inroads into reducing poverty. Unfortunately, though, the restrictive Argentine currency regime could not adjust after the Brazilian devaluation, and the peso soon became overvalued, exports collapsed, and unemployment soared. Wary investors held back as they lost confidence that the government could hold the line with parity. The new administration of President Fernando de la Rua was unable to attract investments to reduce unemployment, and in 2001, the system failed.

The story was similar in Peru. Inflation also raged at almost 3,000 percent after the inept, allegedly corrupt, administration of President Alan García saw prices rise in the late 1980s by almost 1 million percent over a period of five years. As a result, in 1990 an unknown academic of Japanese descent, Alberto Fujimori, was elected president over the famous novelist and conservative, Mario Vargas Llosa. The economic chaos also had fueled a strong insurrectionist movement, the Shining Path (Sendero Luminoso), that now controlled much of Peru. Each year, almost five thousand persons were killed in political violence. Antidrug efforts were stymied by allegations that Peruvian government officials themselves considered the income from cocaine sales necessary to support the economy.

In Nicaragua, the virtual collapse of the economy under the weight of the civil war fought between the Sandinista regime and the "contras" left the country with an $11 billion debt, the highest per capita debt of any nation in the world. Given the opportunity for elections, the Nicaraguan people rejected the Sandinistas and chose as president a moderate, conciliatory woman, Violetta Chamorro. She brought peace and civility to the political discourse. In succeeding elections, the Nicaraguan people continue to chose new presidents from the right of the political spectrum, from Arnoldo Alemán in 1998 to Enrique Bolanos in 2002. Alemán declared that he intended to "run Nicaragua like a business, not a private estate,"[1] a statement that has been the subject of much controversy.

These changes must be seen in the context of the economic evolution of the last forty years. When President John F. Kennedy assumed the U.S. presidency in 1960, Latin America had a rural economy firmly in the control of a regressive rural oligarchy that was land rich but capital poor. There was virtually no entrepreneurial private sector, no reliable banking system, and no tax system. Only a small group of taxpayers, mostly multinational companies, and import duties were underwriting entire societies. Argentina, for example, had fewer than twenty thousand people on the tax rolls. The private sector saved little and had no significant capital accumulation, both necessary for domestic investment.

The roller-coaster history of Latin America in the last half of the twentieth century was the shared responsibility of the region's unrealistic ambitions and the greed of a complacent, protected private sector. In the 1970s, Latin America was the favorite place for U.S. commercial banks to send their money. Chase Manhattan Bank's president, David Rockefeller, repeatedly extolled Latin America as the world's most promising market for U.S. business. Walter Wriston, president of

Citibank, was equally ecstatic. He never tired of telling the U.S. banking community about the benefits of the global financial markets and how Citibank was taking the lead with ever larger portions of its annual profit derived from its Latin American business. Indeed, in 1976, Donaldson, Lufkin and Jenrette, a Wall Street investment-banking firm, commented that "lending in and to the lesser developed countries has accounted for a significant portion of the asset and earnings growth for Citicorp, BankAmerica, First Chicago and other large U.S. banks in the last five years."[2] Not only did they earn large commissions and fees which fattened their balance sheets in the year the loans were made, but Latin America's financial record in the 1960s seemed relatively safe.

Under President John F. Kennedy's Alliance for Progress, the countries began to put into place strong measures to help move their economies into a constructive development cycle. They all agreed to have their economies reviewed annually by a group of donor nations and the international banks who would provide external resources. At the time, only Europe, using the machinery established for the Marshall Plan, had done anything comparable to this extraordinary and elaborate procedure. The so-called Inter-American Commission for the Alliance for Progress (CIAP, for its Spanish acronym) was given the authority to evaluate each year each country's economic performance and external financial requirements. This became known as the annual country review and also became the fulcrum of the Alliance and the principal mechanism that gave it multilateral substance.

The reviews brought together representatives of all the national and major multilateral lending agencies to hear the presentations by the countries' top economic teams. Each country presented specific projects that would benefit development. Government expenditures were held in a tight grip, and there was hope that corruption would be discouraged if not prevented. The Alliance was a revolutionary development in international transparency and responsibility, and its recommendations deeply influenced the decisions of lending agencies such as the U.S. Agency for International Development, the Inter-American Development Bank, and the World Bank. In 1966, the United States adopted as part of its Foreign Assistance Act a provision that a recommendation from the CIAP be mandatory for bilateral loans under the Alliance. The most impressive aspect of the procedure was that it was accepted by all the countries with little fanfare. The U.S. public, however, was hardly aware of the revolutionary procedures under way.

At the beginning of the Alliance, most of Latin America's borrowing went into relatively productive enterprises. In Brazil, dams, power stations, and roads were built. In Argentina the money went to automobile plants, new farmland, and housing. In Mexico, roads, communications, schools, and housing all were paid with project-oriented loans. Led by teams of development experts, the infrastructure for modern industrial states quickly began to emerge. New projects, new investment, new middle classes, and new entrepreneurs were sprouting everywhere. Ted Moscoso, who ran the Alliance for President Kennedy, repeatedly emphasized the importance of the economic infrastructure that was being built with the borrowed money. It would pave the way for accelerated investment by opening new territories and providing energy and transportation links. Most of all, the infrastructure would help build a middle class that was expected to be the bedrock of Latin American democracy and social change.

By the 1970s, largely as a result of the investments during the Alliance years and the confidence that the United States had finally become a dependable partner, Latin America had the highest growth rate of any area of the world. The confidence generated by the Latin American economies' strong performance excited everyone. But then they became reckless. The period that began with so much promise soon deteriorated into huge fiscal deficits and public mismanagement as money poured in and the Alliance for Progress disintegrated in the wake of the Vietnam War. Leaders began to indulge in economic fantasies that disregarded the fact that their economies were moored in primary commodities, always dependent on the demand of the developed economies which swung between cycles of boom and recession. Leaders and lenders alike failed to accept that because the economies were still insufficiently diversified or integrated into the value chain of the productive cycle, indebtedness in hard currencies was risky. As Enrique Iglesias, president of the Inter-American Development Bank, pointed out, this was a period in which Latin Americans were far too tolerant: tolerant of mismanagement, tolerant of inflation, tolerant of lack of productivity. Another observer commented about the time that "we were not underdeveloped countries; we were badly managed countries."

THE DREAM DISSOLVES

The real legacy of the Alliance, which is frequently overlooked, was the enormous confidence it inspired in the financial community. But this confidence was ultimately the Alliance's undoing. Commercial banks began to flood the region with loans. In the rush to recycle the petrodollars coming from the Middle East after the oil price rise in 1973, all the disciplines and cooperative mechanisms were jettisoned, and the Alliance for Progress was dismembered.

> Now the elaborate infrastructure for national planning and cooperation established as part of the Alliance was no longer necessary. No one had to go to any inter-American conferences or meetings. No inter-American agencies, integration of markets, or national plans were required. All that an astute minister of finance had to do was to go to his neighborhood bank and sign a loan. It literally rained money in Latin America in the 1970s. In short, with the influx of commercial loans in the 1970s, the inter-American infrastructure of the Alliance went down the drain, not because of its failures but because it became irrelevant.[3]

Projects that had started with prudence and planning under President Kennedy's Alliance for Progress, which allocated the then unprecedented sum of $20 billion over ten years, were suddenly awash in new, unanticipated finance from commercial banks. Latin America received $200 billion over the next decade, as the ensuing debt attested. The new money came with no objective other than to earn commissions. Too much money was chasing marginal projects, generating enormous waste, and leading to corruption. According to Antonio Ortiz Mena, who was president of the Inter-American Development Bank during this period, "Never before had any region benefitted from such a large scale infusion of financing—a good part of it on very liberal terms."[4] The entire infrastructure that was built with such care under the Alliance soon fell into disuse.

In the 1970s, two events destroyed Latin America's economic policies. First, the oil price shocks of 1973 and 1979 radically changed the economic picture. Countries that formerly had a relatively balanced economy, as was the case in Central America, suddenly were no longer economically viable. The products they exported could not pay for the goods they had to import just to keep the machinery running. Second came the inflation and soaring interest rates in the United States. In the bountiful days of the 1970s, Latin America had agreed to the new concept of "floating" interest rates on their loans. Before 1970, banks made loans at fixed rates. If they made a loan at 6 percent and the cost of money fell to 4 percent, the banks made extra money; and if the cost of money rose to 7 percent, the banks lost money. Debtors could calculate their exposure, and the banks were subject to the normal business risks of their lending decisions. Then in 1972, President Richard Nixon cut the dollar loose, and all exchange rates began to float. So did interest rates.

At first, it seemed to make little difference. But when interest rates rose to 20 percent in the late 1970s, Latin America had to borrow ever more furiously to maintain what became an unrealistic standard of living. Suddenly, Latin America governments were caught in an impossible squeeze. Almost all their hard currency earnings had to be used to service their debt. In the mid-1980s, the official transfer of capital out of Latin America to banks in the developed countries just for debt service reached a negative balance of $30 billion per year. The World Bank reported that between 1983 and 1988, Latin America paid $160 billion more to the developed world for debt repayments than it received from it in new credits. In other words, instead of investing in development, Latin America's limited resources were being paid out to the developed countries. And this did not even include flight capital.

Attempts to achieve economic stability came at the price of social stability. At one point, the percentage of Latin America's gross national product committed to debt service was 8 percent, triple Germany's 2.5 percent which sank its economy after World War I. In Latin America, factories were being closed overnight without any notice to the workers at the same time that the U.S. Congress was debating a new law requiring a sixty-day notice before a factory could close. Latin American workers also had no social safety net or unemployment insurance.

At the same time that most of Latin America's new loans were going to pay interest on their old loans, their trade surpluses were evaporating as oil price hikes put their trade accounts into deficit. Instead of adjusting to the new realities and trying to live within their income, the Latin American nations continued living as though they were still rich. They kept their currencies overvalued and insisted on maintaining the expansionist development policies they had adopted in the 1960s.

Before the collapse in the 1980s, dollars were the cheapest thing anyone could buy in Latin America. As local prices and profits increased because of domestic inflation, exchange rates were kept fixed at artificially high rates. This meant that foreign products could be purchased for less and less of the local currency. Rodrigo Botero was the finance minister of Colombia in the early 1970s while the country tried to adjust to the exchange rate to keep up with internal inflation. He explained that the psychological reaction to devaluing the local currency was so negative that it was political suicide to take it on. Countries like the Dominican Republic and Guatemala, which for decades had prided themselves for keeping their currency at par with the dollar, began to suffer severe distortions. The Dominican Republic's coins were the exact same size as U.S. coins and so would work in U.S. vending machines. Suddenly a thriving business emerged in buying cheap Dominican coins and selling them in the United States.

The distortions from overvalued money pervaded almost every country and brought new windfalls to the elites. Imported luxury goods became cheaper, requiring less local currency, and exports became uncompetitive because they required far more dollars to cover the rising cost of the peso. For example, in Argentina in 1982, one U.S. dollar was worth two thousand Argentine pesos. Given the inflation rate in Argentina, the true value of the dollar was closer to five thousand pesos. When the Argentine industrialist Amalita Fortalbat shocked the art world by buying a painting by Turner at auction in New York for the record-breaking price of $7 million, it was more a reflection of the exchange rates than of the value of the painting. In proportionate terms in Argentine money, it was the equivalent of about $2.5 million, calculated in overvalued pesos. Argentines thought little of shuttling back and forth to Europe and the United States on shopping sprees. I began to suspect things were awry when I suffered the reverse phenomenon. I received only two thousand pesos for my U.S. dollar, which translated into five dollars to launder a shirt in a Buenos Aires hotel in 1982. If a more realistic exchange rate of five thousand pesos to the dollar had been in effect, that same laundered shirt would have cost me two dollars.

Historians may argue about the reasons for the demise of the Alliance for Progress but the United States' interest in it quickly faded after President Kennedy's assassination. President Lyndon Johnson made Latin America a low priority as his attention became monopolized by the Vietnam War. President Nixon adopted what he patronizingly called a policy of "benign neglect," an effort to distance himself from any of Kennedy's policies. He totally discarded the carefully built machinery of the Alliance. In my view, however, the real dagger in the heart of the Alliance was wielded by the commercial banks that swamped Latin America with money and turned a blind eye to accountability. They bear the major responsibility for the ensuing debacle. It was like taking an alcoholic to a free bar. The banks knew that the governments were weak and that enormous quantities of money were flying out of Latin America almost as soon as they signed their loans with the governments. They knew because they handled the money coming out on the round trip. In a discussion on debt relief proposals in the 1980s, after the collapse, one banker told me that he would never agree to debt forgiveness. He knew that Latin Americans had plenty of money because his bank handled much of it. Donald McGough, at the time the senior vice-president of Manufacturers Hanover Bank, was vehement. He was familiar with the accounts that some of the Latin American government and military officials had in his bank. There was no way he would agree to concessions that would adversely affect his shareholders and depositors when these people had the wherewithal to alleviate the conditions in their countries. The United States knew this. The central banks and the private sector of Latin America knew this.

The debt negotiations with Latin America were less about finance in Latin America than they were about power and the financial condition of U.S. commercial banks. The banks were loath to submit to strong-arm tactics by countries they felt had mismanaged their economies and showed no signs of better management. At the same time, the countries chafed at the banks' intransigence. In retrospect, the fiscal performance of Latin America's leaders was better than that of the commercial banks in the years preceding this period. The countries had accepted unprecedented discipline under the Alliance for Progress. Although the Alliance's goals were overly ambitious and many fell short of their lofty aspirations, the region began a profound transformation because of them. Roads were built; schools and health programs accelerated; and training programs provided skilled workers. The trends were going in the right direction. The banks, on the other hand, made loans for questionable projects without regard to fiscal discipline, accountability, or ability to repay.

By the 1980s the fragile balance was overwhelmed by the severe recession that hit the United States, combined with soaring interest rates to stop what was called *stagflation*. Ballooning fiscal deficits and rising inflation spurred by the oil price shocks of the 1970s were aggravated by public mismanagement. The greatest shock came in 1982 when Mexico announced to a stunned financial community that it was unable to service its debt. Depression, both economic and psychological, gripped the region. The middle class collapsed, and poverty rapidly spread.

With the economic depression of the 1980s, everything imploded. The new international terms of trade dictated by rising oil prices destroyed the economic equilibrium of the small countries of Central America and the Caribbean. In an attempt to maintain a standard of living that had suddenly become untenable, they borrowed even more. Drained of all hard currency to service its debt, the region received almost no new capital inflow in the 1980s. In addition to debt service payments, capital flight left the governments virtually bankrupt. Byzantine structures that were built to prevent the outflow of capital also discouraged the inflow of capital for investment. Worse, capital controls and the need to get government approval for currency transactions opened the way for unprecedented bureaucratic corruption, which undercut all enterprises, among the poor and middle class as well as the rich. The tighter the rules were, the higher the bribes that were needed to get around them.

CAPITAL FLIGHT AND PEOPLE FLIGHT

There is an old story about a company that calls in management consultants to find a way to increase its lagging productivity. The consultants advise that providing background music for the workers would improve production. The company marvels at this easy and inexpensive solution. Remarkably, productivity increases almost immediately. After a few months, however, it slacks off to its old levels. The company calls in another expert, who tells it that the music has become distracting, that the company should shut it off and that then productivity would increase. The company does, and productivity goes back up again. But once again, after a few months, it returns to its old levels. In desperation, the company calls in yet another consultant who tells it that music generally works but that it was probably playing the wrong kind. The company changes to more lively music, only to find the same result, that productivity soars for a few months and then slacks off. The company finally catches on. Change it seems—any change—captures people's attention and increases activity. But once they get used to it, old habits reemerge and take over.

This tale is a backdrop for what happened in Latin America in the last half of the twentieth century. The increased demand for raw materials in World War II saw a spurt of economic activity which almost immediately diminished when the war ended. Then the end of colonialism in the 1950s and 1960s again spurred investment in the emerging economies. Because many of the nations were just gaining independence, they sought a fire wall against being overrun again by their former masters under the guise of free flows of capital. The newly independent states thus adopted systems of rigid state controls. The new leadership perceived foreign capital and open markets as very real dangers that would perpetuate the foreign domination they had fought so hard to overcome. The mentality that gripped the developing world rapidly spread to Latin America. Even though every kind of bureaucratic control and governmental intervention were imposed on the economies of the developing nations, the economies seemed to thrive. For a while. But once the novelty was gone and the initial profits were skimmed off, capital flight began.

Ironically, as in the case of the music in the manufacturing plant, Latin America enjoyed one of its greatest economic growth spurts under the now reviled protectionist policies of the 1960s. The changes in that period were made by a group of economists led by Raúl Prebisch of Argentina, who gave his policies the shorthand name of *import substitution*. The concept was not new but simply meant that Latin America's infant industries were to be nurtured and protected from competing exports until they were financially stable. Every industrial country in the world, including the United States, had adopted similar policies in the early stages of industrial growth.

The "import substitution" policies, like the music in the factory, did help the domestic private entrepreneurial class establish a foothold. At the beginning, the protected economies sparked a positive reaction from the multinational companies and generated investment by companies that could no longer export to the local market. The multinationals showed themselves remarkably adaptable, and many new brands were sold under local names. In Brazil, the British American

Tobacco Company began marketing Souza Cruz cigarettes; Esso petroleum was Creole in Venezuela; and food and consumer multinationals began to produce under local brand names.

Infrastructure had a similar story. Major investments in roads and power were needed, but the local private sector had neither the accumulated capital nor the skills to make them. The decision to put government into the infrastructure business was made for two reasons: first, with no local capital markets, local capital accumulation was insufficient to finance the projects, and second, in theory it could be managed more equitably. For better or worse, the Alliance for Progress and the commercial banks also helped the Latin American governments create government-controlled industries that required massive capital inputs. Moreover, the foreign banks actively encouraged the state's role, insisting it give them guarantees that no private group in Latin America could offer. Ironically, because of this need, the foreign commercial banks played the most important role in forcing the Latin Americans to centralize power in the hands of the government, since they insisted on guarantees from the central government. With the central government guaranteeing every project, the predilection toward total state control was easily reinforced.

The impact of the new music wore off almost as quickly as it began. Overtones of the cold war soon crept in and infected perceptions. Protectionist policies became enmeshed in a quixotic fad to cast Latin America's lot with the newly independent states of Africa and Asia. Latin America chose to join up with the so-called Third World composed of other underdeveloped nations in the "nonaligned nations" and to restrict foreign investment. The basic mathematical precept that one hundred multiplied by zero equals zero had not been learned. The combined effect of the decision to make the law more inhospitable to investment has to rank with some of the greatest blunders of history. Before long the combined policies of import substitution and barriers to foreign investment virtually shut off all industrial modernization. It abdicated the developing countries' market share of the evolving global economy to the newly aggressive Asian tigers. The expansion of the Latin American economies came to an abrupt halt.

The real tragedy was the way that the wealthy Latin American private sector colluded with the new class of technocrats in the 1970s to keep out foreign investment. The rapid convergence of such disparate interests was unanticipated by the reformers of the Alliance for Progress. The new technocrats moved into office determined to reverse the local private sector's failure to modernize. They were obsessed by Latin America's adverse historic experience with their oligarchies and private sector, which they considered self-centered and corrupt and which they blamed for plundering Latin America's economy. Foreign investors, however, were considered even worse. They were seen as sharing the same greed and corruption and, in addition, making business decisions relating to their own shareholders that took no account of the country's needs. Serious articles were written about how the average Latin American would get up in the morning, brush his teeth with American toothpaste, eat American breakfast cereal, watch an American-built TV, call his office on an American-built phone, drive to work in an American car, use an American typewriter, and so and so on. The technocrats were concerned that local economies would be dominated by foreigners, that local entrepreneurship would be stifled, and that decisions concerning local production would be made in foreign boardrooms.

The reactions of Latin Americans at this time were not unlike those expressed in the United States in the 1980s against Japanese investment. The Latin American technocrats, however, took action to centralize control even more firmly in the hands of the state, helped, as we have seen, by the foreign commercial banks that needed the signature of a finance minister.

An unnatural alliance was gradually forged between the local business community and the bureaucrats. Under the guise of creating an environment more conducive to domestic investment, they established a new goal of keeping out the more efficient foreign and multinational companies that could produce at more competitive prices and were considered inimical to creating local employment. José Martínez de Hoz, Argentina's finance minister in the 1970s, argued against that view and asserted that Latin America would suffer in the long run from the most protectionist laws in the world: "There was no real competition. Manufacturers could get away with producing shoddy goods at exorbitant prices. They reaped huge profits with relatively little effort." To make matters worse, the banks gave them with loans so they did not have to put their own money at risk. The result, Martínez pointed out, was rich entrepreneurs and poor companies.

PROTECTIONISM IN LATIN AMERICA

In the late 1950s, a brilliant young economist from Argentina, Raúl Prebisch, appeared on the scene. Soon to become the towering figure of Latin American economic thinking, Prebisch was the father of "import substitution" policies. He conveyed his ideas as director-general of the United Nations Economic Commission for Latin America (ECLAC), arguing that "the only way Latin America could industrialize in an already technologically advanced world was to follow a path of substitution of imported goods with local manufactures." New industry would take hold in Latin America only if it were given relief from more highly developed foreign competition. He pointed to other industrialized nations that had had similar policies in their early years, including the United States.

At that time, Latin America and, indeed, most of the developing countries earned their living by exporting raw materials to the more industrialized countries, where they were fashioned into manufactured products. Prebisch predicted that this trend would accelerate under the prevalent economic patterns, with an increasing share of the value added in the industrialized countries. The plight of developing nations in a highly industrialized world, he believed, was substantially different from the development of the pioneering nations in the Industrial Revolution, which had had no competition from more efficient producers. The developing nations, he argued, might never be able to get a foothold in the industrialized world and were in danger of being shut out. The argument seems quaint in contrast to our current fears that with free trade, industry will fly to the developing countries where labor is far cheaper. When Prebisch spoke, the transportation and communications revolution that gave rise to dramatically different patterns and opportunities for the developing nations still had not taken place.

Prebisch's perceptions of the world's growing industrialization led him to believe that before long, the trend toward new materials and new production techniques would sharply reduce the demand for the raw materials produced in Latin America. His view of trade practices in Europe with its cartels and in Japan with its closed markets reinforced his thinking. The new phenomenon of the multinational or transnational corporation being pioneered by several giant U.S. corporations also was unpredictable. Thus, Latin America would lose on two counts. It would easily be blocked from industrializing, and the trends in the world economy would make less and less valuable the few products it depended on for an income. While he advocated capitalism, he called the condition of Latin America *periphery capitalism*, doomed to remain on the fringes and to be second rate, at the beck and call of the large concentrations of capital centered in the United States.

Prebisch's theories swept through business, intellectual, and governmental circles like wildfire. Give local industry a chance, he seemed to be saying, by closing out competition as soon as local production began. Thus, when a Brazilian company began to produce air-conditioning units, huge duties—sometimes 100 percent—were levied on all imports of air-conditioning units, which made attractive the price of the local product, inefficient though it was. In many cases, imports were simply shut off altogether. In other cases, such as the automotive industry, special incentives in tax and social legislation made the inducement to produce locally even greater. Indeed, it was hard to find a Latin American industry in the 1960s and 1970s in which one could not invest and make huge sums of money.

At the beginning, Latin America made considerable progress. With closed markets and profits virtually guaranteed, the international commercial banks came running to finance the new plants. The international bankers liked the closed, protected markets almost as much as did the Latin American entrepreneurs. The loan spigots were opened. Equity capital was minimal. Moreover, many of the plants were outfitted with older and competitively obsolete equipment sent from U.S. and European factories that were upgrading their own production. After all, if the market was closed and protected, the old machinery would work perfectly well. Thus, the system benefited everyone. No one considered that one day the markets could open and the profits would disappear without major refitting into more efficient and competitive operations.

The major flaw with Prebisch's analysis, with which he was beginning to come to grips at the time of his death in the early 1980s, lay in the remarkable changes that began to take place in the global productive chain, largely as a result of the revolution in transportation. It was totally unforeseen in the devastated post–World War II world that the much feared multinational companies would begin to formulate multinational production systems. Similar to the Marxists who embraced his theories, Prebisch did not—and could not—foresee that the multinational corporations would seek more competition for their components through global outsourced production and would adopt more progressive employment standards. International managers learned quickly that their stock prices were sensitive to labor or safety problems no matter where they occurred, whether it was in a sweatshop in Central America or a chemical plant in India.

Prebisch made another fundamental, and this time predictable, error. He totally underestimated the greed of the Latin American private sector once it was protected. Modernizing working conditions and production methods were disregarded with impunity. Inefficiency was rewarded with greater profits. Masked by the veil of Prebisch's economic theories, business leaders paraded behind the curtain of nationalism. The lucrative profits they reaped in closed, captured markets gave them plenty of extra cash to bribe public officials. Under a nationalist banner, they struck an unholy alliance with the far left. The cry of "keep out the foreigners" suited everyone, especially the protected entrepreneur. To the surprised satisfaction of many of the old-fashioned oligarchs, the left became their major ally in championing laws to prevent foreign ownership of businesses. In Mexico, fueled by its inherent fear of the United States, foreigners were prohibited from owning more than 49 percent of any businesses and could not own any property at all within twenty miles of Mexico's borders. Mexicans regarded these measures also as protection against a repetition of their experience with the loss of one-third of their territory to the United States in the nineteenth century.

Another element was equally decisive: a controlled media. In the strong, family-oriented, insular Latin American societies, each nation's small elites dominated its economic and political life. In these days before CNN, journalism was rudimentary as a profession, and the media were owned by members of the same elites. Public pressure to change conditions was nonexistent.

To be fair, Prebisch always insisted that his import substitution policies were meant to be for the short term, only until the basic elements of an industrial base were in place. But he suspected, as we all did, that once granted, these privileges would be extraordinarily hard to withdraw. They were hard to withdraw for the same reasons they were hard to withdraw in the United States and Europe in the earlier part of the twentieth century: the political interests they created as well as the hardships and unemployment that would result if economic adjustments forced open competition. Thus, instead of a first step on the road to "takeoff," the countries remained mired in primitive capitalism that continued in full force and vigor until the debt crisis made it implode.

Given the small and tightly controlled international capital markets at the time, import substitution cannot be called a complete mistake. It was a phase of development and it failed because of its unholy mixture with small, elitist, mercantile societies and because it did not insist that the societies use the time they were gaining to redress appallingly bad income distribution and social conditions, especially in education. The demise of import substitution came when the policies overstayed their usefulness.

In short, the protectionist polices engendered by import substitution became exhausted. Rather than altering them to open economies gradually once the industrial base began to take root, the small entrepreneurial elites which the policies had nurtured maintained their privileged protected position. They took advantage of the traditional statist approach to convince the bureaucrats that they needed more, not less, protection to survive. The result was the most protected economies in the world, which became increasingly uncompetitive and fostered a self-perpetuating, incestuous network of privilege and corruption.

At the same time Latin America was becoming more restrictive, the Asian nations were becoming more hospitable to business, providing all sorts of incentives and attractions for investment and export industries. The difference in the results was dramatic. In 1982 South Korea was more indebted on a per capita basis than the worst Latin American debtor. Yet its incentives for investment did not create a capital flight problem, and it steadily repaid its debt. That is, South Korea's policies created wealth inside the country, not outside it.

Latin America went in the opposite direction. The leftist rhetoric that its countries had been plundered by the foreign multinational companies caused Latin Americans to adopt increasingly stringent laws circumscribing investment and limiting the remission of capital and payments for royalties on patents and technology. Pedro Pablo Kuczinski, then cochairman of First Boston International and more recently the finance minister of Peru, blamed much of the problem on basic structural weaknesses such as the lack of capital markets or mechanisms to ensure the efficient allocation of capital. "Instead of encouraging investment," he said, "we did everything in our power to repel it. Investment policies were run by people who never made an investment in their lives, inadequately trained government officials who had learned about the world from books." Whether or not Latin Americans agreed, the reality of the markets was unchangeable. Investments are extremely sensitive to price and cost. The rules governing the ease of doing business as well as local taxes and other "payments" and corruption costs all figure prominently in the price competition calculated by every investor.

These were years of fantasy throughout the world, not only in Latin America. Academics and intellectuals everywhere talked about the north-south agenda and the north-south stalemate.[5] Neutralism and nonalignment, the catchwords of the 1960s, produced the "economic voice" of the poorer nations. The theory was that the world had to adjust to the needs of the poorer nations or be overwhelmed by the wave of resentment. Mexico's President Luis Echeverría took the lead in advocating a new international economic order, which became the subject of countless articles, conferences, and chest thumping throughout the Third World. New magazines appeared emblazoned with the word *South* and maintained that the industrialized North had to reverse its economic policies in order to address the concerns of the developing countries whose growing population would make them an irresistible power. In other words, the people who were inventing technology, and the companies that owned it, should channel it to the inefficient, corrupt bureaucracies of the poorer nations, as if pouring more resources into failed systems would somehow make them work. The naïveté of the perceptions for a so-called modern age was astounding.

In a remarkable performance demonstrating the new hubris, Mexico's finance minister, Ricardo García Sainz, came to the United States in 1978 and described Mexico's tightening of its foreign investment laws, which limited foreign investors to no more than 49 percent in any major company and restricted payments for royalties and licenses. "Yes, gentlemen," he proudly announced, "there are new rules to the game." He honestly believed that investment would come no matter what he did. The result was predictable. Those who owned the technology stopped going to Latin America.

It was a harsh learning experience. As their debt increased, the developing nations sank further and further into economic stagnation. They ignored the need to adjust to the evolving global economy and to penetrate the markets of the developed nations. They failed to in-

sist on more responsible and responsive and less corrupt governments. No amount of foreign aid could help under these circumstances. Unemployment soared, education deteriorated, new housing
ground to a halt, roads crumbled, health services collapsed. The
scarcity of hard currency prevented manufacturing plants from importing needed spare parts, much less modernizing. The stage was set
for a major overhaul of all aspects of governance and economic pre-
sumptions.

"THE WINGBEAT OF CAPITAL FLYING"

At the same time the commercial banks were increasing their cash flow
to Latin America, the wealthy of Latin America were taking theirs out.
The first wave was related mainly to a lack of confidence in the local
banks, the lack of alternative local investment vehicles, and the thin
capital markets. Savings in Latin America were at high levels at this
time; it was just that people put their savings abroad where their money
was safer and secure from currency devaluation.

The issue of capital flight is attributed to various forces. The first
was the lack of faith in the domestic banks' integrity. The second was
lack of confidence in the currency's integrity. Even with high interest
rates, a deposit could lose value if the currency was devalued at a
higher rate. The third force was the general perception of future risk. Alberto Grimoldi, an Argentinean investment banker, described the Argentinean economy in the 1980s as one in which no matter how money
came in, from either exports or foreign aid, as soon as it made its way
through the economy and wound up in private hands, through either
wages or consumption, it would flow out. The reason, he told me, was
that "so long as people think the future will be worse than the present,
they will protect their capital. The minute people feel that tomorrow
will be better than today, they will stop. The moment they regain confidence, it will start flowing back."

In the beginning, however, the capital did not fly. It was pushed.
The increasingly militant leftist nationalism generated insecurity in the
local markets. Several phenomena interacted to produce the downturn.
The bureaucracies' voracious and growing appetites led to greater government controls, putting a damper on entrepreneurial activity. New
political leaders like Fidel Castro in Cuba and old populist demagogues

like Juan Perón in Argentina inflamed the atmosphere, and authoritarian military governments began to experiment with the national socialist model of Egypt's Gamal Nasser. Anyone who had any money had only one choice: protect it by sending it abroad. The alternative was to see it gobbled up by insatiable bureaucracies or evaporate in surging inflation.

In addition, the prevailing policies advocated expropriation and nationalization based on the perverted theory that if the state owned the enterprise, the profits would stay at home. Draconian laws complicating foreign investment discouraged even the most loyal of Latin America's supporters. Latin Americans themselves could not invest. One Venezuelan businessman I knew wanted to invest in Ecuador to take advantage of the new economic integration incentives in the Andean Group. He lamented that the amount of paperwork to be filed for his small cross-border investment was so overwhelming that only rich companies and foreign multinational companies could afford the lawyers and accountants required to do it. The very laws designed to encourage Latin American investment were, instead, keeping it out.

As the nationalist policies gained momentum, the laws even restricted royalty payments for the importation of technology. Little thought was given to the fact that people and corporations, not governments, invented and controlled technology. Risk versus reward governed investors' thinking. In Latin America at this time, the risks were enormous and the rewards were diminishing. As a result, investments in technology turned to Asia.

These attitudes were not helped by the general perception throughout the hemisphere that the U.S. government did not care what happened in the Americas and, indeed, that many U.S. businessmen were in collusion with the corrupt Latin politicians. The legendary role of the United Fruit Company in Central America and the sordid stories of International Telephone and Telegraph (ITT) abetting the 1973 coup d'état in Chile rang true to most Latin Americans. Skeptics in the private sector figured that if a crisis came, the United States would do nothing. Ironically, it was evident even then that the real stabilizing force was U.S. policy, which had a profound effect on the private sector's attitudes and motivation. When the United States was involved in economic development, the private sector felt secure and kept up a reasonable flow of investment. When it felt that the United States was willing to let Latin America go down, it opted to avoid risks.

Everything happened so fast that few people were able to foresee what was coming. Almost all experts underestimated how price competition in the developed countries would keep forcing new capital investment in capital goods and an unending search for greater productivity. With Latin America closed and inhospitable to foreign investment, the large corporations turned to Asia. With little effort, Latin America could have had that investment if the governments had wanted it.

By the early 1980s in Latin America, any money that could not be used immediately in business had to be protected abroad. Any money left in banks would either depreciate rapidly or be vulnerable to the increasing appetites of the bureaucracies. There are no reliable numbers on the amount of capital that left Latin America in this period. In 1985 U.S. Secretary of State George Shultz told the Organization of American States General Assembly that the U.S. government estimated the amount of flight capital from Latin America had exceeded $100 billion since 1980.[6] By 1990, the estimates for the major countries were as follows:

Mexico	$84 billion
Argentina	$30 billion
Venezuela	$50 billion
Brazil	$25 billion

Source: Bank of Mexico, *Annual Report*, 1989,
cited in *Diario las Americas*, July 2, 1989

This adds up to $189 billion from just four countries.

To blame Latin America for its behavior here would be hypocritical. Nationals of every country try to protect and diversify their capital holdings. In the developed countries, it is called "investing" abroad. Moreover, for every Latin American who wanted to protect his capital, a U.S. bank was ready to take it and a U.S. law firm was ready to help. Many top bankers and attorneys in the New York financial community made a good living from helping Latin Americans get their money to the United States or Europe. Most of the schemes involved procedures that stretched, if they did not break, the law. Exports were overbilled and imports were underbilled, with the differences going into foreign bank accounts. One of the most common schemes took advantage of the accepted practice of paying commissions to "export sales agents" who were actually dummy corporations that Latin American exporters set up themselves. These so-called commissions went into their own pockets. Domingo Cavallo, the former finance minister of Argentina, never tired of pointing out that the more regulations that governments enacted to prevent capital transfers, the more fear they engendered in the private sector and the more ingenious ways that were found around them. Many of these ways pointed to public officials using the regulations for individual transactions and remittances abroad.

Throughout Latin America, bewildered politicians scrambled for solutions or colluded in corruption. Latin American governments listened to foreign and domestic experts of every stripe; they controlled prices, then they decontrolled them; they subsidized exports, then they took away the subsidies; they controlled exchange rates, then they went to floating rates; then back again. Peru simply stopped paying its foreign debt. One observer commented *in 1889* that

> Argentineans are always in trouble about their currency. Either it is too good for home use, or, as frequently happens, it is too bad for foreign exchange. . . . The Argentineans alter their currency almost as frequently as they change their finance ministers. No people on earth has a keener interest in currency experiments that the Argentineans.[7]

Norman Bailey, senior adviser to President Reagan for international economics on the National Security Council, quipped that it was a time in which any Latin American businessman had to be "schizophrenic, paranoic, psychotic, almost catatonic" to try to plan economic activity.[8] Government policies lurched from one extreme to another. The reality was that no one, neither banker nor economist, had the slightest idea of what to do to protect their capital. So they sent it abroad.

The United States' huge trade deficits pumped liquidity into the world markets and allowed many countries to run trade surpluses to help repay the ballooning debt. Brazil, Mexico, and Argentina all tried to enlarge their trade surplus by exporting more and importing less. At the beginning the banks put up more money. When the debt crisis erupted, Walter Wriston, the chairman of Citibank, noted that countries do not go bankrupt and recommended patience to see the crisis through. The logic of his accounting mentality could not be questioned. If the crunch was temporary, the banks could wait out the storm and keep their balance sheets looking good. New loans would be disbursed to Latin America, and the Latin Americans would use the proceeds to repay the banks, which would register their own funds now in their profit account. The game enabled everyone to gain time and keep the banks' shareholders' temperature down. But like a Ponzi scheme, it could continue only so long.

The loser was Latin America, which saw its $200 billion in debt in 1982 balloon to $400 billion by 1988 and got absolutely nothing out of it. Negative transfers of funds—the flow from the poor to the rich countries—reached almost $200 billion for the decade of the 1980s, with the high point of $50 billion in one year, 1988. Jesús Silva Herzog, a former Mexican finance minister, commented that at that rate, Latin America would have owed more than a trillion dollars by the year 2000 without having received one extra dollar to invest in development.

The major impediment to a more responsive policy was the overextended position of a few large U.S. banks, as can be observed in table 5.1. In 1982, the total equity capital of the major U.S. banks amounted to slightly more than $70 billion, in the face of the outstanding Latin American debt of $215 billion. The ratio of debt to equity was more than 300 percent. By 1987, the banks' equity capital had grown to $129 billion while their debt exposure had been reduced to virtually the same amount. The smaller banks were better at reducing their risk to manageable proportions. Most of the non–money center banks sold out their entire positions in Latin American debt, establishing their reserves and taking their losses. During this period, the smaller U.S. banks increased their capital to $78 billion while reducing their exposure to $32 billion. Professor Jeffrey Sachs of Harvard University strongly advocated the write-down: "The U.S. investing public doubted that the debts would be repaid in full," and he pointed out that the stock markets gave a much higher value to the shares of those banks that wrote off their debt.[9] Banks that wrote down their debt saw their shares on the stock markets valued at nine to fifteen times earnings, whereas those that did not were valued at only five to six times earnings. U.S. investors were not fooled. Minister Silva Herzog of Mexico explained that the Latin American finance ministers understood what was going on and were willing to cooperate in order to allow time for the adjustments to be made. But it had to be an interim solution until an equilibrium was established.

Table 5.1

Latin American Debt Exposure of U.S. Commercial Banks ($ billions)

| | 1982 | | 1987 | |
Type of Bank	Total Bank Capital	L.A. Debt	Total Bank Capital	L.A. Debt
Nine major U.S. banks	$29.0	$176.5	$51.5	$97.0
All other U.S. banks	41.6	78.6	77.7	31.9
Total	70.6	255.1	129.2	128.9

Source: Jeffrey D. Sachs, "New Approaches to the Latin American Debt Crisis," unpublished paper presented to Harvard University symposium, Cambridge, Mass., September 1988.

A closer look at the U.S. banks' predicament during this period is even more revealing. Of the $240 billion owed to the commercial banks, $200 billion was concentrated in five countries: Mexico, Brazil, Venezuela, Argentina, and Chile. All the other thirty countries of Central and South America and the Caribbean owed about $40 billion to the commercial banks, distributed almost equally among the United States, Europe, and Japan, hardly a life-threatening danger. Pedro Pablo Kuczinski commented that the banks selected their risks—they thought—carefully and put their money where they thought they would have the greatest gain and the least risk. This was in booming economies of Mexico, Brazil, Argentina, Venezuela, and Chile, all of which were developing capital markets. The banks paid scant attention to the other countries.

For the smaller countries, it was not the commercial banks but the governments of the developed countries that held most of their debt. Bolivia, for example, owed a total of $6 billion to foreign governments and international financial institutions (IFIs), while its debt to the commercial banks was only $600 million. The English-speaking Caribbean nations had a total of $8 billion in debt. Of this amount, $6.6 billion was owed to the official governmental institutions, and only $1.4 billion was owed to commercial banks. The Central American countries, excluding Nicaragua—which was a special problem because of its civil war—owed $11.7 billion, of which only $3.4 billion, or 25 percent, was owed to commercial banks.[10]

Ironically, the U.S. banks made another move during this period that helped the Latin American governments become even more statist and exercise greater controls over the private sector. In policies that would never have been tolerated in the United States, the U.S. government openly pressed the Latin American governments to assume responsibility for their private sectors' debts. In 1981, almost one-third of

Latin America's debt was private debt without state guarantees.[11] The Latin Americans agreed to the policy, understanding that the U.S. Federal Reserve would lose its flexibility if the U.S. banks had to write off the private-sector portion of their debt. By 1984, the governments had assumed responsibility for almost 100 percent of the private-sector debt. Colombia was the only country that did not bow to the pressure. The U.S. government was insisting that the Latin American taxpayers pay for the follies of their own private sector. It is not hard to imagine what would happen if anyone suggested that policy in the United States.

The guarantees of the Latin American governments came in many forms, but all had the same result: the governments took the most active intervention in the private sector in their history. Wherever it happened, corruption escalated. The Latin American bureaucrats, ever eager to dominate the private sector, were given a new instrument to extract graft, and they did not hesitate to use it. In Venezuela, for example, the government guaranteed a more favorable exchange rate for businesses to pay their foreign debt, on the rationale that the debt had been contracted at a lower exchange rate (4.3 Venezuelan bolivars to the dollar) and should be repaid at the same rate at which the debt had been contracted and thereby avoid raising internal prices and aggravating inflation to cover the increased amount of bolivars needed for repayment. In the interim, however, the currency had depreciated more than 300 percent to more than fifteen bolivars to the dollar. It was as if when President Nixon devalued the dollar in 1972, the government exempted U.S. companies from the devaluation and allowed them to repay their foreign debts at the exchange rate existing before the devaluation.

With the potential of a 300 percent profit or loss, bribery ran amok. Businesses had only to prove to the local bureaucracy where and how they contracted its dollar debt. If they succeeded, they could send $1 million abroad at a cost of 4.3 million bolivars. If it was a legitimate debt, the dollars would go to their creditors. But if, as in many cases, they retained control, as in the case of intercompany debt, they could shortly turn the money around and send it back to Venezuela on the free market and get 15 million bolivars. The jockeying among the Venezuelan businessmen to take advantage of this subsidy predictably created one of the worst scandals in Venezuelan history, the so-called RECADI scandal, in which huge payoffs were allegedly paid to top Venezuela officials in order to get approval for below-market exchange rates. While such a policy would hardly have been permitted in the United States, the U.S. government looked on benignly as the U.S. business community joined its Venezuelan counterpart in pressuring for this policy.

COSTS BUT NO BENEFITS

The vicious circle gained momentum, becoming a vortex and aborting Latin America's attempt to build a viable modern economy. The vaunted "takeoff" of the developing economies, a term made popular by presidential adviser Walt W. Rostow in his 1960s book *Stages of Economic Growth*, never happened. The more inflammatory the rhetoric of the politicians and the technocrats grew, the faster the dollars flew abroad. And the faster the dollars flew, the more intractable the bureaucrats became. It was a financial travesty rooted in erratic statist policies and the arrogance of the bureaucracies running the Latin American governments. In societies notorious for their lack of social mobility, government positions became the surest way to power and wealth. The more rules the bureaucrats made in the guise of stemming the leakage, the richer they became.

As the difficulties mounted and inflation worsened, the historic gap between rich and poor, always a problem for Latin America, widened even further. The middle class and the poor were hit the hardest. The wealthy moved their money abroad and watched it increase in value in comparative terms as local currency was repeatedly devalued against the dollar. The ranks of the poor swelled as jobs and the opportunity for advancement disappeared, and because of the inflation, the middle class could no longer make ends meet. This was the same middle class that had been hailed as the bedrock of democracy and was the developmental priority only two decades earlier in President Kennedy's Alliance for Progress. Now they saw their earnings disappear overnight. Bankruptcies and layoffs left many out of work, and families sank rapidly into poverty. For a region of the world that had a long history of underdevelopment, poverty, and social inequities, the advances of the 1960s and 1970s were set back a generation and, in many cases, have yet to recover.

The debacle was not without cost to the United States. U.S. exports to Latin America, which stood at $41 billion per year in 1981, fell 25 percent to $30 billion in 1985 before they began to recover. Even so, they accounted for only $43 billion in 1988.[12] If U.S. exports to Latin America had grown at a normal rate during the 1980s, they would have grown to close to $80 billion by that time, almost double.

The debt problem took a terrible toll in Latin America. Political leaders faced an untenable dilemma. Because stabilizing the economies meant destabilizing the societies, they opted for indecision. The military, which was in power during much of this period, decided to abandon its governing role when the treasuries emptied. It was not adverse to governing when the treasuries were full but when economic development came to a halt, the military abdicated its role as power broker, and the political spectrum began to change to democracy. It was almost democracy by default. The old autocrats gave up. They simply did not know what to do.

THE UNITED STATES STEPS IN

The United States' role in the debt crisis matched that of the Latin Americans, measure for measure in misdiagnosis, lost opportunities, and partial solutions. Despite the increasing evidence of deep-rooted problems in the structure of the Latin American economies, the Reagan administration insisted on avoiding the central issues. At first, the Latin Americans did not take the Reagan administration seriously. While preaching to the Latin Americans about balanced budgets, the United States was running deficits of unprecedented magnitude. President Reagan was converting the United States from the world's largest creditor nation into the world's largest debtor while pressing the governments of Latin America to raise taxes to balance their budget in order to reduce their deficits.

U.S. policy toward Latin American debt was the victim of a serious misdiagnosis of the problem.[13] Secretary of the Treasury Donald Regan called it a temporary problem of liquidity and scoffed at the possibility of debt relief. His assessment was that with time and patience, Latin America would resume its growth and be able to repay its debt. Such inconsistent policies took their toll. Latin Americans, who were long accustomed to the moral posturing from the United States, felt them most. In 1984, President Miguel de la Madrid of Mexico was one of the first to acknowledge that his country incurred the debt and would pay for it. It was clear, though, that the price would be enormously high in both human and financial terms. President de la Madrid put it bluntly, asking, "How can we explain to our people that the developing countries are being told to reduce their public expenditures while other countries make use of a growing deficit as an essential lever in their recovery?"[14]

There was another anomaly, whose import was not lost on Latin Americans. While the Reagan administration vehemently denied any policy to bail out the banks, it did everything it could to make sure the crisis did not irreparably impair the banks' capital structure. The administration protested strongly that the Latin Americans should not join together to negotiate with the banks, on the grounds that each country had a different problem. However, it did not object to the banks' getting together to form a bankers' cartel, even though the situation and solvency of each bank was different—and becoming more and more different each day.

One person, Federal Reserve Chairman Paul Volker, understood the perils and stepped into the vacuum with a "back door" foreign assistance program not found in any textbook.[15] Immediately upon learning of the severity of the Mexican financial crisis in August 1982, he provided a $3.5 billion U.S. government bridge loan to give Mexico time to deal with the immediate pressures and to allow the U.S. government to demonstrate to the private sector and the banks that it would not let Mexico down. None of the traditional U.S. government agencies, the State, Commerce, or Treasury Departments, had any response. Nor could the international community get its act together to agree on a practical strategy to deal with the debt. The result was that Volker's farsighted move was for naught.

By the end of the 1980s, debt fatigue began to affect both U.S. and Latin American negotiators. As the danger to the commercial banks subsided and their balance sheets improved, the banks became less intransigent. One reason for the changing equation was instructions from the U.S. bank regulators that the banks would have to write off increasing portions of their Latin American loans. By that time, eight countries were not paying anything on their debt.[16]

By 1990, attitudes changed substantially in Latin America as well. The reason was that it had no more options. Governments traditionally get money from three sources. They tax, they borrow, or they get foreign aid. Latin American governments did not like to tax; they could no longer borrow; and foreign aid had dwindled. They tried printing money to fill the gap, but that was even more disastrous, compounding the debt problem with one of the most devastating and demoralizing combinations of inflation and economic depression in Latin America's history. The governments finally concluded that since the world was not going to adapt to them, they had to adapt to it. The only source of meaningful investment money in the world was in the hands of the private sector, and the only source of trained management ability to compete in global markets was in the private sector. Both had to be attracted to Latin America if the countries were to progress, and the new presidents of the region understood this. Chile, under General Augusto Pinochet, had shown the way in the late 1980s and was rapidly accelerating its economic growth. Newly elected Presidents Carlos Salinas de Gortari in Mexico, President Carlos Menem in Argentina, and President Alberto Fujimori of Peru all had the courage to begin acting.

As the banks accelerated their write-offs, selling their loans in the secondary market, taking their losses, and building up their reserves, negotiations with Latin America became more flexible. The banks had long known that the prospect of loan repayment was begging the question. The heart of the banking business is to have loans repaid so that new loans can be made. Imagine if the banks told all their credit card holders that they must repay their loans and would not get any new ones. Who would go broke, the customers or the banks? Plans to stretch out debt repayment and reduce principal would give the Latin Americans greater capacity to pay what remained—and greater capacity to borrow again.

In 1988, the big break came when Citibank finally faced reality. John Reed, president of the bank, took the world's banking community by surprise when he announced a $3 billion write-off of Latin American debt. Almost every other major bank followed suit. Within a few months, the banks had established almost $10 billion of loan loss reserves. Then the new U.S. secretary of the treasury, Nicholas Brady, announced a new approach in which he recognized the underlying insolvency of the Latin American nations and the need for structural reforms to enable them to become more competitive in the global markets. He also acknowledged that such restructuring would require the Latin Americans to make significant write-offs of obsolete assets and spend considerable money to retool industry. The only way they could do this, which would be to everyone's benefit, was with debt relief. He proposed a new "Brady Plan" to accomplish just that. Debt relief would now be granted to those countries that pledged their commitment to a specific package of economic reforms.

FLIGHT CAPITAL:
THE SOURCE OF LATIN AMERICA'S RENEWAL

At the end of the debt crisis in the 1990s, Latin America was far richer than the data revealed. Citizens of the countries had enormous wealth. It just was not located in Latin America; it was abroad. The capital flight of the 1980s and these people's desire to protect their assets created a tremendous pool of liquid resources in banks in the United States and Europe. That capital was available to return to Latin America for new development if the conditions were right. These vast resources, universally condemned at the time as contributing to the decline of Latin America's economies, actually made Latin America one of the richer areas of the world. Indeed, the region's true net worth was greater in 1990 than it was in 1980.

The evidence of this reality was quick in coming. Both flight capital and flight people did return to the region when the conditions changed. The return of flight capital to Latin America became evident early in the case of Mexico. Data from the National Bank of Mexico show that reflows were beginning to take place as early as 1991, even though the reforms of the new president, Salinas, had barely begun. The return of capital was greatly accelerated by the opportunities for those Latin Americans who had kept their capital abroad to repurchase the debt of their own countries that were trading in the open markets at highly discounted prices. According to the terms of their debt instruments, the governments were forbidden to repurchase the debt, but they could encourage their private sector to buy it. Enormous profits were made on what was called "round tripping." As they regained confidence that the new Latin American governments were serious about economic reform, these private citizens used part of their large dollar holdings in the United States and Europe to buy their country's debt in the New York markets at steep discounts. They then turned around and traded it for local currency for new investments in their home countries. The process was economically useful to the Latin American countries, which shared in the discounts by offering less than one hundred cents on the dollar of repatriated debt and benefited by having their debt canceled. The investors made considerable profits, and the countries received new investments in local currency. The music was turned on and the economies began to grow again.

Considering the severity of the hardships during this period, the region as a whole came out remarkably well. There were no massive defaults, no debtor's cartels, and no revolutions, although on several occasions, riots resulted in many deaths. The societies did not disintegrate into populism and chaos, as some pundits predicted. The restraint showed by the leaders generally enhanced the standing of Latin America in the world's financial community. Moreover, Latin America's own capital abroad had been revealed to be its greatest source of liquidity. Latin America's growing realization that its interests were best served by adapting to the realities of the world instead of insisting that the world adapt to it began to create new opportunities to reverse decades of neglect, misguided policies, and stagnation.

6

Where the Puck Is Going

The World Changes

"It's a changing world," lamented Adam to Eve as they left the Garden of Eden.

WAYNE GRETSKY, the famous Canadian hockey star, ascribed his success to his ability to "keep his eye on where the puck is going, not where it's been." Successful entrepreneurs would agree, and the same principle holds true in our relations with the other nations of the world. The great vision of our forefathers in building our nation related not only to their perceptions of human nature but also to the future world to which the United States would have to relate. Strengthening our own economy and building friends and allies were as important as weakening enemies. The wisdom of this approach was evident in the farsighted response of the generation that formulated our policies after World War II. The positive results of their pragmatic decision to help former enemies regain stability stood in sharp contrast to the disaster resulting from the policies of the retribution and anger after World War I.

In the twenty-first century, the United States' vision of where the puck is going relates to the importance of consolidating democracy, resolving disputes peacefully, and succeeding in global competition. All will be greatly influenced by our ability to adopt farsighted policies right here in the Americas.

As we look ahead, it is helpful to remember the insight attributed to Yogi Berra that predictions are dangerous, especially about the future. In international affairs, predictions about impending apocalypses are a cottage industry and are generally as accurate as the legendary economist who predicted six of the last two recessions. In September 1994, right before the collapse of the Mexican currency, the *Financial*

Times proclaimed that "recession is dead and world output is set to expand." The World Bank's forecast for the global economy in 1997 was that "growth in developing countries would accelerate over the next decade and that the five biggest emerging economies—China, India, Indonesia, Brazil and Russia—would become economic powerhouses by the mid-quarter century."[1] The bank continued to predict that growth would surge to an average of 5.4 percent annually through 2006. It reverberated like the classic story about the economist who announced to his colleagues the results of his tracking the growth of his thirteen-year-old son. "At this rate," he predicted, "I project that he will be close to eight feet tall by the age of eighteen," contemplating the life of retirement as a multimillionaire on his son's professional basketball earnings.

Fortunes in international economics change rapidly. Little more than a decade ago, the United States was considered a basket case with old industrial plants, an annual $200 billion deficit, and a national debt of $4 trillion. The Japanese model was the rage. President François Mitterand of France showed his prescience in a 1990 interview, before the 1991 Gulf War. He observed that in the twenty-first century the world economy would be dominated by two great superpowers, the United States of Europe and Japan. When asked about the United States of America, he replied that in the twenty-first century, "the United States would no longer be a factor." Before the financial collapse of 1998, East Asian leaders joined the chorus crowing about the Asian alternative to "decadent Western capitalism."

Forecasts about Latin America of the last three decades prove the point.

- In the 1960s, pundits predicted that President John F. Kennedy's Alliance for Progress would not have a significant impact. Within a decade, however, Latin America had the fastest-growing economies in the world, far outstripping the virtually unknown Asian cubs.
- In the 1970s, when the Latin American economies were soaring, the experts reversed themselves and predicted that the region's accelerating growth made it the best risk in the global economy. The commercial banks proceeded to pour money into the region indiscriminately, with the result that before long Latin America was $400 billion in debt and riddled with widespread corruption as the private banks discarded all safeguards on the use of funds.

- In the 1980s, analysts predicted that it would take a generation for Latin America to recover from the devastating depression caused by the debt debacle and that the hardships of stagnation and inflation would touch off widespread social unrest and even revolution. Instead, the region rushed to embrace democracy and open-market reforms to regenerate their economies within a decade.
- Today Argentina's highly touted pegged currency board, which produced stability and growth for a decade, has resulted in one of the most rapid and devastating financial collapses in the country's history.

In short, the only reliable prediction is to expect the unexpected. Few experts foresaw that by the mid-1990s Latin America would have overcome its debt problem and reduced inflation to single digits. Today, economists still grapple with different theories about the impact of technology on the global economy, and Latin America is positioned to apply new technology to leapfrog into world of the twenty-first century: wireless communications are set to become pervasive, in most places replacing wired phones instead of supplementing them; fiber-optic lines are being built into households in many countries, covering that "last mile" in a way that is far more costly in the United States and Europe; new power generation plants are being constructed throughout the hemisphere; new roads are opening new territories; and new investment is bringing in the most advanced technology. The furious pace of the movement of international capital, information, and technology in the 1990s set the basis for rapid swings in winners and losers. How does one predict the evolution of a global economy in which every major corporation must invest hundreds of millions of dollars annually to upgrade computer systems because they become obsolete in three years?

NEW DEMOCRACIES, NEW REALITIES

The long-term trends in Latin America and the Caribbean are complemented by several trends that will affect the U.S. economy in the coming decades. After 2010, as the baby boomers retire, the number of new entrants into the U.S. job market will be smaller than the number of jobs being created. We will be facing an acute labor shortage. Throughout its history the United States has depended on the influx of immigrant labor to meet its continually expanding need. The coming shortage, however, and resultant tight labor markets will dwarf all others because of the suddenness with which it will take place. The great U.S. workforce, which in the last few decades absorbed the influx of the baby boomers, women, and illegal immigrants, now faces a new phase in its economic evolution. The United States has undergone a great demographic change, as have most prosperous industrialized nations. In 1790, more than 50 percent of the U.S. population was under age sixteen. By 1970, the median age was thirty-three, and by 2050, it is expected to be fifty. The aging of the populations in other developed countries such as Japan and France is even more dramatic than in the United States. By 2025, Japan, with one of the highest life expectancies in the world (today, seventy-six for men and eighty-three for women) will have one of the world's oldest populations, with more than 25 percent of its people over sixty-five. While the United States is faced with the prospect of only 3.3 workers per retiree in 2025, France will have only 1.7 and Germany 2.3.

The reality is that the U.S. economy continues to create more jobs than an aging population will be able to fill. This evolution is debated today in our discussions of the solvency of Social Security and our ability to maintain a comfortable environment for an elderly population. The other, less discussed side of that coin is that the number of workers entering the U.S. job market will begin to fall sharply behind the economy's capacity to create jobs. Signs are already apparent as the unemployment rate in the United States moved below 5 percent for the first time in decades and, even in the recent recession, remained below 6 percent. If the U.S. economy continues to create jobs at the present rate, the curve of new workers to that of job creation will cross as soon as 2010.

In the past, legal and illegal immigrants filled the gap. The 1990 census data show that in the 1980s the United States accommodated the largest influx of immigrants, more than in any earlier period and a percentage equivalent to the great wave of the early 1900s. Today almost 12 percent of our hi-tech workforce is foreign born.

In the future, a labor-short population will require us to rely on offshore production for more labor-intensive activities as we place even greater emphasis on capital-intensive production within the United States. This evolution will alter the relations between the United States and the countries of the Americas, as it will for all developed countries of the world. This evolution will be especially apparent here in the Americas, where the pressure to migrate to the United States until prosperity spreads more evenly in the region will mean that the percentage of Hispanic and Caribbean workers will grow more rapidly than the overall labor market.

In the 1990s, attitudes changed toward democracy and open markets throughout the Americas. Informed by the global information revolution, larger numbers of the world's population are beginning to understand that creativity and capital come from the motivation and innovation of private citizens, not from government. We have seen the emergence of democratic leaders who place a high priority on reversing the counterproductive practices of the past. They know that only productive jobs can bring sustainable economic prosperity to the region, and they appreciate the enormous investment needed to build the infrastructure for production. Without it, there is no escape from intractable poverty. Without a source of income, the poor migrate to cities, intensifying pressures on social services and increasing crime. The more ambitious ones migrate to the ultimate big city, the United States. Some make it legally, but many are motivated enough not to let immigration laws stop them.

Much has to be done to make up for centuries of underinvestment in public infrastructure and social services, but the trends are moving in the right direction. Supplementing national budgets, international financial institutions are today the prime source of capital for this purpose. While progress is slow in many areas because of the complex pressures on the new democracies, many leaders of the Americas are nonetheless conscious of what they must do. The problem is the tension resulting from dealing with both political and economic transitions at the same time. The political transition requires building a consensus through democratic processes, but democratic decision making moves at "democratic speed." Leaders like former President Carlos Menem of Argentina and President Alberto Fujimori of Peru were able, by force of personality and strong leadership, to move more rapidly. Huge and diverse countries such as Brazil must act more slowly and patiently to gain consensus among its regional and sectoral interests. Most of the current democratic leaders understand, however, that investment is the key to job creation and that investment will not come until the country makes private capital feel secure. Peter Drucker noted that "Latin

America [will be] easier to turn around than the former Soviet bloc countries. It can feed upon itself and has a business infrastructure, rickety as it may be."[2]

The prospect of enduring democracy is based on two other transformations now sweeping the continent. First, the attitudes of senior military leaders have been deeply influenced by the commitment to democracy they found during their training in the United States and Europe. They also recognized that competing in a world of rapidly evolving high technology requires expertise that can be obtained only from a healthy private sector. Not only did the military mismanage their countries' economies when they were in power, but their incompetence in their own affairs was dramatically portrayed in the catastrophe of Argentina's Falklands/Malvinas War with Great Britain. Indeed, the miscalculations of the 1980s irreparably damaged respect for the military throughout Latin America.

The second phenomenon is the transformation of the church. The former monopoly of the Catholic Church is eroding as Protestant and evangelical groups are beginning to attract more adherents. The new activism of the evangelical Protestants is also affecting the electoral dynamics, as for the first time in many countries, they are playing an important role in getting out the vote. In fact, the evangelical influence was so great that in Peru in 1990, the opposition candidate to Alberto Fujimori (of Japanese descent) warned the country that a Fujimori victory would allow foreign "sects" to take over the country. The following year in Guatemala, Jorge Serrano Elias, who had become a Pentecostal Protestant when he was in his twenties, openly campaigned for president as such and won 68 percent of the vote. A similar phenomenon is being felt in Brazil where Protestant and evangelical movements not only are exercising a greater influence in the country's cultural life but also are openly campaigning for electoral office. It is reported that Protestant sects in Latin America have increased in number from 15 million members in the 1960s to more than 40 million today.[3] The purported influence of Reverend Sun Young Moon in Uruguay show that ideas are competing in the continent as never before. Even in the Catholic Church a movement called liberation theology is changing the views of the faithful toward political activism on behalf of the poor.

The significance of these developments for the future of the Americas is best understood in the context of the dominant trends in the region. The bases for the growth of pluralistic, responsive democracies are slowly moving into place. But as we noted earlier, many bridges still have to be crossed. After a decade of political and economic reform, democracy is still struggling to achieve its promise. Income inequalities continue and poverty remains a tinderbox. Latin America has had periods of progressive, liberal governments earlier in its history. Will today's push toward democracy be different? Is it an isolated phenomenon or the harbinger of a major shift in Latin America's historical development? The predominant trends affecting the political landscape convince me that the region has crossed an important threshold and that its commitments to democracy and open markets will last. There is ample evidence that democracy has struck a responsive chord among the people. The decisive issue now is whether it can deliver a better life for the people who have the votes. Coming in the midst of a sweeping global communications and transportation revolution, the competing pressures of an abstract desire for progress and a tendency toward avarice make the transition difficult. Overcoming these obstacles is the main reason Latin America will need the attention, understanding, and collaboration of the more developed nations, both the United States and Europe. If these commitments are nurtured, I have every confidence that Latin America and the Caribbean will become a major force for democracy in the twenty-first century.

THE THREE MAIN TRENDS IN THE AMERICAS

The three main trends changing the Americas today are rooted in the waves of information and volatile capital that now leap over national borders at will. They are largely managed by private, nongovernmental actors. Inter-American relations and the future of the nations therefore depend more on private-sector actors than on government policies. Investment, nongovernmental organizations, the media, and computer connectivity all interact in a way that far exceeds the influence of official policy. National laws and regulations and international arrangements written in another era for other historical realities can neither deter nor cope with the new dynamics.

In the nations of the Americas these trends are manifested in the diffusion of political, economic, and civic power, a diffusion that marks a radical break with Latin America's past. It has made it almost impossible for the old-style statist regimes to return, although new forms of authoritarian control are always hovering on the horizon. The raging conflicts in Venezuela pitting a vociferous civil society against an autocratic president is a prime example of the irrepressible forces that have been unleashed. If they are encouraged, the new diffused centers of power will become the core of a sustainable democracy.

In the private sector, the diffusion of power is rooted in the privatization of infrastructure and pension funds and in the growth of small businesses. In the public sector, it is in the devolution of new responsibilities to municipal and local governments and in the drive for regional economic integration. In the past, the objective was to sell products across borders. Now the objective is cross-border investment in various countries' production and commerce, which creates material stakes in other economies and favors governments promoting integration.

The trends promising to change the face of the hemisphere are evident in three areas: the diversification of economic power, the decentralization of civic power, and the growing infrastructure for local, self-sustaining, and self-reliant democracy.

The First Trend: New Centers of Economic Power

The trend that promises to reverse the economic stagnation and to release the entrepreneurial talent of the Americas today is the diffusion of economic power. After centuries of closed societies and tight control by small oligarchic elites, the countries of Latin America are suddenly and rapidly shifting to a widening base of capital and production. While income distribution remains skewed, the composition of the elites is being transformed. An analogous phenomenon is sweeping the Caribbean as people become more self-reliant after centuries of colonial rule. Ironically, in Latin America, the transformation is based in the so-called capital flight of the 1980s. At that time those people moving their capital out of the countries were widely berated as disloyal. But as we have seen, they were prudently managing their assets amid the inept government policies that brought rampant inflation. Latin America was never the poor continent that many commentators bemoaned. The assets held abroad by Latin Americans not only maintained their value but, in many cases, appreciated considerably. That capital constituted a captive pool of resources with a strong potential to be reattracted to the region under the right conditions.

The most telling characteristic about the capital flight was that the businessmen who owned the capital continued to live in Latin America. They maintained their businesses in Latin America and kept their families in Latin America (except in Central America, where a civil war undermined confidence). These people always believed that if government policies changed and confidence was restored, they could bring back their money. And this is what happened. As we have seen, the repatriation of capital fueled the great capital flows in the 1990s as governments returned to more sound fiscal management policies, inflation subsided, and the environment for foreign investment dramatically changed. This reservoir of flight capital became the main source of funds that now provided Latin America with a stronger asset base on which to grow. That base was far stronger than is evident from analyzing the countries' misleading domestic savings rates. As we noted earlier, Latin Americans save, but they do not save at home. They save abroad. No one who has any alternative would keep savings in a country with a government whose fiscal policies undermine the currency and with poorly regulated banks that are vulnerable to collapse from insider dealing. In those circumstances, rational citizens and corporations seek safer havens abroad.

The three external financial shocks that Argentina suffered in the 1990s proved that changing policies can change behavior. The "tequila" effect of the Mexican financial crisis in 1994 created an immediate run on banks in Argentina and Brazil. As interest rates soared, practical businessmen foresaw the coming crisis for a banking industry as a result of more business failures, an inability to repay loans, the ensuing liquidity crunch, and bank failures. Within a matter of weeks, billions of dollars left the country. Local entrepreneurs and multinational companies with working capital in the country worried primarily about local banks collapsing under the pressure of bad debts as the economies contracted. Everyone knows the story of the millionaire who, when confronted with a bounced check, protested that he had ample balances to cover it. "It's not you, sir," he was told, "it's the bank."

After the 1994 crisis threatened Argentina's recovery, the government of President Carlos Menem reacted immediately and forcefully by asserting that there would be no backtracking on fiscal policy and that the free and full convertibility of currency would be maintained. With the help of the international financial institutions through the Inter-American Development Bank and the World Bank, the government cleaned up its domestic banking sector and strengthened its capital base. The result was evident during the 1998 Asian financial crisis. Bank deposits in Argentina not only did not contract, they expanded.

Then came the Brazilian devaluation in 1999 which undermined all that the stable currency was trying to build. We will discuss this in more detail later. In sum, there was no way that Argentina could survive the evolving economic patterns of increased trade within the Mercosur common market with one currency floating and another fixed. The result was a gigantic economic implosion as Argentina lost all capacity to export to its new markets in Brazil.

The event of the 1980s that is most important to the economic future of the Americas is the emergence of new centers of economic power that are far more diffused and more closely tied to international capital markets than ever before in the region's history. The new entrepreneurs who had kept their capital abroad entered into a new dynamic with the global investment community. As a result of their new relationships, Latin Americans got to know international investment bankers on their home turf, and the investment bankers got to know the more dynamic Latin American entrepreneurs. They became comfortable with each other. The business ties established in these years changed their outlook and sense of confidence. Latin Americans learned about the global economy, and investment bankers grew to respect the business acumen—and insider information—of the Latin American investors. Contacts that were once the privilege of a select few became far more widespread.

The trend accelerated as the entrepreneurs, with their money in the United States, sent their children to U.S. universities. Their understanding of the market continued to grow. They were joined by the many young people who were educated in the United States under the Fulbright fellowship programs and scholarships available during the period of the Alliance for Progress. This generation has been exposed to entirely new influences in the business and engineering schools of the United States. They have strong management skills and are comfortable in the global markets. They are not afraid of competing, and unlike the landed oligarchy that preceded them, they do not depend on the military for their political power.

There is an old saying that anyone who questions the value of education does not know the history of the Jesuits. Now we could say that anyone who questions the value of education in U.S. universities does not understand what is happening in the Americas today or the economic energy that will be unlocked when Latin America begins to provide quality education in its own countries.

The galvanizing force for the real diffusion of economic power, however, was privatization. The widespread movement to sell badly managed state-owned companies that were draining state treasuries and providing indifferent service to the public was the vehicle for Latin American capital to return home. The return began when Latin American entrepreneurs with resources abroad began to buy their countries' debt obligations at deep discounts in the New York markets. That debt was repatriated when the governments gave them credit in local currency of double or triple its value if the dollar debt instruments were converted into shares in privatized companies instead of claims on the government. At the beginning, it was a risky transaction, as the entrepreneurs had no guarantee that the governments would keep their commitments or that the new economic reforms would stick. Those investors who took the risk, however, reaped huge rewards. And as investment bankers in the United States and Europe saw the Latin American businessmen whom they had grown to respect repatriating their own capital, they began to follow their lead. As a result, the floodgates of the investment community were opened. Multimillionaires were made overnight in both Latin America and the United States in a harbinger of what occurred a few years later in the technology markets.

Privatization had many collateral benefits. Aside from the well-documented increases in the productivity and provision of services, it opened the door to new capital markets and to the participation of the middle class in wealth accumulation. In the past, the only investments available to the middle class were real estate and government bonds. Innumerable condominia were built in postwar Latin America because they were the only source of stable investment for the region's growing middle classes. Today, with open capital markets and privatized pension funds channeling money into the domestic stock exchanges, new investment vehicles are being created for the region's middle classes for capital accumulation that never existed before.

The impact of privatized pension funds on the diffusion of wealth has been enormous. In the past, people considered their social security payments as a tax, expecting that most of what they paid would be wiped out by either inflation or corruption. Now, however, they regard the payments into their funds as an accumulation of wealth. The result is that they are providing an amount of investment capital never before seen in the region.

In short, "the wingbeat of capital flying," as we described it earlier, created a more diversified economic base. It is a more accurate vision of the economic realities than Ross Perot's graphic "great sucking sound." Capital moves to where it is safest, not necessarily where costs are cheapest. The new capital of the Americas is far more liquid and integrated into the global pool of private capital than was the former wealth of the landed oligarchs that once dominated Latin America. More important, the process of influencing government policy is now more varied and sophisticated.

Today, all governments acknowledge that private capital dwarfs government resources. As a result, private capital has a great influence on economic policy in Latin America, just as it does in the rest of the world. Policymakers in democratic governments recognize this, and even President Hugo Chávez of Venezuela, who took office in 1999 with many populist ideas, had to learn to take it into account.

Latin America is still in a period of transition. High unemployment persists as economic adjustments are made far too slowly. Unfortunately, the difficulty is that economic reforms are not effective when made piecemeal. A critical mass of mutually reinforcing reforms must be in place or the remaining loopholes leave markets vulnerable to manipulation, as the United States learned in the case of the collapse of Enron in 2001. Because of the spotty implementation of reforms, the new democracies still have much to do to create an environment for healthy, competitive market economies. To that end, governments must keep a close eye on how the market perceives their performance. Failing to do so can rapidly ruin the economy. It happened in Asia, the United States, and Europe, and as we have seen in Argentina, the still dependent economies of the Americas remain extremely vulnerable.

The Second Trend: New Centers of Civic Power

The second force shaping the new Americas is the centers of civic power that are challenging the hierarchical authoritarian controls that defined the region's past. The emergence of new civil society organizations (CSOs) is attributable to the same growth of the private sector's self-confidence that has permeated industry. These organizations are, in fact, the private sector of the social sector, the embodiment of private citizens acting for the public welfare. Combined with the accelerating trend of handing over national governmental functions to local and municipal governments, more meaningful citizen participation in decision making is becoming possible at all levels of government throughout Latin America and the Caribbean. CSOs are also one of the best hopes for combating the type of corruption that has allowed the narcotics trade to flourish.

Part of the problem of democracy in Latin American countries is related to the absence of a political and civic tradition committed to fairness and the rule of law, as is found in the legal and political institutions of the United States and Europe. That tradition, rooted in John Locke's political philosophy, is the commitment to both equality before the law and equality of opportunity. The sense of a right to justice and to the impartial application of the law produces a commitment to civic responsibility on which democracy can grow. It has weak roots in the Spanish tradition. Democracy cannot thrive without a culture of civic responsibility, and civil responsibility cannot grow unless it is nurtured by the freedom of expression and responsiveness that is inherent in respect for the rule of law. Its underlying premise is respect for the individual. In politics it is the government's commitment to be responsive to its citizens. In justice it is the concept of fairness to treat all citizens equally regardless of social rank. It is the basis of confidence in a responsive and fair government.

For centuries Latin American culture tolerated far too much passivity in the face of abuses of power. The traditional lament heard throughout the region for any social ill was that it was the government's responsibility or the government's fault. The concept of civic responsibility did not even have a meaningful translation in Spanish. Private philanthropy was almost entirely through the church. The wealthy otherwise shunned responsibility for the welfare of the society in which they lived. Civic responsibility for providing education, health services, or even for paying taxes was in short supply. The notion that common citizens could organize to press the government to take action, or even to take action themselves, was almost nonexistent. The oligarchy had its own special form of private-sector influence to get its desired results from government.

The historically weak civic organization in Latin America stands in sharp contrast to the traditions in the United States where, as Alexis de Tocqueville noted, "Americans of all ages, all conditions, and all disposition constantly form associations. . . . Wherever at the head of some new undertaking you see the government in France, or a man of rank in England, in the United States you will be sure to find an association." The absence of this type of citizen action in Latin America deprived it of a major force for social change.

The signs are that this, too, is beginning to change. The number of civil society organizations is growing. Similar to the history of capital flight, the civil society movement also owes its origin to the traumas of the 1970s and 1980s. The flight of people caused by the human rights abuses of reactive military dictatorships became the soil in which the seeds of a new civil society germinated, analogous to the way that flight capital reacted to inept economic management. Just as financial instability was the catalyst for new economic consciousness, the many Latin Americans who emigrated to escape both political repression and dwindling economic opportunities from stagnant economies are now returning with a new civic consciousness. Many educated Latin Americans who fled abroad found jobs in nonprofit organizations interested in Latin American issues. Many of the uneducated and illegal were protected by civic organizations who advocated for their rights. These are the people now creating civil society organizations. An awareness of civic responsibility may have been the United States' most important export to the region at the time.

In a break from past, the informal citizens' associations and the increasing awareness of citizens' rights spawned by the human rights abuses were supported by an international support network that was rapidly learning how to take advantage of the global communications revolution. With the new and accessible international contacts, leaders became more vocal in rejecting the abuses of their leaders. New internal communications networks outside the control of the central government gathered wider political support. Graciela Fernández Mejide, one of the leaders of Argentina's famous Mothers of the Plaza Mayo protesting the disappearance of their children, gained so much exposure that she became a senator in Argentina and a serious presidential contender. The "market ladies" of Nicaragua were a mainstay of the battle against the Sandinistas who sought to establish state stores in rural communities. The market ladies would not yield to any government interference in their informal farmers' markets in which they sold produce in the village plaza. Their resistance spread to many other sectors and deeply affected the attitudes of the Sandinistas. In Panama, the people banged on pots and pans to protest the dictatorship of Manuel Noriega. Venezuela's marathon strike against perceived antidemocratic practices was an unprecedented nonviolent civic protest. These forms of spontaneous citizen action are the real manifestation of democratic stirrings.

The first generation of civil society organizations (CSOs), born in the battle for human rights, soon expanded into environmental advocacy, motivated by international attention to the deterioration of the rain forests and an innovative way of addressing debt relief. Many Latin American countries have allowed their debt to be purchased by nongovernmental environmental organizations and traded for land that would be then reserved for national parks. Many CSOs jumped at the opportunity and created well-financed international networks. Their principal activity was advocacy. Many Latin American governments remain dubious about the growth of the CSOs because of their brazen challenges to governmental authority and support from foreign CSOs. But as the CSOs evolve from their first-generation role of advocacy, the second generation is turning more to the delivery of social services in education, health, and poverty alleviation.

In the Americas today the impact of civil society on the social sector is analogous to what private enterprise is to the productive sector. The CSOs have become the major hope for reversing the abysmal record of the delivery of social services and demands for accountability in government. It is no secret that government-operated social service agencies were grossly mismanaged and rife with political patronage, favoritism, and inefficiency leading to corruption. Many Latin Americans cynically joked that the only function of the social service agencies was to provide social security to the people they employed. Evita Perón's legendary abuses of social services for her personal agenda were not unique. Rather, the lack of accountability and a tolerance for inefficiency and corruption were the rule.

Today, private-sector CSOs are beginning to fill this void, just as they have in the industrialized countries of Europe and the United States, where foundations and private-sector associations are the principal sources of research and services in heath care and humanitarian relief, education, and community services.

The recent role of citizens in detecting the abuses of and ousting President Fujimori of Peru and in counterbalancing the authoritarian predilections of President Chávez of Venezuela are recent examples. Consultation with citizen groups is now a standard requirement for all loans from the World Bank and the Inter-American Development Bank that will affect the community. The *Financial Times* reported on a mining venture in Peru: "By the time Aguaytia Energy's $250 million integrated gas and power project [financed by the Inter-American Development Bank] goes into commercial operation in Peru's jungle . . . $10 million will have gone into what U.S. consortium's general manager, Rex Cannon, calls environmental and community issues." The experience of the Yanacocha mining venture was similar. After "several internationally funded NGOs fueled the fires," Yanacocha now "has the best developed community assistance program in Peru, spending some $3 million a year on . . . installation of water systems and latrines, construction of schools and medical posts, and training in agricultural and stock raising techniques."[4]

When I was at the Inter-American Development Bank, I was always amazed at and gratified by the growing awareness of community organizations in pressing environmental and community development issues. They brought up issues and facts that otherwise never would have come to our attention. The most mail I ever received came from the Mayan Indians in Belize regarding the protection of their property rights vis-à-vis a proposed road that would pass through their tribal lands. I also participated in a dispute among Indians in Bolivia, a large U.S. multinational power company, and Brazil's state-owned oil company over the right of way for the Bolivian-Brazilian gas pipeline. While the indigenous communities had been organized by CSOs from abroad, their imprint was indelible. The young people of the communities watched avidly, absorbing everything that was going on, learning techniques that no schoolteacher or book could teach. The Mayan communities in Chiapas, Mexico, and the recent stirring of Indian communities in Guatemala, Ecuador (where they helped force the resignation of the country's president), and Bolivia demonstrate the changing dynamics.

The growing citizen action is also beginning to affect social services in the cities. A Brazilian CSO active in helping the "street children" of Rio de Janeiro has made an important contribution to changing public opinion and attitudes. These street children became a major problem in the 1980s when impoverished families lost their jobs and governmental authority broke down as budget cuts undermined police morale. Children abandoned by their parents roamed the streets fending for themselves, living by their own wiles on whatever they could beg or steal.

Violence and banditry exploded in the city streets. Bankrupt governments were incapable of addressing the need. Today, Brazilian CSOs have stepped in to organize support groups for the homeless children, providing education and health services. In another example, an inter-American volunteer corps, the "White Helmets," launched by President Menem of Argentina and endorsed at the recent presidential summit, is a clear recognition of the value of citizen participation in social development in the style of President John F. Kennedy.

The importance of this evolution in democracy in the Americas cannot be underestimated. Its impact on the role of women is sweeping aside social and political barriers that have long left women helpless without education and vulnerable to domestic violence. In most countries of Latin America—except for Ecuador, Brazil, El Salvador, and Uruguay—women were accorded the right to vote only after World War II. Today, the contrast is dramatic. Argentina has a law requiring 30 percent of each party's electoral lists to be allocated to women. In the Mexican legislature in 1997, 87 of the 500 deputies and 18 of the 128 senators—more than 15 percent—are women, compared with 13 deputies and 2 senators as recently as 1962.

New research on domestic violence has shown that the subordinate role of women has undermined economic growth. Recognition of this problem has spurred CSOs to press for educating both men and women about its corrosive effect on society's social and economic fabric. International financial institutions have found the evidence sufficiently convincing to begin seeking ways to address it. The Inter-American Development Bank has sponsored several conferences on women's role in economic and social development and is providing grants to CSOs addressing the issue, and the long dormant Inter-American Commission of Women of the OAS is displaying new energy and activity.

In another important role, CSOs have become the central force for accountability in government. In recent years the battle against corruption has gained new momentum as citizens' groups and the media have grown increasingly bold. Several presidents have been called to account by electorates in Venezuela, Brazil, Peru, and Ecuador. If anything can reverse the historical attitudes toward corruption, it is an alert citizenry unwilling to tolerate the abuse of public power and unafraid to challenge it. In the same way that private enterprise drives the productive sectors, the CSOs embody a reservoir of motivation, energy, and creativity. Their presence, not governmental action, is making the trend to democracy irreversible.

The Third Trend: The Growing Infrastructure for Democracy

"The only enduring solution to the problems of democracy is more democracy" is a time-honored refrain. The conditions are vastly different, however, in different parts of the Americas. In the Caribbean, democracy and open markets were a strong legacy of British colonial traditions. In the countries of Latin America, the growth of democratic institutions is the third major trend changing the face of the Americas.

Governmental reform is neither easy nor cheap. Consultants are needed to redraft laws and procedures. Funds are needed to procure and show how to apply information systems technology, pay the severance costs of large numbers of redundant bureaucrats in the accompanying restructuring, and train personnel in new systems and new ways of dealing with the public. In Argentina, for example, when the finance ministry was reduced from seventeen thousand to seven thousand employees, almost $30 million was needed for severance pay in the downsizing. Fortunately, funds for these purposes are available to the countries through the international financial institutions such as the Inter-American Development Bank and the World Bank. Without these external resources, the process would take decades and possibly might never be implemented.

Another evolution providing even more opportunities for civil society is the trend toward decentralizing governmental functions and electing rather than appointing local officials. Elected mayors have created new, independent sources of political influence, with the result that government policy can be changed without having to deal with the national party elite's centralized political power structure, thereby giving the urban poor a stronger voice in national politics. Gary McCaleb, the mayor of Abilene, Texas, who deals as much with his counterparts across the border as he does with other cities in the United States, observes that in Mexico the result has been that the mayors "are younger, better educated, and more concerned about workaday problems." Similar changes are cited in other countries where elected mayors lead the community in demanding better water and sewage systems. In Bolivia, the mayor of Pucarani championed the community's desire to build an automobile racetrack. A former Bolivian president, Gonzalo Sánchez de Lozada, who spearheaded the movement to elect local officials, remarked that "a moron close to a problem usually makes a better decision on how to solve it than a genius a thousand miles away. One might not be in total agreement with their priorities," he said of the race track decision, "but they are their priorities."[5]

The movement toward decentralization is converting city halls into a new kind of political base. It is playing out in different ways in the large countries of Argentina, Brazil, and Mexico where decentralized power is a strong counterbalance to national government, in contrast to the smaller countries, where mayoral posts in the capital city are generally the second most important public administration position in the country. In the larger countries, local authorities have become new forces to contend with in national politics, creating new dynamics and complexities in consensus building. In Brazil, for example, the unilateral action by a state governor on taking office in January 1999 to repudiate his state's debt obligations to the national government spread fear among investors and triggered the financial crisis that forced the devaluation of Brazil's currency and prevented the national government from taking corrective action. As it struggled with the economic adjustments necessary to contain the fallout from the Asian financial crisis in 1999, President Fernando Cardoso of Brazil, an ardent democrat, learned that decentralization and democracy can be a difficult combination, requiring attention and consensus building among widely disparate interests.

Central America is experiencing the same phenomenon in a slightly different fashion. Mayoral posts in the capital cities are becoming the principal platform for building a political power base and projecting a national identity. All the recent presidents of Guatemala, Nicaragua, and El Salvador had been the mayor of a large city. Hector Silva, the candidate of the former guerrilla forces, became the mayor of El Salvador's capital city and was, for a short while, favored for the presidency. The current mayor of Managua, Nicaragua, is a Sandinista, placing that party in a position of renewed strength to gain the presidency. In South America, similar platforms were used by President Fernando de la Rua in his campaign for president of Argentina, and Jamil Mahuad, a former president of Ecuador, both of whom became president after being the mayor of their capital city.

One of the most important reforms for democracy is the judicial system. Thomas Jefferson's admonition that confidence in the administration of justice was the heart and soul of a citizen's confidence in his government was rarely a maxim of governance in Latin America. Indeed, judiciary systems were largely regarded as another instrument of government to be manipulated in the interests of the oligarchy, and they were historically plagued by corruption and inefficiencies. Underpaid judges, arcane procedures, and the rigidities of the civil law system made the rule of law a matter of rhetoric rather than deed in many countries. Criminal and civil codes dated back to the nineteenth century. Governments refused or were unable to spend money on court reforms and frequently packed the benches with political allies.

Attitudes toward the judiciary are changing in almost all countries of the hemisphere, even though the process is slow and erratic. Seminars explaining the role and responsibilities of the judiciary are being financed everywhere by the Organization of American States (OAS) and the Inter-American Development Bank. A new Justice Studies Center of the Americas was established by the OAS General Assembly in 1999. Money is pouring in from international financial institutions to bring the systems up to date. Scandinavia, Canada, Taiwan, and the European Union are making bilateral contributions. And the United States' foreign aid program is helping finance judicial reform in order to avoid a weak judiciary that can be forced to succumb to the drug industry. The problems, however, extend beyond the judiciary to the growing criminal influences in the societies. The stories of judges being threatened with "*plata o pluma*" (literally, "take the money or be murdered") convey the essence of the problem. Faced with death threats to themselves or family members, on the one hand, or handsome bribes from drug dealers, on the other, only the most courageous of judges can resist.

The record of judicial corruption is long. Arbitrary political influence and the use of the judiciary for political ends are far too common. Even democratically elected presidents repeatedly remove unfriendly judges and pack courts. The jailing of political opponents on charges of corruption or abuse of power may be based on allegations that are worthy of investigation but that are all too frequently used to distract attention from similar actions by the new political favorites. In my law practice I encountered many corporations from developed countries that refused to invest in Latin America because they had no assurance of respect for contracts or recourse to a fair judicial hearing in the event of inevitable commercial disagreements. There is a well-known joke about the judge who goes to one litigant to ask for $10,000 to balance the $10,000 bribe he has just received from the other party so that he can decide the dispute fairly. The problem is that such anecdotes are not jokes when human rights, illegal criminal activity, or large investments are at stake.

Many political leaders understand and have responded. In the United States, Senator Mike DeWine of Ohio has taken the lead in pressing for judicial reform throughout the hemisphere, emphasizing that it is in the United States' interest to help because

> democracies cannot survive [in Latin America] and economies cannot expand, without law enforcement officers and judges committed to law and order. The hard, day-to-day work of democracy is not holding elections. To institutionalize democracy and nurture prosperity requires effective responses to the current threat and challenges facing the region, including corruption, criminal activity, drug trafficking and violence. Democracies and free markets are not sustained just when votes are cast or goods purchased, but also when those who violate the laws are arrested and successfully prosecuted.[6]

This issue also affects the economy. Investors will not invest unless they are confident that commercial disputes will be resolved fairly and rapidly. Multinational corporations are wary of risking large sums if they are concerned that disputes will be resolved in corrupt judicial systems. They are not asking for special treatment, but they will avoid countries whose judicial system is stacked against them or requires them to indulge in corruption that can involve them in illegal activities.

A symbol of the motivation for change was found in Cordoba, Argentina, two years ago when a new law enshrined citizens' rights and set forth the state's responsibilities to its citizens. It details the state's obligation to provide a full and continuing report of public business and expenditures and measures to reinforce the citizens' control over the state government, including the seemingly simple right to know the name and office of any public official with whom they are dealing.

The result is that a larger community of interests between the United States and the other nations of the Americas is emerging on multiple levels with all sorts of citizen exchanges and mutual support in both commerce and civil society. In the past, declarations of solidarity between United States and other American politicians were never taken seriously by the people of the United States or of the other nations. What is different today about U.S.–Latin American relations is that for the first time the United States is able to relate to the emerging societies with open democracies and competitive markets. In the long term, democracy can be sustained only if it is able to deliver on its promise of a better life. This is a lesson the United States knows well in the abstract. We need more determination to put it into practical use in the Americas.

7

Poverty and the Lack of Education

The Dormant Volcano

ARGENTINA AND INDIA have one thing in common: their landmass is almost the same size. Argentina is 1.1 million square miles compared with India's 1.2 million square miles. The similarities, however, end there. In population, Argentina contains fewer than 40 million inhabitants, a density of about thirty-five persons per square mile. India's population is more than 2,000 percent more, almost 1 billion, with a density of more than seven hundred persons per square mile. In income, Argentina's average per capita income of close to $8,000 in 2000 contrasts with India's per capita income of only $1,500. India is struggling to overcome poverty. But Argentina, with its huge expanse of fertile land, is perceived as one of the world's largest grain producers.

One would assume that Argentina produces more grain than India does, but India produces almost seven times more grain than Argentina. In 1997, India produced 200 million tons of grain, compared with Argentina's little more than 30 million tons. Even more astonishing: India *exports* more grain than Argentina does.

In contrast to Argentina's untapped potential is the enormous entrepreneurial talent found in the Americas. The world's largest multinational industry is entirely owned and operated by Latin Americans. It maintains one of the most intricate logistics and distribution system of any multinational company in the global market, tightly controls its product from fabrication to distribution, and has one of the world's most sophisticated banking and investment networks. More interesting, none of its owners or managers ever went to business school. Its business is the drug trade. Regardless of morality, the drug industry is a complex undertaking that demonstrates that Latin Americans can be enormously enterprising when freed from bureaucratic restraints.

These two examples highlight the paradox and the potential of the nations and people of the Americas and demonstrate the complex, interconnected, and multifaceted forces shaping them. For centuries Latin America was one of the earth's richest areas. But in the twentieth century, the region was not able to keep up with the industrializing world. Today it is an area of chronic poverty, strong protection for local industry, corruption, poor financial management, and a tradition of statist intervention in the economies that has discouraged enterprise, initiative, and investment.

The roots of these problems run deep and have profound implications for the viability of Latin America's democracies. They have important implications for Latin America's ability to realize its promise in the global economy or to become a major player in global politics. The success of democracy depends on citizens' confidence in the fairness of their society, and they cannot feel a sense of fairness when their government ignores the poverty in its midst. Walter Lippmann once observed that it defies logic to expect the poor to respect the property rights of the rich if the rich fail to respect the needs of the poor. Poor education systems, weak ethical standards, and disregard of public trust exacerbate the tension. This is the condition and predicament of Latin America today. The stakes for the political leaders are now even higher because of the ease of communication and diffusion of information.

Almost ten years after economic reform began to sweep Latin America and the Caribbean, promising new investment and jobs, poverty remains the central concern. While the adjustments advocated by economic experts—privatizing bloated state enterprises, stopping inflation, liberalizing trade—led to a surge of capital, in most countries, they have not yet been able to provide a better life. The example of the leading countries—Chile, Mexico, and Brazil—which demonstrate that economic growth has a tangible and demonstrable effect on poverty, has been replicated in few other countries. The UN Economic Commission for Latin America reports that almost half the inhabitants of Latin America and the Caribbean live in poverty.[1] Because of the debt crisis of the 1980s, the per capita GDP in many American countries in 2000 was, in real terms, no greater than that in 1970s.

Enrique Iglesias, the president of the Inter-American Development Bank and one of the hemisphere's leading advocates for social development and attacking the causes of poverty, explained, "This was a period [the 1980s] buffeted by severe . . . social reverses. Investment spending was put off, the institutional fabric became unraveled, and health care and education models capable of offering sustained, high quality service [were] nowhere to be found."[2] It wiped out nearly all the gains in per capita income made in the 1960s and 1970s, when poverty levels had dropped to 22 percent. In Central America in 1975 the average per capita GDP was $1,052 after a sharp increase during the Alliance for Progress years, but in 1995 it had fallen to $1,001. The per capita GDP of the Caribbean nations declined slightly from an average of $2,387 in 1975 to $2,322 in 1995. Only the per capita GDP of the Mercosur countries rose from $2,692 in 1975 to $3,507 in 1996. The per capita GDP of the Andean countries rose marginally over these two decades from $1,849 in 1975 to $2,123 in 1996. In Brazil, the percentage of households living in poverty rose from 30 percent in 1979 to almost 40 percent in 1990. In Peru, this percentage climbed from 35 percent to almost 45 percent, and in Venezuela, from 18 percent to 32 percent. Only in Chile did this percentage drop from 38 percent to 27 percent during this period.[3] Not only did income distribution become more skewed within the nations, but among the nations also. In retrospect, the record of the American nations' GDP growth during this period of global change was anemic compared with the sharp rise in the GDP of the European Union nations from $13,104 in 1975 to $18,381 in 1996.[4]

Other comparisons are useful as well. Before the debt crisis of 1982, Mexican workers' wages averaged 22 percent of those of U.S. workers. After the sharp devaluations of the next few years, the comparable averages put Mexican workers' wages at 12 percent of U.S. workers' wages. Then in 1996, after the 1994 financial crisis, they fell to 8 percent. The climb back was slow as austerity measures to control inflation kept wages down. Compensation for employees accounts for 72 percent of national income in the United States, whereas in Mexico, it is 30 percent. That is, in the developing countries, labor has been "squeezed in favor of business." To have any impact whatsoever, the trickle-down effect "requires steady economic growth, something that has not happened in Mexico in the last 15 years." With the investment surge as a result of NAFTA, this is only now beginning to be corrected.[5]

Unstable economies subject to inflation and prolonged economic downturns are the greatest enemy of the poor. Although economic adjustment and fiscal discipline are painful, their absence is more painful. A strong tax base and internal savings are essential for governments to support education, health care, and poverty alleviation programs. This does not mean higher taxes but collecting the taxes that are due. A strong tax base requires a responsible private sector, and without it, Latin America's and the Caribbean's resources for investment must come from the savings of other countries, in the form of borrowing.

There is no question that the economic reform of the 1990s failed even in the area in which it was supposed to be most effective: generating employment. The economic reforms produced marginal increases in economic growth and huge increases in unemployment throughout the region.[6] Unemployment data in Latin America take into account only that part of the population already in the workforce. While the workforce in developed countries is generally calculated on a base of 50 to 60 percent of the population, in Latin America the base workforce is 30 to 40 percent of the population. The data omit the rural and the informal economy, those people who neither have nor are seeking a job because they are resigned to fending for themselves outside both the legal and the tax system. The omitted part of the population, euphemistically known as the "informal sector," is alleged to comprise about 30 percent of the economic activity of the entire region. Although these people are not counted as "unemployed," they are very much a part of the social fabric. Thus by using its statistical base to hide the magnitude of the problem, the political and economic decision makers failed to come to grips with the real problems. Even with the lower base, unemployment today, after ten years of economic reform, has barely improved over the pre-1980 figures and in many countries is far more severe.[7]

It seems clear that for small economies with large pockets of poverty, economic reform that does not create jobs hinders the growth of democracy. This is the area in which the opening of the United States' markets to the Americas can have the greatest effect.

Besides its human costs, Latin America's poverty problem has another downside: it impedes long-term economic growth. In the United States, Japan, and Europe, the high earnings of labor drive the purchasing power of the domestic economy and also are important to exports to the major markets of the developed countries. This example is one that entrepreneurs from Latin America have yet to digest. Although competition and monetary stability help determine wages in developing countries, higher wages are the foundation of the internal market.

The bulk of productivity gains must be passed on to the workers to increase their purchasing power, if only for the enlightened self-interest of the entrepreneurs.

THE FACES OF POVERTY

Poverty has two stereotyped faces in Latin America. One is of urban squalor, and the other is of a rural setting with lazy peasants. Urban squalor breeds violence and contempt. Rural poverty is the opposite: it breeds resignation and indifference. Grossly inequitable income distribution is one of the region's biggest problems. The Inter-American Development Bank reports that Latin America has the worst income distribution of any region of the world. Whereas in the 1960s it was slightly better than Africa's, today it worse than Africa's, worse than Asia's, and worse than eastern Europe's. According to the World Bank's *World Development Report*, the richest 20 percent of the populations of Brazil and Mexico now control more than 60 percent of the wealth, with the poorest 20 percent accounting for 2 to 3 percent of the wealth. In contrast, in the United States the top 20 percent control approximately 40 percent, and the lowest 20 percent account for approximately 5 percent of the wealth. While a gap in wealth has always separated the top and bottom rungs of society, it is nothing like the extremes in Latin America, where recent economic reforms have not narrowed the gap. Indeed, Latin America's failure to sustain economic growth has more to do with skewed income distribution, weak domestic consumption, and corruption than it does with anything else.

The inequities that thrived under Venezuelan democracy are a good example. The country is one of the world's richest in natural resources. Nevertheless, 14 million Venezuelans, 60 percent of the population, are poor. Despite earnings from the oil wealth that exceed $500 per person annually, the country has been unable to address urban squalor or create a system of quality education (half of Venezuela's citizens have no more than a primary school education). The country spends only 25 percent of its education budget on primary and secondary education, compared with an average of more than 65 percent in industrialized countries. There is no real escape from poverty without education. The lack of quality education hurts not only the poor but also the rich entrepreneurs, who have been incapable of creating meaningful value-added industries to develop the country's natural resources and provide productive jobs.

The tensions resulting from such inequity came to a head in Venezuela in the 1998 presidential election. For forty years, two political parties dominated Venezuelan politics, but in this election, the two parties were not only thrown out, they received only 6 percent of the vote! Independent candidates received 94 percent, and a former colonel, Hugo Chávez, who had led a coup attempt several years earlier, allegedly to throw out corrupt democratic leaders, was elected president by a landslide.

The complexity and the paradox of Venezuela are compounded in the tragedy of its private sector. Throughout the 1960s, Venezuela's private sector was held up as an example for all of Latin America for at least its verbal commitment to assist the country's social development. When Rómulo Betancourt brought back democracy after the 1950s dictatorship of General Pérez Jiménez, it was hailed a model of democratic reform. The Betancourt government and the private sector expressed a commitment to social and economic development. A 1968 book on philanthropy in Latin America cited almost fifty foundations created by Venezuelan businessmen, led by Eugenio Mendoza, a close friend of Nelson Rockefeller, to assist social causes. Two percent of corporate profits were committed to social causes in a "Voluntary Dividend for the Community." Action programs and microenterprises were initiated in many slum areas. Rockefeller, who promoted the involvement of the private sector, cited Venezuela as model for the future and sponsored several inter-American conferences throughout the country in the 1960s and 1970s on the topic of socially conscious philanthropy.

Thirty years later, the Venezuelan private sector has sunk to inglorious depths with a reputation as one of the least enterprising and most corrupt nations. In 1994, the banking system collapsed, looted of more than $10 billion through corruption and mismanagement. It cost almost 20 percent of the GDP for the Venezuelan taxpayers and the poor, who footed the bill with the contraction of credit and the economy. Yet not one person landed in jail. What happened in Venezuela? How could such a promising beginning crumble into such a ruin? Not only did the private sector abdicate its role in developing the nation, but it also missed out on the wave of investment capital that swept the Americas in the 1990s. Venezuela, rich in oil, gold, aluminum, and other natural resources, could have become a major global power. Israel, a country that did not even exist fifty years ago, with a population of only 5 million and education as its only natural resource, today has a larger gross national product than does resource-rich Venezuela.

Throughout Latin America, this story of poverty is repeated with minor variations, with important exceptions in some countries, such as Chile, Costa Rica, and Uruguay. While measurements of poverty levels are, to say the least, inexact, the general figures are not in question. The World Bank estimates the number of people living below the poverty line as close to 40 percent in urban areas and more than 60 percent in rural areas.[8] The situation is far worse for indigenous groups, which comprise more than 30 percent of the populations of Bolivia, Ecuador, Peru, and Guatemala—and are a significant minority in countries like Honduras, Colombia, Mexico, and Panama. While the absolute numbers of urban poor people are far greater, those in the rural areas are in a more desperate state.[9] In urban areas, the hope of finding productive work exists. In rural areas, it generally does not.

This reflects another harsh reality concerning the issue of poverty, the large difference between poor people in a wealthy country and poor people in a poor country. While poor people in wealthy countries can benefit from the diversity of their societies, those in poor countries have no such option. When disaster strikes a poor country, as it did in Honduras with Hurricane Mitch in 1998, there is no place to turn. There are no domestic reservoirs of support, only assistance from the international community. This is especially true of countries that are poor because of their meager geographical or natural endowment. In the long run, however, the success of a society in overcoming poverty depends on the motivation of its leaders to mobilize resources for this purpose, meager as they may be, and to provide incentives for free enterprise. Governments mirror the values of its society and its citizens who earn the wealth and manage the economy. Citizens who ignore the poverty around them generally have governments that ignore poverty, and societies that mismanage national economies usually mismanage poverty programs.

The principal support mechanism for Latin America's poor is still family networks, as it has been throughout history. Neither the state nor industry provides a meaningful social safety net. Although Latin America was a pioneer in legislating social security systems in the early twentieth century, erratic fiscal policies, corrupt administration, and inflation made the benefits worthless.

Many apologists contend that Latin America today is struggling not only to modernize but also to undo the attitudes bred in a culture inherited from a colonial past—a heritage, as we discussed earlier, of inequality and poverty derived from its Spanish colonial structure. As a result, many countries of the Americas are really two nations. At the top, mostly those of European descent, are those who move easily in international markets and are able to obtain foreign capital for their ventures. At the bottom of the ladder are the rural poor, often of mixed race, who are isolated from the basic services of education and health care. These differences also reflect the underlying issue of race. While there may be little open discrimination, illiteracy rates among indigenous peoples and Afro-Americans are almost double those of the white population, and their access to clean water and sewage disposal is far below that of the white population.

Latin America's colonial heritage tells only part of the story. The societies are also caught up in attitudes motivated by self-interest and corruption. Even where the physical and economic infrastructure is competitive, little progress has been made in the battle against poverty because too many public officials—at all levels—have only a marginal allegiance to their public trust. In too many cases, allocations of resources reflect the personal interests of public officials rather than a sense of social responsibility.

In short, poverty is unquestionably the greatest obstacle to democracy and economic growth in the Americas. How long will it take before it corrodes the integrity of the new democracies? Despite their best efforts, under the current conditions, Latin America and the Caribbean are in danger of falling further behind. In the early days of President John F. Kennedy's Alliance for Progress, it was said to be "one minute to midnight" in Latin America. In the brutal depression of the 1980s, predictions of imminent social upheaval were rife. But even when led by men no less ambitious than Fidel Castro and Che Guevara, midnight never arrived, nor did the populist reactions. To the contrary, the people rushed to embrace democracy. But they are not catching up to the rest of the developed world. Our greatest enemy today is not social upheaval but society's inability to consolidate institutions that promise an even application of the law in the face of self-interest and greed.

THE WAGES OF POVERTY

Shimon Peres, a former prime minister of Israel, once asserted that "crime comes from poverty; terrorism comes from poverty; fanaticism comes from poverty; fundamentalism comes from poverty. No society can succeed when large numbers of its people are mired in poverty." He might well have added the enormous cost to society to fight the violent crime, kidnappings, and guerrilla warfare bred in poverty. In Colombia, for example, the cost of private bodyguards and security measures is said to exceed the amount paid in income taxes by many wealthy families.[10] But the greatest threat comes from the alienation that widespread poverty and squalor generate among educated youth and the middle class. Terrorists and revolutionaries are created by educated elites who have been alienated by a sense of unfairness and helplessness in the poverty they see daily around them.

According to the Inter-American Development Bank, in Latin America, 33 percent of the population live on less than $2 per day, or $500 per year. If the income distribution were the same as in Asia or eastern Europe, less than 8 percent would be in this condition.[11] When combined with rapid population growth and low economic growth, such a skewed income distribution makes it almost impossible for the new democracies to make inroads in the problem of poverty. In this context, Latin America's periodic forays into populism, with its message of redistribution of wealth, only breed cynicism and a sense of hopelessness among the poor. There is no evidence whatsoever that populist rhetoric has ever helped resolve the underlying issues of poverty.

Here again, the issue is partly rooted in a colonial legacy that hobbled the state's efforts to impose systems of fair taxation and thus to build the infrastructure necessary for a modern economy. Albert Hirschman, an economist during President Kennedy's Alliance for Progress initiative, addressed the issue of property taxes:

> The powerful landowning groups seemed to be unwilling to submit to a graduated land tax . . . of sufficient magnitude to mobilize the land market and improve the tenure distribution. By the time the balance of power [shifts] . . . it is too late for such evolutionary and gradual measures . . . [and] owners and non-owners of land are frequently separated by . . . racial and cultural class barriers. The system reinforces the status quo and confers power upon those with inherited position and

wealth. [As a result] [f]arm investment is low, demand for consumer goods restricted, and large segments of the population are held at the margin of the economic mainstream in the countries. Political democracy and social mobility are greatly circumscribed. . . . If one were to superimpose the effects of the other institutional factors—which . . . include access to capital and access to markets, the tax structure, education, local government and other related topics—the situation would appear even darker.[12]

Admittedly, pervasive poverty is not limited to Latin America. In its 1997 report, *Human Development in the World*, the United Nations noted that 800 million people around the world still do not get enough to eat, and 1.3 billion, almost 25 percent of humanity, live on less than $1 a day.[13] Latin Americans represent only 8 percent of the global poor; Southeast Asians account for 39 percent; and Africans number 17 percent. Latin America's 8 percent of the global total, however, comprises nearly one-third of its total population. This is one of the highest percentages of poor as a proportion of the total population of any region of the world and is the greatest difference between the wealthiest and the poorest 5 percent. While the impact of poverty varies, some countries, as in Southeast Asia, have made steady progress while Latin America has regressed.[14]

The good news is the progress being made in ameliorating some of the worst aspects of poverty. Between 1960 and 1995, infant mortality fell from 107 deaths per 1,000 live births to 38 in 1995. Clean water is now available to 75 percent of the population, compared with only 60 percent in 1960. And life expectancy in 1994 averaged sixty-nine, compared with fifty-five in 1960.

The international financial institutions have played a major role in these changes. The Inter-American Development Bank lends an average of $7 billion a year to Latin America and the Caribbean, and the World Bank averages about $5 billion a year. This means that more than $12 billion in external resources is invested annually in development programs, which is $12 billion a year more than the region was able to mobilize in 1960. Almost half goes directly to social-sector projects. When the money from the private sector invested in infrastructure development—as a result of the privatization of power, water, sewage, and transportation facilities—is included, it adds up to a real opportunity for change.

The difficulty of reducing poverty in order to create a solid base for sustainable democracy in Latin America should not be underestimated. In the old Latin America, the state was immobilized by favoritism, patronage, and self-dealing. In recent years, many of the old inefficient state enterprises have been privatized. But the state continues to be unable to provide the fundamental services of security, education, justice, and health. Respect for the rule of law, with full disclosure and transparency, the enforcement of tax laws, a fair system of justice, and progressive labor practices—essential to create a sense of confidence in government as well as to sustain economic growth—are still far too weak.

The lack of progress in reducing poverty during the economic reforms of the 1990s is now creating a strong backlash. Argentina is a good example. On the surface, the economy looked solid for many years. After extensive reforms, Argentina tamed inflation, reduced its budgetary deficits, maintained its currency's parity with the dollar, and cleaned up its banking system. But it was increasingly plagued by the highest unemployment rates in its history, reaching 18 percent in 1999 and a staggering 23 percent after the financial collapse of 2001. As a result of their past trauma with inflation, the Argentinean people remained patient for many years. But their patience wore out in late 2001, and the long simmering resentment at the political establishment and the elites exploded into one of the worst social crises in the country's history. Part of the problem was that in their effort to ensure a sound macroeconomic policy, the U.S. government and the International Monetary Fund (IMF) completely overlooked the impact the crisis would have on the confidence of the people in all of their institutions—political, economic, and judicial. The final chapter of this debacle, loss of trust in government, has yet to be written.

The conclusion is that economic reforms will succeed in consolidating democracy only if they become far more sensitive to social realities. To achieve its goals, democracy and open markets, the reforms cannot be haphazard or piecemeal. They will lose credibility unless matched by social reforms as well as parallel progress in institutional reforms for a more evenhanded and transparent application of the law. Many leaders of Latin America, led by former President Fernando Cardoso of Brazil, recognize this. But their power to address it is weak. If the United States, Canada, and Europe are not prepared to help, the slow pace of today's piecemeal approach is almost certain to fail.

EDUCATION

According to former President Cardoso of Brazil, "Education has to become the essential element in the entire process of development. . . . Otherwise all of the talk of social inclusion is pure hypocrisy."[15] Education is, indeed, the *only* road out of poverty. Yet Latin America's record in the field of education is one of centuries of neglect. The issue is not money. Latin America spends as much on education as do other developing countries measured as a percentage of GDP, almost 4.5 percent.[16] Rather, the issue is quality. Inter-American Development Bank and UNESCO studies place the quality of education in Latin America among the lowest of developing nations. While education experts were concentrating on enrollment rates, they overlooked what was happening in the schoolhouse. There, political as well as bureaucratic infrastructure has become more important than the students. Although ministries of education were given adequate budgets, few politicians paid attention to how it was being spent. In countries where jobs were at a premium, teaching was, at least, a job. One Argentinean minister was quoted as saying, "the number of people teaching is very small compared with the number of teachers."[17] Twenty percent of the teachers are said to be "ghost" teachers who never show up.[18] Examples are legion of school construction contracts awarded to political backers or teachers recruited in return for political patronage. Textbooks arrive at rural destinations only rarely and often not because they were not paid for. The *Financial Times* reported that one mayor in Brazil closed a local school because the teacher there opposed his election.[19] Social-sector ministries such as education are the most notorious repositories for political patronage.

The causes are many. Low salaries for teachers, especially in rural areas, lead to political agitation for increases, which are given priority over teaching materials or training. Poor teacher training makes whatever education is available to the poor only marginal. In many countries, school lasts for only a half day in order to accommodate a second job for underpaid teachers. After about fourth grade, many of the teachers, especially in rural areas, are barely a grade ahead of their students. Adequate teaching materials are almost nonexistent. Too much money is spent on administration at the expense of books, equipment, and teacher training. More than 40 percent of the budget of Venezuela's Ministry of Education is for bureaucracy. The moment any money becomes available in the national education budget, the teachers' unions press for it to go to salary increases. Textbooks and teaching materials take second place. The teachers' unions also protect the teachers from being accountable to national testing or to their communities. Even in Chile, where literacy is among the highest in the region and educational reforms are the most successful, teachers' unions oppose the creation of "schools of excellence" and performance-based pay. Teachers' strikes are one of the most disruptive political weapons.

The worst problem is the gap in schooling between the rich and the poor. Inter-American Development Bank studies show that the lowest 10 percent of the population receive four years of schooling, sometimes for only three or four hours a day, while the highest 10 percent average twelve years, full time. Research shows that programs to improve education and health stimulate economic growth and are among the best investments for a developing country. They provide a clear return on investment, estimated at 24 percent for the primary level and 15 percent for the secondary level. While many factors go into the analysis, it is interesting that the positive correlation between the decline of poverty and the increase in education holds true for almost every country examined.[20]

I had the opportunity in Haiti to observe at first hand the results of inattention to education. Thirty years ago, I went to review what seemed to me at the time to be important technical assistance programs. The Organization of American States and the International Development Bank were working on agriculture, irrigation, small industries, and road building. But with almost 70 percent functional illiteracy in the country (President Jean-Bertrande Aristide told me it was really closer to 90 percent), there is little hope of developing the economy or a cohesive political system. Sustainable democracy in Haiti is a fantasy without a better educated citizenry. Nor is there much hope for progress in the economy for a workforce largely without skills. The impact of illiteracy affects every sector of a country's social and political life. Take a simple matter like forestation. Thirty years ago, 50 percent of Haiti was forested, and deforestation was proceeding rapidly with the growth of the population. Enormous amounts of international aid were included in many programs to help reforest the other 50 percent. Yet today the country is virtually 100 percent deforested. In retrospect, I believe that if we had done nothing else in Haiti for the last thirty years but concentrate on education, it would be far better off today. Uneducated subsistence farmers in an overpopulated country think only of their immediate needs. For them, long-term concerns are what their next meal will be.

In contrast, educated people have different expectations of their political leaders and for their communities, especially regarding their children's education. The example is clearest among women. Because educated women have fewer children, education also is central to slowing the population growth. Education also makes a tremendous difference in a country's health practices, with the education of girls the most influential factor. Educated mothers have healthier children and are far more conscious of the importance of clean water and sewage disposal. Educated mothers also are less likely to have uneducated children. And yet UNICEF reports that women still comprise almost 70 percent of the world's functionally illiterate people.

In addition, education raises the output of workers and farmers, and educated workers earn higher incomes. East Asia today is witness to the direct, positive correlation between education and sustained economic growth. For example, in 1960 South Korea's primary school enrollment of 94 percent stood in stark contrast to the average 60 percent enrollment rates in Latin American countries with comparable income levels.

The urban-rural divide is another sign of the skewed allocation of resources. In Mexico, at least 50 percent of the rural youth do not go to high school, and in most of the smaller countries, the percentages are even higher. Inter-American Development Bank studies of children found that standardized test results from schools in rural areas are at least 15 percent lower than those from private schools in urban areas. Brazil raised its literacy rate from 50 percent to 82 percent between 1950 and 1990, but the rural northeast still is 60 percent illiterate. The statistics are even worse for graduates of elementary school. In northeast Brazil, the Inter-American Development Bank reports that only 10 percent finish the eighth grade.

Development planners greatly underestimate the thirst for education. There is a real market for learning. The poor and the middle class are willing to pay for it if they think it will help them earn more money. Indeed, there is hardly a city or town in Latin America in which a small private school to teach secretarial, computer, or language skills cannot be found. Both politicians and private-sector leaders should take heed.

THE PRIVATE SECTOR AND CIVIC RESPONSIBILITY

As a practical matter, overcoming poverty is vital to all sectors of society but most of all to the private sector. Growth depends on investment, and as Lawrence Summers, former U.S. secretary of the treasury, pointed out, private capital flows thrive on stability and prospects for continuing economic growth. Markets have little tolerance for the social instability that results from events such as Chiapas, the civil conflict in Colombia, the Sendero Luminoso in Peru, or the riots in Venezuela. The social dangers in the recurrent financial crises and their potential effect on the flow of investments were immediately recognized by the international community. In the 1990s, the Inter-American Development Bank and the World Bank mobilized resources specifically to relieve the pressures that enforced economic austerity would have on social services so that the poor did not bear the brunt of the budgetary cuts as they did in the 1980s. With the roots of democracy now spreading, consensus building and attention to all sectors of the electorate are mandatory. Without them, a heavy price will be paid in electoral loses, the reversal of market openings, and the destabilization of democracy.

In this regard, the role, the attitudes and motivation of the private sector are important to the future of democracy. They are a critical link in a tightly closed circle. No democracy can ensure a stable government without meaningful social development. It cannot ensure social development without economic development to promote growth and provide jobs. It cannot have economic development without investment, and it cannot attract investment unless investors have confidence in political stability. The circle thus closes because political stability is not possible without social development.

The role of private capital in financing the infrastructure and investing in facilities that produce prosperity cannot be underestimated. Only the private sector has pockets deep enough to do this on the scale needed. Governments do not have sufficient capital to maintain the flow of investments needed to keep up with technological changes because of the high demand on its limited resources to provide education, health, and security.

But it will take a while before people regain trust in the private sector in Latin America. In the late 1960s one of the causes of the technocrats' turn to state enterprise was the almost universal dismay at the pervasive corruption of Latin America's private sector. Regardless, every society must come to terms with the role of the private sector. It comes down to a simple equation:

- Poor people cannot escape from poverty unless they have productive jobs.
- They cannot have productive jobs unless they have skills and can produce value-added goods.
- They cannot produce value-added goods unless they can get them to market.
- They cannot get them to market unless there is adequate infrastructure in the form of roads, ports, power, and communications.

In short, developing countries thrive only as their industry thrives, and their industry thrives only as their domestic purchasing power grows. Without productive jobs, we may try to develop the economy, but there will be no domestic foundation. Without productive jobs we may try to temper the effects of poverty, but we are not providing an avenue of escape. When they have jobs, the poor people of Latin America spend their money on products that drive domestic industry. When they do not have jobs, they are a source of perpetual instability. When they do not have jobs, the poor of Latin America are becoming increasingly mobile. They move to their own urban areas looking for work. Many of the best and most ambitious emigrate to the United States, legally or illegally. It is in the interest of the private sector to reverse this cycle in order to achieve sustainable democracies and sustainable open markets.

The elites of Latin America, however, have failed to demonstrate that they understand that the purchasing power of the poor is the missing link in the Latin American economic growth chain. They have not learned the lessons from the United States and Europe about the need for a broad and deep domestic market as the bedrock of a national economy. The masses of poor people in their midst are the potential market that will consume their products and drive the domestic economy. When poor people earn better wages, they do not stuff the money into their mattresses; they spend it. Better wages, better education, and a motivated workforce attract investment. When they emerge from poverty, the prospective purchasing power of the poor will be the real engine for domestic economic growth. These factors have been the motor of the great U.S. job machine. Until they understand and act on these basic laws of economics and politics, the region's prospects for new democracies and economic prosperity will remain uncertain.

BOTTOMS UP

Credit for productive enterprises is the most direct means to enable the poor to lift themselves out of poverty. Credit programs, whether to start a business or to improve a community, have proved enormously successful. Known as *microenterprises*, such programs today can be found everywhere. The *Financial Times* reported on an entire town in Mexico, Chipilo, that "today resounds with the clatter of hammers, saws and industrial lathes . . . with 68 furniture and metal workshops, many of them erected beside family cow sheds," which are producing furniture for export financed with microloans from an antique reproduction factory that itself got its start as a microenterprise.[21] This is the informal economy that operates beneath the surface of the formal economy.

Hernando de Soto of Peru described the informal economy in his book *The Other Path*. He showed how another economy, entirely self-contained, operated outside society's normal rules and regulations. Street vendors, back-alley workshops repairing cars and producing shoes, and small merchants of all kinds comprise this economy. It operates outside the legal structure, partly because of the complexity of incorporating and creating a legal entity. De Soto illustrates his point by showing how someone could incorporate a business in Florida in four hours but that in Peru it required more than two hundred separate steps and took more than six months. Another reason for the shadow economy is the people's distrust of government. They do not want to be on any local authority's list. They do not want the government to know about them, especially those agencies that collect taxes or charge for the use of electricity or water.

Borrowing for an microenterprise, however, is different. Poor people have always been borrowers. They borrow from the usurers, from their friends, from the village store. They pay exorbitant interest rates to usurers, often as much as 10 percent a day. So borrowing for microenterprises is not new. The poor also save money, not in banks but in tangible materials. Instead of putting their money in a bank to save for a house, they build their house, one brick at a time. Every extra penny goes to buy a brick or cement. Throughout Latin America, shantytowns formerly made of cardboard and tin are now cement and brick, transformed slowly, brick by brick, over many years.

Credit programs for the poor were pioneered in Latin America as long ago as 1966, when I took part in an experimental program to offer small loans to poor communities to install village improvements such as water pumps and small schoolhouses. The program was under the auspices of the Pan American Development Foundation of the Organization of American States. We asked the poor communities, "Do you want to wait years for the government to come and install a water system, or do you want us to provide the money for you to build it yourself?" The answer was unequivocal. They wanted to do things for themselves. The only proviso was that each family receiving a loan had to chip in a few pennies each week to repay the revolving fund so that others could benefit as they did. Indeed, one of the first foundations was called the Penny Foundation. In 1965 the U.S. Agency for International Development (USAID) rejected a request for $25,000 to launch such a program, so we had to organize it as a social program and charity because no one believed that poor people would ever repay their loans. The Organization of American States provided the initial funds, although it, too, considered it a charity because it never expected the funds to be repaid. Little did we know then, but this was the beginning of what has evolved into microenterprises.

Today, USAID, the World Bank, and many bilateral aid programs favor microenterprises. Women's World Banking, organized by a former investment banker, has a program to provide microloans to women around the world who often find it impossible to get any kind of commercial credit. Microlending programs can now be found throughout Latin America in something many observers have hailed as "changing the face of foreign aid," with Acción International, Banco Sol of Bolivia, Community Credit of CARE, Orion of Peru, ADEMI of the Dominican Republic, and many others stepping in to fill the enormous needs of low-income groups. It is no longer surprising to find that the repayment records of microfinance programs are better than those of many commercial banks. Credit to help poor entrepreneurs improve their lives on their own without waiting for the government is one of the greatest hopes for Latin America.

8

Undermining Prosperity

Corruption and Narcotics

Put a genius on the wrong path and he will fly ever more quickly to
the wrong results.

CARLOS HANK GONZALEZ, the son of a German solider who mi-
grated to Mexico, spent most of his professional life in government
posts, including several ministries and as mayor of Mexico City. Before
his recent death he was listed as one of Mexico's richest men, with holdings alleged to exceed $1 billion. Hank Gonzalez's family holdings in-
cluded a partnership with General Motors, Daimler-Benz, and a major
stake in Laredo National Bank in Texas.[1] He proudly proclaimed that "a
politician who is poor is a poor politician." A former mayor of São
Paulo, Brazil, took pride in his slogan, *"Robo, mas faco* [I steal but I
build]." Both were tolerated by both the electorate and society.

Today, there is good news and bad news. The good news is, as a
Latin American friend recently commented, "Corruption is no fun anymore." The issue is openly addressed everywhere. The press—the part
that is not bought off by corruption—is becoming more daring. Citizen
groups are vocal. The threat of exposure and prosecution is real. Av-
enues for money laundering are narrowing. And the patience of an increasingly sophisticated public is running out. Presidential summit
meetings openly condemn the practice, and the nations of the hemisphere have approved the Inter-American Convention Against Corruption which is monitored by the Organization of American States.

The bad news is in two areas. First is the fact that corruption per-
tains to power and spoils, a drive that has not abated throughout history. Second, the civil service remains severely underpaid. As long as
this remains the case, government officials will always be susceptible to

corruption. The absence of strong institutions to enforce the rule of law and secure property rights forces the private sector to bribe public officials to protect them. One Mexican businessman I knew used to call the petty corruption "user fees." Since the Mexican government did not pay civil servants livable wages, he explained, they earned compensation for their services by directly charging the user. "Market forces at work," he would laugh. Another businessman I met during this period made a more worrisome confession. If he did not take part in the graft, he would not be *trusted* by his peers! He added that he would be considered a fool and would certainly get no business.

Corruption has two partners, corrupters and corruptees. The corrupters are generally from the private sector, and the corruptees may be found in both the private and the public sector. The two work in a close embrace, like mesmerized tango dancers. As we noted earlier, the trend toward centralized state controls accelerated in Latin America in the 1960s as a result of the perception of the private sector as the worst corrupter. The dynamics of small elitist societies feed on themselves, and the new technocrat managers were quickly sucked into the process. Helpless electorates had few means to halt the trend with a weak rule of law, controlled media, and no institutional base for accountability.

The incestuous relationship between the private sector and underpaid government officials is an active one. Domingo Cavallo, a former finance minister of Argentina, proclaimed that in societies with weak law enforcement, *every* government regulation is a breeding ground for corruption, and every regulation becomes an opportunity for extortion. Many ministers caught with their hands in the till are not career politicians but people from the private sector. Today, with the extensive privatization and regulatory oversight managed by the same underpaid civil servants, this sordid history has a fertile field to repeat itself.

If any one practice can subvert democracy and open markets in Latin America, it will be the failure to curtail corruption. The lack of transparency and accountability in governmental operations is one of the more vexing problems facing developing countries. Whatever problems the Americas suffer, from housing and health projects to security or government services, the failures can often be traced to corruption. Perhaps the most pernicious problem is not what happens but what does not happen. Countless numbers of entrepreneurial people do nothing because of prevailing attitudes in a corrupt society.

This is a difficult problem for the United States. In the past we had our own sordid record of openly tolerating corruption. During the cold war, our principal concern was countering Communism. We did not choose our allies for their honesty. We supported almost any leader who opposed the left, with no compunctions if he was corrupt or if innocent citizens got caught in the web. We gave no thought to breaking up monopolies, opening markets to competition, or penalizing corruption if the practitioners were anti-Communist. As a result, businessmen from all over the world participated in corrupt practices in the Americas while the U.S. government silently observed, in full knowledge of what was going on.

No matter what programs are instituted to combat corruption, the issue cannot be separated from society's respect for the rule of law. The framers of the U.S. Constitution were well aware of the problem of corruption and argued for strong governmental institutions to protect against the "greed, avarice and obstinacy of their fellow citizens."[2] In Latin America today there is a paradox between the pressure for respect for the rule of law and the corruption of the judicial system itself, which allows contractual obligations to be disregarded and corrupt criminals to escape prosecution—for a fee.

Even today, the way that corruption is addressed in Latin America is disconnected from reality. Polls confirm that most important to citizens is security from crime on the streets, better education, and a fair system of justice. But when asked whether they would be willing to pay reasonable salaries to judges, police, and teachers to help make this happen, the answer is generally negative. As an old saying goes, when you pay your public officials peanuts, you'll get monkey business.

The temptations are legion. Customs officials and government procurement employees are responsible for processing millions of dollars annually. Yet their pay is paltry, and there are few mechanisms for accountability. In other words, in many countries, the lack of institutionalized systems for disclosure give public officials almost carte blanche to act, with little fear of getting caught.

The ethics depicted in the popular culture acknowledge the pervasiveness of the issue. In the popular *telenovelas*, Latin America's version of the soap opera, everyone takes advantage of everyone else. The husband cheats on the wife; the wife cheats on the husband; the husband cheats on his business; the business partners cheat on one another; the maid steals from the household; the maid returns to her shantytown only to run the gauntlet of petty local thieves. When she gets home, she finds her husband is cheating on her, and on and on. In many countries the poor people are far more afraid of corrupt, unaccountable police than they are of thieves. In Brazil, there is a saying in the poor areas that "if you are in danger, call a thief."

In the long run, efforts to curb corruption are doomed until a more professional, better-paid cadre of civil servants gain respect for the rule of law and society is more open to social mobility. When President-elect Lionel Fernández of the Dominican Republic vowed to "root out corruption" in the mid-1990s, one Dominican friend commented to me about the futility of the effort. He said that the president's party had been out of power for twelve years and that in the Dominican Republic, a government job was the only avenue for social mobility for the middle class. His conclusion was that there was no way the president was going to be able to control his cohorts' determination to take advantage of their turn at the trough.

Corruption takes many forms, of which outright bribery is but one. In Brazil they refer to corruption, clientelism, and *caudilhos*. Corruption is found in favoritism, in self-dealing among the private sector, and in the self-aggrandizement of union officials. Most of it is internal: favoritism in government purchases, monopolies, and laws benefiting certain imports. A pernicious practice among Latin America democracies is for a newly elected political party to divert attention by charging the previous party with corruption while it goes about preparing its own networks of corruption. The worst manifestation of corruption is in the banking system, which has been described as a license for stealing.

Latin America, with its history of bank failures, has to be especially vigilant. Bank failures that result from self-dealing and inept management—not to speak of outright stealing—are one of the biggest burdens the economies have had to bear. In Chile, Venezuela, Mexico, Ecuador, and several smaller countries, bank failures over the last two decades have cost the taxpayers up to 20 percent of the countries' GDP. Compare this with the 3.5 percent that the savings and loan scandal cost U.S. taxpayers in the 1980s. In Argentina, for example, an inquiry into the loss of $67 billion from the Central Bank in 1989 revealed that 80 percent of the money went to bail out failed banks and subsidize private companies selected by favoritism. The governments of developing countries cover these costs by additional international borrowing, the repayment of which falls to the taxpayers and future generations, diverting resources from social projects to cover the expense of rescuing the banks.

Whenever it appears, corruption results in the misallocation of resources. It undermines the rule of law, favors duplicity rather than productivity, rewards inefficiency, and destroys the integrity of the markets. It is wrong and hypocritical to scoff at Latin America's problem. The corporate scandals in the United States with Enron, WorldCom, and others have unmasked the widespread hypocrisy found on many levels in many countries. One former Latin American president said to me that "as long as the Europeans keep spreading money around the way they do, any efforts to combat corruption are futile." Indeed, until recently in several European countries, bribery of foreign officials was not only condoned, it was recognized as a legitimate, tax-deductible expense.

The political dimension of corruption and drugs leaves democracy vulnerable and its future unpredictable. Hugo Chávez's rise to power in Venezuela will have deep repercussions on the future of Latin American democracy. Whatever one thinks of the way in which he manages the institutions of democracy, President Chávez was elected on a platform consisting almost exclusively of resentment of the pervasive corruption. The nerves he touched among the Venezuelan people were evidenced in their initial overwhelming support despite his difficulties in addressing the country's economic issues. His election was not the action of a small elite arrogating power for themselves through arms and repression, like that of Fidel Castro. Rather, Chávez's election was an endorsement by a majority of the people in a democratic election. He conscientiously followed the procedures and institutions of democracy in order to achieve almost absolute power. For two years, he moved slowly, step by step, referendum by referendum, adhering to every constitutional process. First he won a referendum for a new constitution in which his supporters received 121 of 135 seats. This was not a rigged election; it was carefully monitored and verified by international observers. The result was so overwhelming that there was no question about the results.

The magnitude of the political void that Hugo Chávez moved to fill revealed the tremendous loss of credibility of democratic institutions over years of mismanagement and the rule of greed. But the grossly mishandled attempt to overthrow him in 2002 revealed Chávez's failure to understand and accommodate the diverse interests of democ racy. Even as opposition grew to his stewardship and alleged corruption within his own administration, however, the people's frustration with corruption continued unabated. With a term of six years and re-election possible, Hugo Chávez could be around for twelve years. If he survives the current onslaught of opposition, within a few years he could become one of the more experienced presidents of the hemisphere, and with Venezuela's huge oil resources at his disposal, he could become a major voice in shaping Latin America's policies and political attitudes.

The closest recent analogy to President Chávez is the momentum that brought Juan Perón to absolute power in Argentina in the 1950s. In Perón's case, his own corruption and favoritism destroyed the country's infrastructure, which required twenty years to rebuild. In Venezuela, the wealth from its petroleum and other natural resources far exceeds that of Argentina. If Hugo Chávez had the ability to address the issue of corruption while managing the economy, he could make a difference. But if, like Juan Perón, he uses the populist banner of anti-corruption as a mask for indulgence, future generations will inherit a country shrouded in cynicism.

The most damaging impact of corruption is on the revenue side of governmental operations, where it contributes to the region's anemic tax collections and budget deficits. In many cases, money is just stolen by the tax collectors. In 1997 in Bolivia, the Chamber of Commerce estimated that uncollected import duties and other taxes amounted to $450 million, the same amount as the country's budget deficit. In other cases, the contempt for corruption in government discourages the private sector from paying taxes. In Guatemala, citizens on all levels oppose taxes on the grounds that "government cannot be trusted to use the money properly."[3]

While Argentina began to address the problem of petty corruption—to the extent of turning over responsibility for customs inspection to private companies, "to curb rampant tariff evasion, contraband and dumping"[4]—the people of Argentina strongly attribute the collapse of their economy to the corruption of the entire political establishment, including legislators and judicial officials. Argentina's case is not an isolated one. The sale of favors by relatives of high officials was the center of the controversy surrounding former President Carlos Salinas of Mexico, whose daring moves to open Mexico to NAFTA and the global economy were overshadowed by scandals involving his brother. The

recent president of Brazil's legislature, Jader Barbalho, is being prose-
cuted, along with several Brazilian legislators and governors.

Corruption flourishes where there is weak political accountability,
a lack of transparency in finance, no requirement for disclosure for the
private sector, and the absence of competitive procurement practices.
As part of his New Deal in the 1930s, President Franklin D. Roosevelt
considered disclosure to be the best way of discouraging the manipulation of private finance and discouraging corruption. The principal instrument of the then new Securities and Exchange Commission (SEC)
was disclosure. Competitive bidding for government purchases was
ensured by the establishment of a centralized agency, the General Services Administration (GSA), which oversaw competitive procedures for
all government purchases. To address the issue in foreign markets, Congress passed the Foreign Corrupt Practices Act (FCPA). U.S. companies
at first complained that they were being severely handicapped when
"competing" (note: corruption was part of competition) with foreign
businesses because of the law, and for several years they fought for its
repeal. Finally, however, they realized that their efforts were futile, and
so they joined the crusade to help the U.S. government persuade other
governments to adopt similar laws. In 1997, the European governments
agreed to outlaw bribery and to adopt provisions similar to the U.S. legislation. Today, a new European Union agreement prohibits paying foreign bribes in the same manner that the Foreign Corruption Practices
Act does in the United States. Relentless U.S. pressure on governments
around the world, aided by the World Bank and Inter-American Development Bank in insisting on transparency in their international bidding, is beginning to show results.

The major global accounting firms have a strong responsibility in
this effort. Although the recent corporate scandals in the United States
suggest they, too, have been part of the problem, they have a key role in
finding the solution, as they are the principal watchdogs for enforcing
transparency rules and adhering to generally accepted accounting prin-
ciples (GAAP). Progress is being made slowly. Today the issue is at least
openly talked about, whereas ten years ago hardly anyone mentioned
it. The fight against corruption reminds me of the fight for human rights
in the early 1960s. As the first U.S. staff member of the Inter-American
Commission on Human Rights, I impatiently argued for all sorts of activist programs. "No," was the wise advice of Luis Reque, the commission's first director. "Our first task is to let the governments and the peo-

ple get used to the fact that we are here. Let's first set the precedent that we can shine a spotlight on the issues. In a few years our presence will be irreversible. Then we can be more active." Soon that spotlight generated its own heat, and ten years later when the commission was really needed, it was a solid, firm, irreversible institution. Today the same thing is beginning to happen in the battle against corruption. The spotlight is now on, and we can hope, as my friend remarked, that before long, corruption will definitely not be fun anymore.

THE DRUG TRADE

Colombia's present battle against drug-financed armies is the culmination of a long, tragic history. I was in Colombia in 1986 when drug thugs invaded the supreme court and took the justices hostage. Nine of them were murdered, and roomfuls of irreplaceable records were destroyed. The cause of the atrocity was the possible extradition of narco-criminals to the United States. In 1989, when the drug lords were at the peak of their power, three Colombian presidential candidates were assassinated. Thousands of mayors, judges, police officers, and journalists have been murdered. A reliable estimate is that more than 30,000 people are killed each year and that the violence has created more than 100,000 refugees. The price being paid by Colombian society for their toleration of the drug trade in the 1980s is inconceivable to U.S. citizens.

For every murder or kidnapping that reaches the public's attention, however, countless more are not reported. For every drug bust that comes to the public's attention, scores of people—public officials and peasants alike—participate in the trade undetected. Once targeted by the drug mafias, public officials have an unimaginable dilemma. Judges and mayors who have the misfortune of getting in the way of drug traffickers too often are confronted with the choice of *"pluma o plata,"* previously noted as an option to either take bribes or bullets. The drug cartels are far more omnipresent and exacting in their demands than the U.S. attorney general, and they do not give their targets trials and due process of law.

Next to corruption, one of the greatest threats to democracy is the drug trade and the violence against citizens that it engenders. When the United States invaded Panama and kidnapped General Manuel Noriega in 1989, it highlighted the fact that Panama had become the first country virtually controlled by the drug mafias. Mexico's continuing battle against the drug shipments shows the extent of the mafias' penetration of the police and security forces. The mafias' ability to bribe, corrupt, and extort from public officials would stretch the imagination of the most violent TV drama writers. Few American governments have the financial wherewithal to combat the wealthiest criminal organizations ever known in the history. In several countries such as Bolivia and Peru, they became a major threat to the government's stability before the leaders took action. Today, Bolivia has set the target of becoming drug free, at a huge cost. It is suffering from severe political unrest at the same time as the well-financed drug industry underwrites civil disobedience among the poor indigenous farmers, who make a better living producing coca than anything the other part of the free market offers them.

The complexities of addressing the issue are evident from the amount of money involved. U.S. Senator John Kerry estimated that the global revenue of the drug trade is more than $400 billion annually. In 1999, *Fortune* reported that the value of Mexico's drug shipments "have climbed to an estimated *$120 billion a year* [emphasis added] . . . equal to a third of Mexico's official GDP of $360 billion and more than twice the value of its exports of legal goods such as oil." According to this same article, the net worth of the principal Mexican drug peddler, Juan García Abrego, was thought to be approximately $15 billion. It is significant that the drug barons' influence in Mexico reportedly originated in the financial crisis in 1982. The Mexican government, humiliated and rebuffed in its quest for financial aid from the United States is alleged to have made a secret pact with the drug kingpins to deposit their money in Mexican banks to help alleviate the growing economic crisis. Similarly, the Colombian economy was one of the best performing in all Latin America throughout the 1980s, an achievement that many people attributed to the influx of drug money.

The success of the drug mafias results from the juxtaposition of the world's largest consumer of illicit drugs, the United States, and its operation under governments that are both poorly equipped to contain it and under severe pressure to apply their limited resources to address social problems and poverty, not to fight drugs. During the 1980s, political leaders of Latin America openly expressed their cynicism of the United States' position. They pointed to the hypocrisy of its policy toward Mexico, which was, at the time, the leading supplier of marijuana to the United States. With intense U.S. pressure and assistance, Mexico significantly reduced its production of marijuana. Within a short time, the leading supplier of marijuana to U.S. consumers was California. These huge quantities are not grown in small family plots and transported by bicycle but are major growing and transportation operations. Indeed, the U.S. interdiction of Mexican marijuana became known as the most effective trade protection program this country ever instituted.

The difficult issue for the Americas is the continuing "metastasizing" of the problem. Drug organizations are not being eradicated; they are simply forced to move to different areas of a vast unpoliced continent. If leaders are arrested, the operations find new ones. Demand in the United States is so strong that every time production is shut down in one area, it reemerges in other areas or other countries. When the Colombian cartels in Medellín and Cali were broken, 60 percent of the drug production was handed over to small "boutique" syndicates. The growth in Colombia was given a further boost when both Peru and Bolivia began to cooperate extensively with U.S. enforcement agents and nearly shut down the drug producers. Peru shrank its producing areas from more than 100,000 hectares in 1994 to less than 50,000 in 1999. Bolivia, under a series of three presidents, has now eradicated all drug production. But the cost to the poor has been enormous. The United States has helped with millions of dollars for eradication, but only pennies for the alleviation of poverty.

At the same time that Peru and Bolivia were successful in controlling production, Colombia increased its planting. Satellite photos from the UN's Drug Control Program (UNDCP), estimates that in 2000 Colombia's coca fields covered more than 400,000 acres, despite the claims of the Colombian police to have sprayed 143,000 acres. The capacity of such extensive planting is estimated to exceed 800 tons of cocaine (U.S. consumption is estimated at 270 tons a year). Bruce Bagley, an expert on Colombia, reported that

by 1999, Colombia had become the premier coca-cultivating country in the world, producing more coca leaf than both Peru and Bolivia combined. Between 1989 and 1998, Colombia coca leaf production increased by 140 percent, from 33,900 to 81,400 metric tons. Even more remarkable, 1999 production levels more than doubled the 1998 totals, reaching an estimated 220 tons. . . . This explosive expansion occurred in spite of a permanent Colombia National Police Eradication program that sprayed a record 65,000 hectares (145,000 acres) of coca in 1998 alone.[5]

The United States' myopic policies between 1994 and 1998 during the presidency of Ernesto Samper so weakened the fragile Colombian government that those insurgents who planted coca thrived. But the United States considered its policies a righteous defense of democracy and accused President Samper of selling out to the mafias in accepting campaign finance. Bowing to the pressure, President Samper's record in combating the drug trade soon became better than that of his predecessors. Colombia maintained a vigorous drug eradication program during that period, chemically destroying more than 25,000 hectares a year. U.S. moral indignation, however, was implacable. Harsh measures against the Samper administration, including its unilateral "decertification," undermined Colombian political institutions during the period, discouraged investment, and created a fertile environment for the real drug industry to thrive.

The cost to Colombian society has been enormous. Dissension among the governing elites weakened the governing institutions and controls over the police and the bureaucracy. The government was almost totally exhausted from fighting the left-wing insurrection, and the ability of the underfinanced police to maintain law and order collapsed. Unable to stop the kidnappings, bank robberies, and extortion, criminal activity soon grew into an industry of its own. The guerrillas' coffers overflowed. They were able to strengthen their forces, recruit their own mercenaries, and form an alliance with the drug industry that made both even richer. They had far more resources and were far better equipped than the legitimate security forces. In the face of a government deprived by the ill-advised U.S. policy of the wherewithal to fight the insurgency, wealthy entrepreneurs began to defend themselves by financing vigilant paramilitary organizations. Respect for human rights and the rule of law collapsed—on both sides.

As a result, the United States and other nations are now forced to pour enormous amounts of money into Colombia to help the beleaguered Colombian government fight the drug lords and insurrection militias, as well as to revive its battered economy and strengthen the institutions of justice and democracy. The new "Plan Colombia," approved by the U.S. Congress in 2000, will cost a minimum of $7.5 billion, of which $4 billion will come from Colombia, $1.3 billion from the United States, and the balance from other cooperating countries. Preventive measures would have cost a fraction of that amount, and the outcome of the battle is far from clear. Unlike the battles against insurgency that were waged in Central America in the 1980s, the alliance of the guerrilla forces and the drug industry gives the insurgents an unprecedented ability to finance themselves.

The worst aspect of the conflict is the spillover of criminal activity into the countries bordering on Colombia, especially Ecuador, which had long been an oasis from Latin America's narco-trafficking. As a result, small countries with small tax bases are hard pressed to meet the social pressures of democracy, much less strengthen its security forces along the border. A far wiser U.S. policy would be either to create multilateral security through an effort, modeled on NATO, by all American countries or to provide direct assistance for the countries to maintain their own security forces.

One of the more embarrassing aspects of the drug problem is that most of the profits from the narcotics traffic remain in the developed countries where the narcotics are sold. It is estimated that less than 20 cents of each dollar returns to the producing country, of which only pennies go to the producers. The real profits are right here in the United States where most of the money laundering takes place. Unfortunately, the United States itself has been derelict in enforcing the recommendations of the Financial Action Task Force, as stock brokers and insurance companies are not required to comply with reporting requirements for suspicious transactions, leaving a significant loophole in efforts to stem money laundering.

One of the most bizarre elements of the drug story in Latin America was the civic-minded behavior of some of the first drug barons. The Cali cartel, for example, was well aware of the importance of "corporate social responsibility." *Fortune* magazine reported that "over 20 percent of the population in certain rural areas is employed by the narcotraficos, who have built schools and hospitals for their workers and invested in local banks."[6] In Cali, Colombia, the Rodriguez brothers built housing developments, schools, hospitals, and playgrounds and supported civic organizations in a grand manner. Since they were apprehended, however, their enterprises have been divided among lesser lords whose clandestine activities have been distinctively antisocial in every respect.

The only way to win this battle is through the cooperation of all the hemispheric nations. Until now, the isolated, unilateral efforts to criminalize participants, dismantle organized cartels, and eradicate and interdict production have yielded conspicuously poor results. To be successful, inter-American collaboration cannot be piecemeal. It requires better-paid and -trained police forces and economic support to create new employment and economic opportunities. It must be multidimensional to deal with the many areas that feed on the criminal activity, from controlling traffic in armaments and the substances used to manufacture narcotics to laundering money. Only the United States has the financial resources to wage this war against the drug trade in the Americas. Success will require the same degree of organizational focus, determination, and collaboration that NATO used in the cold war. Not only is it time for such an effort, but the war cannot be won and democracy cannot be sustained without it. If the United States pressures the Latin American and Caribbean countries to act without offering them commensurate economic resources, we will force them to curtail education and social development. It would be a self-defeating and contradictory policy.

There has been progress. The elements of hemispheric cooperation in this area are beginning to be recognized. A multilateral evaluation mechanism (MEM) to review each of the American government's policies in this area was recently launched by the OAS. This mechanism is important to the United States, as it goes to the heart of the thesis of this book: that full and responsible collaboration of democracies in the Americas is strongly in the United States' interest. Many people in Latin America and the Caribbean are taking a stand against drugs at a far greater risk to their lives than the average U.S. citizen can imagine. They need a meaningful support mechanism. The hemisphere needs a comprehensive, real safety net for all those in the battle.

In the long run, this battle, which pits the world's largest consumer of drugs against poor countries that produce or transport them, will be won only by building the bases of economic prosperity. Small countries with vulnerable economies and enormous social pressures need the collaboration of the United States to be successful. If the United States fails to respond with effective policies, it will, at best, make the task of consolidating democracy far more difficult. At worst, it will result in the failure of democracy, with tremendous setbacks in the battle against international crime. If we do respond with a comprehensive program and a NATO-like mobilization, history suggests that we will see the emergence of a meaningful system of mutual support that will be an essential building block for the realization of Greater America.

PART II

THE AMERICAS IN THE GLOBAL ECONOMY

Building a Greater America

9

Commerce and Foreign Policy

BILL GATES gave us a hint of the world to come in his observation that he did not consider Microsoft a United States corporation; he considered it a global corporation that happened to be headquartered in the United States. Alfred Zeien, the CEO of Gillette, commented that thinking of business in terms of national boundaries was obsolete. "We treat the world as a single nation," he said.[1] Enterprising companies have set up systems in Latin America that enable people to buy from amazon.com and bid on e-Bay without paying duties. The Internet has made global companies out of businesses that were nonexistent a decade ago. Unlike the past when trade consisted of self-contained products exchanged among nations, new production cycles rely on products composed of components from many different sources. Production interruptions in one country thus directly affect jobs and production in others. This means that business investment will increasingly be directed to locations in which stability and access to resources and efficient infrastructure can be assured.

Economic and commercial interests have always been one of the primary defining forces for foreign policy. Throughout history, access to resources or land or domination of trade routes has been a major strategic consideration determining national interests. In the twentieth century, these factors have been subordinated to tangible threats to our security. In the new world emerging at the end of the cold war, military alliances that were required for physical defense are being replaced with commercial alliances to ensure market share in commercial competition. Battlefields are being replaced by boardroom battles. Free-trade zones will be to the new world order what NATO was to defense policy. Economic competition will dominate global politics in the twenty-first century.

In the past, the principal factors affecting the United States' economic well-being were largely contained within our borders. Our domestic markets were largely self-sufficient compared with those of the other major world powers, and most of the resources needed by our industries were right here. Until the 1970s, domestic consumption accounted for almost 90 percent of our GDP, with foreign trade accounting for less than 10 percent. Our national economic interests were almost totally self-reliant and depended on internal markets. Not until after World War II, with the transportation marvels of jet airplanes and supertankers that completely revolutionized international commerce did we begin to pay serious attention to overseas markets.

It began slowly. After the Marshall Plan helped Europe recover after World War II, the principal strategy of U.S. corporations was to build plants abroad to produce U.S. products close to the consuming market. International transportation was still too slow and unreliable to allow production cycles in the United States to be based on supply chains in different countries. By the 1980s, though, our industries had manufacturing outposts around the world. This was dramatically different from the rudimentary "globalization" of previous times which was based principally on trade. The new movement toward global penetration rooted companies in the social, economic, and political life of foreign nations. But U.S. trade statistics never really reflected this important fact, reporting only the proportion of our foreign trade that is shipped directly from the United States. They do not reflect the products of U.S. corporations manufactured in plants abroad and sold in foreign countries. The profits from those sales, however, are a vital part of our international trade and directly benefit U.S. taxpayers. Today, companies like Citibank, GE, Hewlett-Packard, Caterpillar, AIG, and many more all earn more than 50 percent of their revenues from sales abroad.

In commercial relations, the world is coming full circle, although under vastly different circumstances from which it began. For centuries, for geographical reasons, production was largely decentralized and local. In a world with only primitive transportation and communication, each community and economic entity operated only as far as its most effective means of transportation could reach. The market for one community's products was as far away as a donkey or sailing ship could travel before the goods perished. The spice markets from the East thrived because they were not perishable. For the most part, however, the village, not the nation, was the center of economic activity.

After the Industrial Revolution, the centralization of power enabled national governments to control huge economic resources. Efforts to centralize revenue and political and productive power culminated in the twentieth century in fascism and communism. As we approach the twenty-first century, decentralization is again rising to the fore, but this time it comes in a very different package. The decentralization of capital and its mobility are placing economic power beyond the reach of any one state. Instead, individual economic decisions have become the relentless modus operandi of the world.

The global economy that influences decision making at the national level will be different from anything the world has yet known. The principal factors of capital and technology already transcend frontiers. While their target, markets and resources, will still be based on national policies, the decisions to satisfy or employ them are almost always centered in the international policies of private corporations. As the world embraces cross-border production and marketing in the coming decades, the multinational corporations' commercial interests and supply lines will become just as important to our national interests as the military's supply lines were in the last century.

A foreign policy that serves our interests will recognize this evolution and its inherent benefits and contradictions. Policies that generate prosperity for the American people will have to secure sources of revenues for corporations and higher wages for their workers. The dependence of the U.S. economy on global markets and resources will grow, along with a wide range of uncontrollable factors. Building markets for U.S. products will depend more on the fortunes and well-being of other nations than ever before.

For the United States, the other side of the equation is vitally important. The world has to be able to buy our products. Impoverished people are not consumers. Accordingly, it is in our interest to help raise the incomes of other peoples to enable them to buy our products. The more workers prosper, the better they will live and the more they will consume. Consumption drives employment and domestic and international markets.

The markets in the world for the United States' goods and products are enormous and, considering where we stand at this stage of history, virtually insatiable. Economist Paul Krugman pointed out that the nature of consumer demand in the twenty-first century will keep basic materials at the top of the list. In an article in which he imagined looking back on the twenty-first century, he wrote,

> The billions of third world families that finally began to have pur-
> chasing power when the 20th century ended did not want to watch
> pretty graphs on the Internet. They wanted to have nice houses, drive
> cars, and eat meals. . . . It soon become evident that natural resources,
> far from being irrelevant, had become more crucial.[2]

As development spreads throughout the world, more and more
people in Asia, east Europe, and Latin America will be entering the
market. Their purchasing power will be directed first to tangible material goods—houses, appliances, cars—that we take for granted. They
will want to travel, to educate their children, to live in decent housing.
This will create enormous markets for hard goods and for the machine
tools and productive capacity that only the developed nations can supply. The competition to supply those goods to the developing nations
and peoples of the world will be fierce, continuing to put pressure on
commodity prices. The United States can best benefit its own citizens if
it moves now to ensure that it will have a big share in supplying that
market.

The battle for consumer markets has a more worrisome facet. The
dynamics of the development model we are promoting, which empha-
sizes productive employment and consumer economics, will make
heavy demands on natural resources, energy, and the environment.
The competition for the limited supplies of these resources will inten-
sify. In addition to the increasing demand for food production, land
values will escalate, and supplies of fertilizers will be limited. The demand from Asia alone will exert enormous pressure on the world's
food supplies. The production of grain for animal feed has quadrupled
in the last two decades. Either biogenetics will open a new horizon for
human sustenance, or prices will rise. Prices for raw materials will reflect this competition, and disruptions in lines of supply as a result of
political instability will be another source of concern for the growth of
our economy.

The most effective, albeit idealistic, way for the United States to
make decisions regarding our national economy in this environment is
the same way that corporations plan to increase market share. Our policies should be designed to help our productive units achieve strong
markets in the rest of the world. If we do so, the United States' productive capacity will continue to grow.

By becoming part of the huge production cycle originating in the U.S. economy, Latin Americans will ensure their own future prosperity. Given their predilection for the United States and their natural north-south focus in travel and trade, the linkage is a natural one. The United States, Canada, Latin America, and the Caribbean nations are about to join in a free-trade association of the Americas (FTAA) for economic co-operation and development that could change the lives of hundreds of millions of people and dramatically alter the global economic balance of power. The decision to create an FTAA made at the Presidential Summit of the Americas in Miami in December 1994 set a time frame of ten years to complete the task. Free trade in the Americas is scheduled to begin in 2005. At present, nine different intergovernmental committees are at work analyzing legislation, making preliminary agreements, and defining the areas for further negotiation to bring the agreement into effect. A preliminary draft of the treaty was made public for comment in July 2001, and the detailed negotiations entered a more critical phase when President George W. Bush won "fast-track" trade-negotiating authority in 2002.

With the emergence of the European Union as a coherent force and the huge East Asian markets, the markets and access to resources in the Western Hemisphere as a whole could well be decisive both for Latin America and the United States. Canada knows this and is trying to take advantage of it by concluding free-trade agreements with almost every major country of the hemisphere. U.S. companies now face tariffs of 8 to 15 percent in many countries of Latin America, but Canadian goods enter free of duty. Several U.S. companies are learning to take advantage of Canada's nimbleness and are transferring their export sales to Latin America to their Canadian subsidiaries. Both Chrysler and Caterpillar openly considered transferring their export production to Canada to take advantage of that country's extensive free-trade network in the Americas in the event the United States rejects a free-trade agreement. Even a hi-tech company like Cisco Systems complained of the unfair competitive advantages of its Canadian competitor, Newbridge Networks.[3] As a result, Cisco shifted much of its marketing to the Americas from Canada and became the major corporate sponsor of the Presidential Summit of the Americas held in Quebec in April 2001. One does not need to be an economics professor to understand that this means more jobs in Canada and fewer in the United States.

THE EUROPEAN CHALLENGE

The move toward hemispheric free trade comes none too soon. While global free trade is the core concept of U.S. policy, and indeed is paid lip service by the other major regions, the reality is that Europe and Japan are basing their strategy on close-knit arrangements with their neighbors as a foundation for their core trade. Both regions are consolidating their positions to dominate the regional markets in their geographic zones. Europe has already achieved total economic integration, tearing down trade barriers, creating a unified currency, and forming a market of almost 400 million people, the world's largest single common market.

The central European countries, whose sudden independence of decision after the implosion of the Soviet Union stunned the world, are rapidly becoming a mature market. While the United States will have an active role in central Europe to maintain the strategic balance, we should have no illusions regarding trade. The central European markets will be dominated by the strong economies of western Europe, which have an overwhelming historic interest and close proximity. They are already investing huge sums of money to help the nations of central Europe develop market-based institutions. Europe's leaders understand that the money they are spending to reinforce the institutional structure will be returned when the central Europeans buy goods and services that will feed the economies and factories of France, Germany, Italy, and others. Before long, the integration of Poland, Hungary, and the Czech Republic will expand the reach of unified European markets. U.S. goods will then be at a substantial competitive disadvantage. The European parallel to the Great American Common Market is, in the long term, inevitable. It is in our interest to make its parallel inevitable here.

At the same time Japan's economic cooperation with the other Asian nations, temporarily set back by the Asian financial crisis and the prolonged Japanese recession, has strong historic and pragmatic roots in intraregional Asian trade. Indeed, Japan's huge financial assistance to and investment in the East Asian countries are aimed at training its market specialists to focus on its Asian neighbors. While Japan today is struggling with its limited internal markets, it is slowly executing an economic strategy to dominate the markets of its neighbors with Japanese finance and economic power. In short, all the industrial powers know that if their economies are to have a firm foundation, they need first to secure their base in the markets closest to home before they can secure larger markets in global trade.

Europe and Japan are also moving quickly in the Americas. European and Asian leaders learned an important lesson from the Mexican financial crisis of 1994. When Mexico made draconian cuts in imports to balance its trade accounts, the decision affected every country in the world *except* the United States. In the midst of the economic downturn, U.S. market share in Mexico rose from 69 percent in 1994 to 76 percent in 1996, while the Europeans and Asians saw their market share dwindle by 25 percent. This was a direct result of the NAFTA trade agreement. The Europeans are determined not to be caught napping a second time around.

The challenge from Japan in the Americas is multidimensional. Despite economic troubles at home, Japan sees its future relations with the developing world in terms of its larger interest in strong global economic development. Japan has become the world's largest provider of bilateral foreign aid and has replaced the United States as the principal individual bilateral donor to Latin America. Moreover, almost all Japanese aid is what is called "untied," which means awarding contracts through international competitive bidding without directly giving preference to Japanese firms. Most of Japan's aid takes the form of grants and goes to the poorer nations. In essence, Japan is laying the groundwork for its role as a global power. The payoff will come when many countries regard Japanese products as a natural choice.

There is no question that the potential markets of Latin America are in the sights of the rest of the world's industrialized nations. In the last several years newspapers have been full of stories about world leaders traveling to Latin America to position their countries better in the growing Latin American markets. Europe is exploiting the ties of language, history, and economic relations with the region. In 1996 and 1997, the president of France, the chancellor of Germany, and the prime ministers of Japan, China, and Korea all traveled to Latin America. It was the first time in history that so many world leaders have visited the region at one time. Prime Minister Jean Chrétien of Canada took a delegation of more than five hundred Canadian businessmen in his mission to the region in early 1998. Reliable sources reported that one of the more intriguing sales pitches was "Buy Canadian. Get U.S. technology without U.S. hassle."

As part of the offensive, European foreign assistance to Latin America and the Caribbean has also mushroomed, so that today it comprises more than 60 percent of the foreign assistance received by the American nations, for a total of $2.5 billion, far more than that from the United States and in contrast to the global downward trends in development assistance.[4] In the Caribbean, the European presence is even greater. The international agreement that accords special treatment to its former colonies, called the Lome Convention, has promised more than $15 billion in financing from the European Union for the next five years, or $3 billion a year. President Bush has promised to reverse the drop in U.S. assistance, which fell to an all-time low, from 29 percent of total official development assistance in 1991 to 9.4 percent in 1996, but that promise is not to be carried out until 2005.

The purpose of Europe's farsighted policies is beginning to pay off. Although starting from a much lower base, Brazil's trade with Europe has grown more than 300 percent in the last decade. While the United States remains Brazil's largest individual foreign trade partner, today 27 percent of Brazil's trade is with the European Union, 23 percent with Latin America (as a whole), and 19 percent with the United States. Germany's penetration of the Brazilian market has grown so much recently that some wags now consider São Paulo one of Germany's largest industrial cities.

David Hirschmann of the U.S. Chamber of Commerce commented that the European countries "see Latin America as the fastest-growing market in the world for goods and services."[5] President Jacques Chirac of France forecast Europe's future in the region in far broader terms, claiming Brazil for the world: "Geographically, Brazil is part of America. But it is European because of its culture, and global because of its interests."[6] While Europe's protectionist agricultural policies create problems in reaching a meaningful trade agreement with Latin America, recent advances from regular European–Latin American summit meetings have set the course for negotiations for a free-trade agreement. Chile, which waited long and patiently to be the first new U.S. trading partner after NAFTA, concluded a comprehensive free-trade agreement with Europe before its agreement with the United States in 2002.

The overall trade of the South American nations with Europe now parallels that with the United States, with approximately 23 percent going to each destination. The Mercosur countries export 22 percent of their produce to Europe, compared with only 16 percent to the United

States. Imports from Europe also exceed those from the United States by 27 percent to 24 percent.[7] Chile's major trading partner is now Asia. In 1997, European investment displaced the United States as the largest source of direct foreign investment in the country. Significantly, the composition of those exports is markedly different, which bodes well for future trade with the United States. While both are heavy buyers of natural resources, the United States and Canada import far more manufactured goods from Latin America, 24 percent compared with 12 percent for Europe.[8] In the rest of Latin America, the Caribbean, Mexico, and Central America, the figures tilt strongly to the United States. The flaw in this argument, however, is that Europe is still many countries; the United States is one. No other single country competes with United States as a marketing destination.

The leader and champion of this resurgence of interest from Europe is, of course, Spain. Spanish companies today have acquired a dominant position in nearly all strategic financial, telecommunications, and power sectors in Latin America. In a drive that the Latin Americans call the "*reconquista*" (reconquering), the Spanish have assumed a dominant position in the region's financial institutions that ensures a continuing flow of financial opportunities for Spanish interests. The Spanish are not shy about favoring their own businesses. Spain's Banco Santander, Central Hispano, and Banco Bilbao Vizcaya Argentaria dominate the region's financial markets in a way that harks back to colonial days. Banco Santander's consolidated assets are now estimated at $80 billion in Latin America and the Caribbean, followed by Citibank at $32 billion, Banco Bilbao at $28 billion, and Fleet Bank (formerly Bank of Boston) at $24 billion.[9] The *Financial Times* reports that the Spanish banks now have a position of 20 percent or more in the banking markets of Chile, Venezuela, Peru, and Colombia, and a strong position in Argentina.[10] The United States' Hispanic population is also within their strategic sights: Banco Santander assumed a 10 percent interest in First Union Bank until U.S. regulatory provisions proved too complex and it sold out. Banco Bilbao Vizcaya recently opened another flank by acquiring one of Puerto Rico's leading banks, Banco Ponce.

Spain has now become the second-largest investor in the region, regarding Latin America's markets and economic activity as its way to reclaim the status of an important economic power. Spain saw and took advantage of the opportunities in many of the initial privatizations, telecommunications, electric power, and banking industries. It began a new policy of annual "Iberoamerican summits" to include only Spain, Portugal, and the Latin American countries. The king of Spain attends regularly. Spain's cultural links to the region open all doors, its historic record of stripping the region of its wealth gently put aside in favor of the profit opportunities Spain presents to Latin American entrepreneurs. Ease of communications in language and access to the European Common Market are leading rapidly to strong new bonds with Latin America. Spain's emphasis on the strategic industries in finance, infrastructure, and communications has set the foundation for it to be a major long-term player in the region's commerce.

Telefónica was Spain's state-owned telephone company when it began its foray into Latin America. It invested billions of dollars to acquire controlling interests in the telephone companies of most of the Latin American countries, making Telefónica one of the world's largest multinational companies. Privatized in 1997, it is now the region's leading telephone company and largest multinational company with sales of $12.439 million, edging out General Motors' $12.425 million,[11] and is now moving to consolidate its Latin American holdings as wholly owned subsidiaries. Until the recent collapse of the Argentinean economy, Telefónica's investment there was earning an annual return of 40 percent. Equally aggressive moves in the Internet have put Telefónica's Terra network in a strong position to appeal to the U.S. Hispanic market as well. The United States' BellSouth is a distant second.

Spain's publicly owned power company ENDESA is now the leader in Latin America's electric power industry, with annual sales of $5.1 billion and a major interest in the power-generation facilities of almost every Latin American country. In Buenos Aires, the Spanish companies have a virtual monopoly over power generation. While they and Telefónica were hurt badly in the chaos following the implosion of the Argentine economy, they have steadfastly maintained their position. Spain's principal oil company, Repsol, has built itself up to be the seventh-largest multinational company in the region, with annual sales of $8 billion, based largely on its dominant position in Argentina's giant oil company, YPF.[12] In early 1999, in the face of Brazil's financial turmoil and plummeting petroleum prices, it paid $2 billion, a premium of 22 percent over the New York Stock Exchange's market price, for control of YPF. Because of its investment in Latin America,

Repsol has now grown to be the world's tenth-largest holder of proven oil reserves, with a major position in the Mercosur and Peruvian markets.

In automobiles, Volkswagen and Fiat are among the largest-selling cars in the region; in fact, one-third of Volkswagen's production is now in Latin America. Volkswagen's $11.9 billion in sales in the Americas closely follows General Motors' $12.4 billion, with DaimlerChrysler's $9.7 billion making it the strongest player in the truck and bus market. Daimler is now constructing a $400 million factory in Brazil to assemble passenger cars. In the chemical and pharmaceutical markets, Germany's BASF and Hoeschst, recently merged with France's Rhône-Poulenc, are taking major positions. In short, the Europeans are building a strong base to expand their Latin American ties by targeting the financial sector and key infrastructure projects in telecommunications, transportation, and energy.

In June 1999, the first ever European–Latin American summit, in Rio de Janeiro, took the initial steps toward a free-trade agreement. This move is important to Europe, where intractable unemployment and the cost of a population aging far more rapidly than that of the United States have formed a large cloud on the horizon. Europeans know that they must have strong market share in the emerging countries to fuel their economies. In the old world it was possible for second-rate nations to acquire military power. But in the new world, it will be not be possible to feign economic power.

The Asians have been equally determined to cultivate Latin America as both a future market and a source of resources. South Korea's Goldstar built a $1 billion plant in Brazil. Honda and Toyota are now there manufacturing automobiles. Honda's new assembly plant in Brazil builds engines for Civic sedans produced locally as well as for export. Horacio Natsumeda, Honda's Brazil director, said that this decision "is linked to our target to accelerate the nationalization of the Civic sedans manufactured in Brazil."[13] Sony and NEC in electronics and Mitsubishi and Marubeni in power generation are being equally aggressive. Most of Japan's televisions and computer monitors are now produced in Mexico. Finally, China recently won control of two oil concessions in Venezuela.

Attracting companies from all over the world should be a major objective for Latin America. It has important assets, an internal market with great growth potential, locations closer to U.S. markets, and abundant resources. Economic growth is also in the United States' interest. Anything promoting economic development in the region, from wherever it comes, will help alleviate poverty. In the long run, progress can be made only when Latin America becomes a global trader. For the United States, the challenge is to encourage this evolution while taking steps to ensure its market share during the transition.

10

The New Americans

IN 1985, *FORBES* MAGAZINE'S LIST of the world's wealthiest people in the world included seven from Latin America: from Monterrey, Mexico, the Garza Sada family, which built an industrial empire in steel, glass, and chemicals; and from Brazil, Roberto Marinho, a publishing magnate; Antonio Emirio de Moraes in mining and industry; and Sebastian Camargo in construction. The other Latin Americans on the list were three drug lords from Colombia, all of whom are now in jail or dead.

In 1995, this list contained twenty-nine Latin Americans, with Argentina, Chile, Colombia, and Venezuela now included, and no drug lords. The men and women on the list were those who sparked the industrial resurgence of Latin America in the 1990s. The old oligarchs, who clung to land and protected industry, have become history. The new managers are in the vanguard leading the region's efforts to become a competitive factor in the global economy. Most of them were trained in the United States.

Some families of the old oligarchies have been able to retain their power, such as the Votorantim Group led by Antonio Emirio de Moraes of Brazil, the Visa Group of the Garza Sada family of Mexico, and the O Globo Group of Roberto Marinho in Brazil. Each of these groups was established in the twentieth century and have aggressively taken positions in the emerging industries in their economies. But they have done so by demonstrating that they understand the exigencies of new technological revolution. They have shown a respect for modern management, have struck alliances with major multinational companies, and ensured that their children received the best management education, often in the United States.

An entirely new elite now dominates Latin America's economies. They are men who took advantage of the opportunities offered by debt swaps, privatizations, and greater access to international capital markets. At a time when most of Latin America was paralyzed as a result of hyperinflation and recession, these men bought assets. Many are immigrants or children of immigrants, and their attitudes differ from those of the previous generation of Latin Americans. Whereas the previous generation was addicted to protectionism, the new leaders are far more pragmatic and are positioning themselves to compete in open markets. Whereas the previous generation erected high barriers to foreign investment in major industries; the new leaders are trying to attract foreign investment partners. Whereas the old generation tolerated the bureaucracy's inefficiency, the new leaders are supporting the government's efforts to reduce bureaucracy, privatize, and outsource services.

Carlos Heliu Slim, who was unknown five years ago, is today referred to as "Mexico's one-man conglomerate." The sixty-five-year-old son of Lebanese immigrants began his trajectory out of the middle class with the purchase in 1976 of a printing company that specialized in cigarette labels. From that inauspicious beginning, he entered the cigarette industry as a partner of Philip Morris and, in the Mexican depression of the 1980s, used the assets of those businesses to acquire insurance, retail, and mining companies. His major achievement, however, was winning the bid in the privatization of the Mexican telephone company, Telmex, in 1990, in partnership with Southwestern Bell and France Telecom. Most recently, he has acquired a controlling interest in CompUSA and made other acquisitions in the U.S. market. Today, with assets that are said to total more than $7 billion, he is a major force in Mexican and global business.

Benjamin Steinbruch used a family textile company to become one of Brazil's principal industrialists, gaining control of a large part of the iron and steel industry in less than five years. With a small interest gained in the privatization of Brazil's largest steel producer, CSN—a company that was near bankruptcy and run by political appointees—he put together the winning bid on the privatization of Brazil's premier mining company, the Companhia do Vale do Rio Doce (CVRD), the world's largest producer of iron ore, with interests in gold mining, aluminum, manganese, and pulp. Steinbruch turned CSN around, installed modern management and technology, fired almost seven thousand employees, and got the company on the New York Stock Exchange. With a reputation as one of Brazil's most determined industrialists, Steinbruch is bringing the same energy to CVRD, opening it to global markets with partners from many different countries.

Andronico Luksic, the seventy-year-old dynamo of Chile's major industrial and banking conglomerate, was the son of a Croatian immigrant who settled in the mining town of Antofagasta. The *Wall Street Journal* noted his philosophy as looking for "cheap companies that are undervalued and badly run."[1] The family, which was burned when it struck a deal with Chile's Marxist president Salvador Allende, recovered after the Chilean banking crisis of 1982 and launched the debt-for-equity swaps that helped Chile get its economy in order. It bought out companies in industry, brewing, banking, and telecommunications and now owns stakes in one of Chile's biggest telephone companies in partnership with Southwestern Bell and has begun to expand its holdings in banking and breweries in Argentina and Peru.

Gustavo Cisneros is the son of Diego Cisneros who grew the small trucking company his father founded in 1930 into a major bottling company in partnership with Pepsi-Cola and built alliances with major multinational corporations that introduced him to bottling ventures, supermarkets, and retailing in almost all the other countries of Latin America. Today, with interests in business in more than thirty countries, its core businesses are a media and television empire. Cisneros engineered one of the stunning business coups in the 1990s when he abandoned the fifty-year-old Pepsi franchise his father had built, switched to Coca-Cola and then sold out to Panamerican Beverages of Mexico. Venevision, the flagship of the Cisneros media colossus, is rapidly expanding throughout Venezuela and Latin America in direct satellite broadcasting in joint ventures with Brazil's TV Abril, and Hughes Communications. With major interests in AOL Latin America and Univision in the United States, Cisneros has demonstrated his farsighted vision of the future of the Internet and satellite broadcasting. He has formed a joint venture with Brazil's TV Globo, TCI of the United States, Rupert Murdoch, and the late Emilio Ascarraga, who built Mexico's monopoly private television station, Televisa, to launch Sky Latin America and the Galaxy satellite. In addition to Univision, the major Hispanic broadcaster in the United States, Cisneros bought Spalding Sporting Goods and Evenflo and later sold interests in the companies to Wall Street's Kohlberg Kravis Roberts for more than $1 billion.

Jorge Gregorio Pérez Companc, the adopted son of a Buenos Aires schoolteacher, took over the company his stepbrothers founded fifty years ago in construction, energy, banking, and telecommunications. Making his major move in the difficult times that wiped out most other Argentine businesses in the 1980s, the family built its foundation on construction and shipping contracts with the state-owned oil company, YPF. Pérez Companc then teamed up with international giants such as Enron, GE, and France Telecom to assume control of some of Argentina's most productive assets in energy, telecommunications, and banking. The leap to an industrial colossus came with his acquisition of a major interest in the privatization of the former state-owned telephone company.

Eduardo Elsztain and his brother Alejandro, descendants of an orthodox Jewish family, stunned the old landed oligarchy of the Agricultural Society of Argentina with an audacious program acquiring more than 2 million acres of prime agricultural land in the midst of the depressed agricultural sector that suffered under severe government controls. Beginning in 1990 when he was studying in New York, he convinced George Soros, who admired Eduardo Elsztain because "he knew when to sell as well as when to buy," to bet on Argentina. They foresaw the opportunity to restore Argentina's once enviable agricultural production with the new open market policies of President Carlos Menem. They moved rapidly to install the latest equipment and technology. As a result, their holding company, Cresul, became one of the world's largest producers of beef and grain. Their company, listed on the NASDAQ as IRSA, is now acquiring shopping centers and commercial real estate.

Lorenzo Zambrano, from an older, more traditional family, was educated in the United States, and built a sleepy Mexican cement company, Cemex, into one of the world's predominant cement companies, with acquisitions throughout Latin America, Europe, and Asia. Building on holdings in Venezuela, Colombia, and Peru, Zambrano's acquisition of Spain's largest cement producer in 1992 made his company one of the largest cement producers in the world. It soon became even bigger by acquisitions of low-cost producers in the Philippines and Indonesia, so that more than 50 percent of the company's revenues today derive from interests outside Mexico.

In the list of the largest Latin American enterprises with global interests, well over 50 percent are led by children of recent immigrants. The success of Latin America in global markets today has more to do with private-sector actors than it does with governments. Granted, the openings for the private sector in both industry and civil society resulted from major transformations in government policy. The impetus for the 1990s takeoff in industry, retailing, banking, and insurance in Latin America was the stability resulting from better-managed currencies. Investment was spurred by more liberal laws concerning trade and open markets. Even though in the smaller countries, tightly controlled ruling elites still hold the power over government, in the larger countries a new type of entrepreneur has begun the diffusion of that power.

THE NEW CONSENSUS

The consensus in economics and politics that emerged in the 1990s was a historic watershed for Latin America. While the island nations of the Caribbean have always been known for their prudent fiscal management, Latin America's history has been marked by violent swings in economic policy. Three events helped forge this consensus: the shock of the closing of global financial markets to the region in the debt crisis of the 1980s, the dramatic growth of prosperity in Chile (fortified by the remarkable resurgence of the Spanish economy), and the successful efforts of President Carlos Salinas of Mexico to restructure and reorient the Mexican economy to open trade with the United States. In addition, the fall of Communism in Eastern Europe made a profound impact on Latin Americans. The traditional authoritarian oligarchy and military had already lost their credibility with their mismanagement of the economy in the 1980s. Czechoslovakia's "Velvet Revolution," coming on the heels of that debacle, had a chilling effect on the decaying, left-leaning economic theories, and as result, the radical left lost its moorings. There were few alternatives.

The most influential Latin American event, however, was Chile's success with free markets. It made a profound impression on the thinking of the political leaders and the people at the same time that Marxist-influenced centralized approaches failed. Even those who opposed the authoritarian president, General Augusto Pinochet, for his human rights abuses had to acknowledge the positive results of the economic revolution. Chile, which started off the 1980s with the highest debt per capita in Latin America, achieved, with its free economy, the most vigorous economic growth, the lowest rate of unemployment, and the lowest rate of inflation of any Latin American country.

Chile established the model with its firm commitment to open market reforms as early as the 1980s. By the 1990s its economic growth was averaging more than 8 percent annually, for a cumulative growth in the 1990s of more than 100 percent. Internal savings climbed to 27.2 percent on the wave of privatized pension funds, up from 12 percent as recently as the early 1980s. The strategy of opening to global markets increased exports from 12 percent of GDP in the 1970s to 37 percent in 1995. And even though exports continued to be dependent on copper (80 percent of the exports in the 1970s), by 1995 copper's share had dropped to less than 40 percent. Chile made impressive gains in conquering economic volatility, reducing unemployment, and alleviating poverty—an outstanding record for any country. Building on this example, which tamed inflation and opened the economy, a new convergence in economic thinking emerged in the region in three areas:

1. In fiscal policy. Balanced budgets were an extraordinary accomplishment for the new democracies, given the overwhelming demands for social services. In 1998 the rapid action of Argentina, Mexico, and Brazil to slash their budgets to meet the sharp reduction in revenues resulting from the fall of commodity prices after the Asian financial crisis was indicative of their commitment. Government deficits in the region fell to an average of 2 percent from an average of 9 percent in the 1980s. Inflation, which had reached four digits in a number of countries, was reduced to single digits by the end of the 1990s.

2. In financial policy. Freely convertible currencies have helped open capital markets, and independent central banks are pursuing sounder monetary policies. Financial systems are being better supervised and regulated, although there is still a long way to go. Taxes are being converted to indirect value-added taxes to circumvent tax evasion, and most countries, with the help of international financial institutions, are trying harder to collect them. The countries' former dependence on customs revenues is forcing major changes in outlook as trade barriers are lowered.

3. In trade policy. The movement toward more open markets has lowered tariffs from an average of more than 40 percent in the 1980s to 15 percent by 1995. Nontariff barriers were universally reduced as the countries moved toward subregional integration.

Mercosur, the Andean Group, the Central American Common Market, and the Caribbean Common Market all renewed their efforts to resolve regional issues.

As a whole, the widespread consensus that emerged in the early 1990s among the politicians and the people—and even the economists—facilitated a broad restructuring of the economies. Attitudes toward the role of the private sector in job creation changed, as did the understanding of the linkages among trade, investment, and money. As one Latin American wit put it at the time, "As a teacher of popular economics, inflation has no equal."

Surprisingly, the leaders of Latin America's old left led the reformation. Traditional socialists—Presidents Carlos Andrés Pérez in Venezuela, Michael Manley in Jamaica, and Peronist President Carlos Menem in Argentina—influenced by the dramatic market reforms implemented by their socialist friend, Prime Minister Felipe González in Spain, recognized that the old policies were totally incapable of creating the millions of jobs required in the twenty-first century. Chile's record in following Spain's example helped it become the most successful economy in Latin America's history. The determination and conviction with which Mexico's young president, Carlos Salinas de Gortari, adopted a pragmatic approach and opened Mexico's economy to the United States were the final elements that gave impetus to almost universal changes throughout the Americas.

Political change in the Americas in the 1990s was equally as dramatic as the economic reforms. Following the violent conflicts of the 1970s, the nations began to focus on the political structure to allow and listen to dissent. Enrique Iglesias, president of the Inter-American Development Bank, commented to me on the torment that Chile endured in that period: "The best thing they did was to put their anger aside and not let it paralyze them. It did not form part of the national debate. They concentrated on moving the society ahead." Capping off the changes, the dismantling of the centralized state has hastened the decentralization of administrative responsibility to local governments. Mayors, formerly appointed by the central government, are increasingly popularly elected. While democratic institutions are still weak, and economic reform has yet to deliver on its promise, the lessons of recent failures are deeply ingrained in this generation's decision making.

The changes that took place in Latin America during the 1990s have forever altered the political landscape. It is significant, as Enrique Iglesias stated, that "in the recent global upheaval not a single country showed signs of pulling back from the global economy; there have been no controls levied on capital movements and no barriers raised to international trade."[2] Changes in the ownership of wealth have made many of the region's entrepreneurs more confident and mobile. The influx of capital from the multinational corporations have brought training and technical assistance, giving rise to a new class of professional managers. The knowledge base and intellectual linkages of the society are now global, overcoming historical parochial and isolationist points of view. In government, the old interventionist models are giving away to a more passive but productive role of regulatory oversight. The penchant for state control is giving way to institutions favoring disclosure and transparency. Moreover, most leaders of the region now agree that access to markets of the United States is the surest path to prosperity.

Many dangers still lie ahead. The new consensus has changed the dynamics of the old oligarchies but has created new problems in its wake. The region is still marked by the most unequal income distribution in the world. The concentration of wealth from the privatizations has engendered a new variation on the old oligarchies. New faces have appeared, but many old practices persist. Insider favors and corruption continue to plague the interplay of public- and private-sector business. The rapid movement to privatization before the regulatory framework was put into place left many countries vulnerable to abuse from private-sector monopolies, and the governments have neither the skilled civil servants nor the institutional framework to deal with it.

This is where the policies and attitudes of the United States can help. Latin Americans are responsible for organizing their productive system to compete effectively in the global markets. However, the supporters of these reforms must be able to point to a credible record of success and assure doubters that their sacrifices will result in real economic growth. Argentina's collapse after rigorously adhering to orthodox economic policy demonstrates that investment will not come from economic reform alone. It has to come from access to larger markets. If the United States is prepared to open its doors to trade from Latin America and the Caribbean, they can begin to attract the investment they need to create jobs. With it, the forces in Latin America that advocate sound economic and progressive social policies will prevail. Without it, the region's small markets and low education levels will restrain investment and production.

TECHNOLOGY:
FORGING AHEAD OR FALLING FURTHER BEHIND?

With all the reforms gradually taking hold, the pace of change in the rest of the world is also accelerating. Even though the stock market has now retreated from the inflated expectations of profit from the technological changes, information technology offers an unparalleled opportunity for the nations of the Americas. Properly and assiduously applied, this technology will give them a new platform for open, transparent, responsive, and efficient governance. For government, new management tools and telecommunications provide a way to overcome inherited inefficiencies, combat corruption, and give better service to the public. Latin America and the Caribbean have a chance to leapfrog over years of stagnation to create facilities that can compete with the industrialized economies.

As great as the potential of the technological revolution is, the danger is just as great that the nations of the Americas could find themselves falling further behind. For Latin America and the Caribbean, strong and aggressive polices are required to educate and train people in the requisite skills. But there are a number of ominous signs that Latin America is lagging behind in implementing the legislative and regulatory framework that would signal to the technology companies that they are welcome.

To put this into context, compare the current state of the region with Asia. A former senior official of the World Bank, Shahid Javed Burki, reported that in 2000 Asia had 116 million computers in use, compared with 18 million in Latin America and the Caribbean. Cuba restricts its population's access to the Internet, and estimates are that only about 100,000 computers can be found on the island. Of the fifteen countries in which hi-tech accounted for a major portion of exports, seven were from East Asia. No country from Latin America and the Caribbean made the list. The data prove his point:

Information technology [IT] exports by Malaysia to the U.S. account for 45 percent of the total in 2000. For Taiwan, South Korea and Singapore the corresponding figures are 40 percent, 28 percent, and 27 percent. By comparison, Latin American IT exports are of little significance. In 1998, Brazil's share of IT to the U.S. was about $700 million, slightly more than 2 percent of the total.[3]

The demand for Internet services in Asia grew by more than 600 percent in 2000 and by more than 250 percent between Asia and the United States, compared with negligible growth between the United States and Latin America. Burki concluded that one reason why Latin America is in danger of being left behind is that the countries have not invested in the infrastructure required to provide the needed skills. Japan now has 4,900 scientists and engineers per million people, and the average in Asia is now about 2,000 per million, and in the United States, 3,700. In comparison, in Latin America, Argentina has 660, Mexico 330, and Brazil 168 scientists and engineers per million people.[4]

The key to development in this area is through export markets. Despite its large population, the predominance of poverty makes the real domestic markets of most Latin American countries far too small to sustain heavy investment. The inflated expectations of the first phase of the Internet era hit the region as hard as it did the developed countries. In 1999, Argentina had nearly two thousand domestic Internet sites, but in 2001, the number fell to seventy-five. After Global Crossing provided fiber-optic access to all of South America, the implosion of that company as well as many of the major telecommunications companies curtailed investment in the next generation of facilities in Latin America because the body of consumers was too small to ensure a return on the investment. Unless the region pursues aggressive policies to overcome this, it is in serious danger of missing an unparalleled historic opportunity.

MEXICO SHOWS THE WAY

As it enters the twenty-first century, the Mexican economy is booming. Its currency is stable. It is making inroads on its extensive poverty problem, and it is actively addressing its problems in crime and the environment. Its political parties are vigorous and competing fiercely, which are healthy signs of a growing democracy. It was not that way only a decade ago.

The real impetus to forming a new relationship among the nations of the Americas began in Mexico. For decades, Mexico was wary of close relations with the United States. A familiar Mexican lament was "so far from God, so close to the United States." The historic transition to closer relations with the United States was engineered by President Carlos Salinas de Gotari. Following that was another, more difficult transition toward genuine democracy, which was deftly handled by his successor, President Ernesto Zedillo. In his quiet, persistent, but non-threatening manner, Zedillo totally dismantled the oligarchical monopoly by the Institutional Revolutionary Party (Partido Institucional Revolucionario, or PRI as it is commonly referred to), which held power for more than seventy years. Zedillo moved slowly and carefully, one law at a time, each unopposable on its merits, to build an irreversible critical mass of far-reaching political reform. The cumulative effect ensured open and fair elections and the advent of real political democracy in Mexico in 2000. The result was the election of an opposition candidate as president, Vicente Fox. Considering the enormity of the vested interests at stake, only a totally determined and wise president of Mexico could achieve this, and President Zedillo did it.

The transformation into a modern Mexico began in the 1970s. The country was in deep economic crisis at the time when the discovery of huge oil deposits in the Gulf of Mexico changed everything. Suddenly Mexico was awash with oil money. After declaring that they would manage their economy with care and not repeat the mistakes of Iran and other oil-rich countries, the leaders of Mexico succumbed to the same practices. They led one of the greatest binges of spending and alleged corruption of the twentieth century. Despite the almost tenfold rise of government revenues, the leaders burdened future generations by borrowing almost $100 billion and bankrupted the country in 1982.

After trying several different remedies, the new president, Miguel de la Madrid, decided to open the economy, eliminate protectionism, and take Mexico into the General Agreement on Tariffs and Trade (GATT). He kept his promise to reduce government deficits, which he lowered from from an unprecedented 16 percent in 1986 to 6 percent in 1989.

Carlos Salinas de Gortari was barely forty years old when he was elected president of Mexico in 1988 in an election considered fraudulent by most observers. The PRI, which had a historic record of stopping at nothing to win elections, was alleged to have gone further than usual to elect Salinas because of the strong challenge by a popular leftist candidate, the son of a former president, Cuahtemoc Cardenas. Salinas had a double problem. Not only was he relatively unknown to Mexicans, but he also was regarded as a lightweight by the old-time politicos, who saw him as a young intellectual technocrat and inexperienced politically. Inexperienced he may have been, but he was also brilliant, forceful, and determined and had a clear view of what it would take to move Mexico out of the backward, unproductive patterns of the past. Handpicked by the outgoing president, Miguel de la Madrid, who had good reason to appreciate the intelligence of his former minister of economy, Salinas proceeded to make history.

Educated in the United States, Salinas selected a team determined to realize Mexico's latent economic potential as a neighbor of the largest economic power in the world. They began working feverishly to reform the protected Mexican economy and keep up with the daunting population increases. They were convinced that their priority was to create jobs to surmount the devastating poverty of the countryside and open the Mexican economic and political systems. To do this, they had to seek a partnership with the United States. The result was the achievement of the North American Free Trade Agreement (NAFTA) before the end of President Salinas's term and Mexico's definitive turn away from its Third World mentality to that as a member of the industrialized world.

Today, as a result of the strong policies and perseverance of three successive presidents—Miguel de la Madrid, Carlos Salinas, and Ernesto Zedillo—Mexico has changed irrevocably. One of the principal concerns in the Mexican financial crisis of 1994 was that the country might revert to its old anti-American stance and that the serious recession in Mexico could force it to close its markets again. Many attempts were made to blame the financial crisis on the advent of NAFTA, although NAFTA had nothing to do with it.

In spite of the financial crisis, Mexico did not revert to its old ways. President Bill Clinton understood the stakes not only for the recently launched NAFTA but for all of Mexico. He took an enormous political risk when he came to Mexico's financial rescue with an unprecedented $40 billion loan package from the international community. His daring action and the economic promise of NAFTA turned the tide on what could easily have degenerated into financial panic. The rest of the story, when economic growth and stability resulted in the election of an opposition political party and the advent of real democracy, is history.

BRAZIL: THE LAND OF TODAY

A common quip about Brazil is that it is "the land of tomorrow and always will be." It is time to put that old joke aside. Brazil now is the land of today. It is the locomotive of South America and the plum of Latin American trade. The private sector knows this and is acting on it. In 1999 Brazil edged out China as the primary destination for foreign direct investment. In 1998, foreign investors set a record by paying $19 billion in the privatization of the various companies of Telebras, the Brazilian telecommunications conglomerate. In a separate transaction, Bell-South paid a record $2.6 billion for the cellular phone license for part of São Paulo.

None of the private sector's optimism is misplaced. I watched Brazil—a country larger than the contiguous United States, with vast resources and indomitable optimism—grow. The first job I had in Latin America, in 1954, was conducting a preliminary market study of the Brazilian economy to determine whether it was suitable for the manufacture of air conditioning. It did not take much vision to predict that it was. But at that time, Brazil had virtually no manufacturing industry. A crash effort by then President Juscelino Kubitshek induced Volkswagen to begin manufacturing automobiles there in the late 1950s, the first automobile production plant in South America. A number of respected economists predicted that the Brazilian market could never accommodate it. Today, Brazil produces more than a million vehicles a year, and one of Brazil's major automobile parts producers, Metal Leve of São Paulo, owned three plants in the United States before it was bought out by Mahle, a German car parts manufacturer.[5]

Today, Brazil has achieved stability and a growing presence in the global economy. It is the desired location for investment to reach the South American markets and boasts a thriving manufacturing and agricultural export industry. Its aircraft industry, led by Embraer, has become one of the world's leading manufacturers of commuter aircraft, giving stiff competition to the Canadians. It has a vigorous export industry in automobiles and chemical products. Its shoe industry benefits from the fact that Brazil has the largest cattle herd in the world, almost

200 million head. It is now the world's third largest exporter of beef. Brazilian cattle were kept free of the "mad-cow" disease that affected Europe because its cattle fed on grass and not pulverized animal remainders, as they were in Europe. In agriculture, Brazil is now one of the world's largest producers of soybeans. Its recently growing cotton industry could have a huge impact on global cotton markets. Brazil's exports of more than $50 billion a year put it in a league with most of the countries of Europe.

Brazil's policymakers regard intraregional trade among the South American nations, now at about 20 percent and growing rapidly, as the cornerstone of a South American free-trade area. Brazil has been a good neighbor. The history of the Americas has been fortunate in having a peaceful and tolerant country of its size in the hemisphere. Brazil's highly professional foreign ministry has decided on a long-term strategy for Brazil in the evolving global geopolitics by first consolidating its place in South America. For years it did this by pursuing its own trading regime with the other South American countries in an approximation of a South American free-trade agreement before a free-trade agreement for all of the Americas (FTAA) is achieved. If it does, the negotiations for an FTAA will change dramatically. Consequently, Brazil relished the delays and uncertainties of the U.S. Congress in approving trade promotion authority. If it had not faced an election of its own and the financial crisis in the wake of the Argentine collapse, Brazil would be seeking to take advantage of U.S. temporizing to consolidate its own strategy in South America. Some Brazilians have been known to boast that their best ally in the South American strategy has been the U.S. Congress.

The Brazilian economy continues to grow as its currency, stabilized under President Fernando Cardoso, is strained by the continuing consolidation. For many years Brazil was isolated from global markets by a rigid protectionist policy. But manufacturing thrived in a booming domestic market despite an economic environment of high inflation and rigid foreign exchange controls. In global competition, however, Brazilian firms lost out because of their low productivity. The opportunity to position itself in the global economy by increasing productivity and quality was hampered by its unstable currency, which deterred investment. Today, its more stable economy has benefited almost every sector. Brazilian exports grew from $22 billion in 1986 to more than $50 billion in 1997. This growth has produced great wealth but also many dislocations. The Brazilian foreign minister spoke of Brazil's undergoing "an intense competitive shock" as a result of the rapid opening of the economy and steep tariff reductions within a very short period.[6] Nonetheless, optimism abounds throughout Brazil. It was summarized by the Brazilian-born president of the U.S.-based Bank of Boston, Henrique de Campos Meirelles, who cited stabilization as the principal factor in the accelerating rate of growth. "The best," Meirelles said, "is yet to come."[7] Brazil's new president, Lula da Silva, recently appointed Meirelles as the head of Brazil's Central Bank.

The most pressing issue in rethinking U.S. policy toward the hemisphere is recognizing Brazil's role in global economics and politics. Nothing the United States can do anywhere in South America could match the significance of having good relations with Brazil. In the geopolitics of South America, Brazil will inevitably assume a role analogous to that of the United States in North America. Its productive capacity needs larger markets; the resolution of its poverty problem needs new economic opportunities; and its energy needs demand close relations with its neighbors. The United States, however, has imposed unprecedented protectionist measures against Brazilian products. Brazil has begun to penetrate global markets in a number of products, especially agriculture, shoes, and steel, and the United States has erected barriers to or "voluntary" quotas of Brazilian imports for almost all these products. Brazil's former president, Cardoso, repeatedly challenged the U.S. practice that mixes sermonizing on free trade with uncompromising protectionist action, which has been especially hard on Brazil. But Brazil is coming to appreciate that the only way it can overcome the protectionist elements of U.S. trade policy is through a multilateral free-trade agreement.

Contrary to the misunderstanding of many in the U.S. government, Brazil's success in integrating Latin America's markets is very much in the interest of the United States. We both have strong stakes in a successful democracy; we both have a strong need for economic growth; and we both trade globally. Brazil's success is the Americas' success, and Brazil's best partner in its goal of integrating Latin America's markets is the United States. U.S. investment and technology can help production in Brazil and help open the country to global markets. This issue is of primary importance to the two countries' long-term goals and demands far more careful attention than either country has given it to date.

THE CENTRAL AMERICAN DILEMMA

The economic and demographic problems of Central America are dominated by its proximity to the United States, which is both its greatest asset and its greatest liability. A geopolitical observer once noted that the only small states that have prospered in modern history are those that either have a rich endowment of natural resources or bask in the nearby sun of a great economic power. This is the story of Singapore and Hong Kong. So it could be with Central America. President George W. Bush's offer to negotiate a free-trade agreement with Central America even before the conclusion of an FTAA is a strong and positive recognition of the importance of this need.

The economic potential of Central America is vastly different from that of South America. Central America's proximity to the United States gives it easy land transport, ready markets, and an opportunity to develop a strong position in the agroindustry to balance the winter-bound United States. Indeed, the United States is the destination of almost 50 percent of Central America's exports. Since 1996, U.S. exports to Central America have grown 42 percent to $9 billion, more than U.S. exports to Russia and India combined. Its proximity, however, also has its costs. Fortune hunters from the United States have played a major role throughout history in encouraging corruption there.

Holding the region back is its largely undereducated population, which was partially the result of indifference toward the education of the indigenous population and the ease of living of the elites who had little incentive to build an industrial society. Central America is home to two of the hemisphere's poorest countries, Nicaragua and Honduras, and it has one of the hemisphere's most diverse ethnic populations, with a strong influence from its Mayan heritage.

Historically, most countries of the region have had agricultural economies, as little manufacturing or even assembly was possible in the tropical climate before the advent of air conditioning. Moreover, the region is prone to natural disasters like earthquakes, volcanic eruptions, and hurricanes that in an instant can set back economic progress for years. The neglect of education, however, is the most devastating handicap. A former president of Honduras explained to me that his government had great difficulty implementing the International Monetary Fund's recommended economic reforms because the average education of the people in his country's civil service was fourth grade.

Central America's proximity to the United States, however, has other implications in this new century. Ease of transportation means ease of migration, as the flood of illegal immigrants during the Central American civil wars of the 1980s demonstrated. Ease of shipment also means ease of transport of illicit products. For this reason alone, the United States has an important interest in ensuring the growth of more prosperous economies here.

Given its small size, the cost of transforming Central America from an economic backwater to a useful producer would be relatively small. Its assets—rich agricultural land and abundant hydroelectric power—give the countries a base on which to build prosperous societies. Hydroelectric power currently supplies 65 percent of the region's energy. Consolidation of transportation, communications, power, and the water infrastructure makes integration the centerpiece of the political agenda. The Inter-American Development Bank is reinforcing this trend, financing projects to integrate the region's power grids, expand road networks, upgrade airports, and consolidate small, illiquid regional capital markets. The integrated power grid will enable power plants to be built anywhere in the region to serve industries' requirements throughout this century. Within a short time, hydroenergy will be supplemented with natural gas piped from Tabasco in southern Mexico and north from Colombia across the Darien region of Panama.

Recent agreements on a new framework for Central American economic integration and the positive response to President Bush's offer of a free-trade agreement indicate that the region's new leaders are well aware of the core issues for economic development and job creation. Central America, *The Economist* reported in 2000, is "integrating faster and further than ever before . . . with common macroeconomic policies in deregulation and taxes." Tariffs have been reduced from an average of 80 percent in the 1980s to 8.9 percent in 2000, and trade and exports are growing at close to 25 percent a year.[8] The reluctance of the richer but still vulnerable economies of Panama and Costa Rica to join with their poorer neighbors is an impediment, but the promise of a free-trade agreement with the United States will change everything. The countries are moving ahead with all democratic speed to harmonize their legislation in areas relating to trade and have now agreed on a plan for a Central American customs union.

The region has had a spate of damaging and embarrassing bank failures as a result of allowing privatization to advance ahead of the governments' ability to enforce regulation of the financial system. The integration of the region, however, will be accelerated by the carrot of free trade with the United States. The offer of Mexico to collaborate with the region in a development program, which President Fox calls the "Plan Puebla-Panama" to signify its reach from the poorer areas of southern Mexico throughout the Central American region, also will help the nations plan together to provide needed infrastructure projects in power and transportation.

The development of Central American countries has been uneven. Education-conscious Costa Rica provides free and compulsory primary and secondary education to all its citizens as well as a strong network of health care. Today its 94 percent literate, skilled, and healthy population is the greatest reason for its newfound ability to attract major investments from hi-tech companies such as Intel. Intel's exports alone helped spur economic growth of more than 7 percent in 1999, a year that saw the rest of the region mired in recession induced by the Asian crisis. Dramatic economic advances are also taking place in El Salvador, which has unilaterally slashed tariffs, reformed tax and social security regimes, adopted the U.S. dollar as its legal tender, and is considered to have one of the world's most open economies. Together the two countries show that it is possible for the region to compete in the global economy.

THE CARIBBEAN SUN

In 1972, Eric Williams, the prime minister of Trinidad and Tobago who led the movement for independence in the Caribbean, made his famous observation that "ten minus one equals zero." His comment was aimed at Jamaica's refusal to join a union of the Caribbean nations. Since the 1960s, the ten Caribbean colonies had been joined in a federation, and as full independence loomed in the late 1960s, they discussed establishing a formal union. Without Jamaica, however, the largest and strongest economy of the region, the other countries considered union not to be viable, economically or politically. It was a fateful decision. Ever since, Caribbean leaders have been trying to patch together their thinly populated, thinly capitalized countries into a workable trade alliance. Committed to democracy with fiercely individualistic people, each has been trying to come to grips with its vulnerabilities in a competitive global economy and its near total dependence on generating income from its relationships with the powerful industrialized economies of Europe and the United States.

For the island nations of the Caribbean, shifts in production and services generated by the combination of an open global economy and the revolutions in technology and communications are offering as many new opportunities as they are closing down the traditional mainstays of their economies. For centuries, the sun was their principal— and, in some cases, almost only—natural resource. It enabled a plantation economy of sugar and bananas. In recent years this has been supplemented by sun-and-surf tourism. As the market for low value-added sugar and bananas becomes increasingly untenable, the small economies have been struggling to find a new place in a competitive global economy. During their centuries of colonial rule, they had little choice. They were, as they said, "the butterfly on the horse's back." Since independence, however, they can now fly on their own, and with a strong sense of self-reliance they have struck out in many new directions.

The size of the economies belies their importance to the United States. As recently as the cold war, the island nations were viewed as giant aircraft carriers anchored offshore the United States' east coast, bases from which attacks on the U.S. mainland could be launched if they fell into the hands of a hostile power. Today, with governments that cannot afford an efficient coast guard, the myriad secluded harbors of the Caribbean are natural transportation hubs for the narcotics trade.

President Ronald Reagan's 1983 Caribbean Basin Initiative (CBI) was hastily passed by Congress when a left-leaning regime took control of Grenada and the influence of Fidel Castro suddenly threatened again to spread throughout the region. The unilateral CBI was hardly a free-trade agreement, however. It was set to last for only twelve years and had several critical exceptions such as textiles, leather goods, and petroleum products. Nevertheless, the initiative was an enormous success at a nominal cost to the United States. It gave birth to a wide range of new assembly plants and a new sense of entrepreneurship among the leaders. It gave the region a significant advantage over other countries more than a decade before NAFTA was signed. For a region that formerly exported only sugar and coffee to the United States, the exports now included garments, electronic products, and shrimp. Jamaica, whose exports to the United States before 1984 were almost 70 percent aluminum ore, has doubled its exports to the United States, and aluminum now counts for less than 10 percent of the total. The tax bases are strengthening, and much of the frustration and discontent that had been growing in the region gradually subsided. After its successful beginning, however, the CBI act expired, and its renewal was delayed several years before being renewed in 2000.

One of the best-kept secrets of the United States' trade patterns is that, at present, the Caribbean nations are among our top trading partners, as President Bush has recognized in his "Third Border Initiative." The record of the Caribbean after independence is impressive. First, it made a major thrust in the 1970s into tourism, which greatly increased per capita income. Then a move into financial services accelerated growth even more. In 1972, for example, the newly independent Cayman Islands were dirt poor with no resources, a population of ten thousand, and a per capita income of $300. Thirty years later, between tourism and financial services, per capita income has risen to $10,000. In Antigua and Barbuda, the United States–educated prime minister, Lester Bird, declares that he wants his people "to know how to handle spread sheets, not bed sheets." He launched a major drive to attract information technology companies to the island. The Internet's gaming industry in the island nation has become so prosperous that it has sponsored a new private-sector hi-tech university. Blazing a similar path since its independence, Barbados now has one of the world's highest literacy rates, at 99 percent, as well as the highest longevity and per capita income levels in its history. Prime Minister Owen Arthur has put computers in every school, achieved integrity in government and monetary management, and is making steady progress in reducing poverty. Grenada raised its per capita income to more than $4,000 by eliminating all income taxes, building good roads, and putting computers in every school. While it may be a dubious model of the business potential, the combination of modern communications and the impeccable English of its population has made "telephone sex" in Guyana one of its largest export earners.

At present, the region is fighting several political storms. First, NAFTA has severely undermined the region's limited economic base. The growth of U.S. apparel imports, one of the Caribbean's principal labor-intensive industries, declined substantially as Mexico's increased. These exports are critical to many nations. Honduras derives 35 percent of its GDP from apparel exports; the Dominican Republic, almost 15 percent of its GDP; and the other countries of the region, from 5 to 10 percent. While Mexico's apparel exports now dwarf those of the other countries, they amount to only 1 percent of Mexico's GDP.

The second debilitating storm comes from the drug trade. With the dismantling of their narco-traffic centers, the Colombian cartels have decentralized their operations in keeping with the best practices of modern multinational management. Recent reports on the increase in drug traffic cite that more than 60 percent of South American cocaine now moves through the Caribbean, "fueling corruption, violence . . . and threatening the political and social fabric of the region."[9] As the countries moved into the financial services area to increase income, suddenly its vulnerability to money laundering became apparent. Ironically, it was the bank confidentiality laws modeled on the Swiss codes, which many of the nations adopted to help develop their financial services industry, that opened the doors to the mafias. But the Caribbean nations have been trying as best they can with their small staffs to cooperate fully with the developed countries' financial officers to clean up the situation.

One day, the Caribbean will be buffeted by another storm that could further slow its economic momentum. Sooner or later the Cuban economy will open up. When it does, its impact will be like the force of a tropical hurricane. It will affect tourism patterns with newer hotels, marvelous beaches, greater accessibility, and, at the beginning, curiosity. An extremely affordable Cuba, with a highly educated workforce, will become a strong contender for assembly plants and new production facilities. Compared with the high-income countries like Barbados and Trinidad with more than $4,000 per capita GDPs, Cuba's current per capita income of less than $1,000 will be very attractive. Rechanneled flows of foreign aid and capital will divert investment and tourism from other Caribbean countries, at least in the near term, after the normalization of relations.

The most recent irritant in our troubled policies toward the Caribbean was the decision of the United States to contest through the World Trade Organization (WTO) those European policies favoring Caribbean bananas with the trade preferences. The Europeans, concerned about the economic vulnerability of its small economies, had set up a system of tariff preferences to give the Caribbean a larger share of the European banana market. Unfortunately the production of U.S.-owned Chiquita Brands (the former United Fruit Company) in other countries of Central and South America was adversely affected. Even though the United States itself produces no bananas, it decided to use the case to test the new WTO rules. The WTO decision in favor of the U.S. position hurt banana production in almost all the small Caribbean nations. More than 50 percent of the export earnings of the Windward Islands and almost all the agricultural exports of Dominica and St. Lucia are from bananas. Europe at the time was more concerned than the United States with preserving the income streams of these small economies.

Even though the United States finally won the case in the WTO and the Europeans were forced to terminate their preferences, the United States would have been better served by using another product instead of bananas as its test case. The struggle did considerable psychological damage to U.S. relations with the region. Significantly, President George W. Bush recognized the damage and, as one of his first acts, informed the Caribbean that the United States would allow a transition period of five years, about all that was requested in the first place.

Alternative economic strategies for the Caribbean nations to find their niche in the global economy are now being pursued. In 2000, the U.S. Congress passed the Caribbean Basic Trade Partnership Act, restoring trade preferences. This will help considerably but still leaves the region vulnerable and far behind the benefits that were accorded to Mexico by NAFTA. Nevertheless, the highly educated, English-speaking population is attractive to the emerging information service industries. The British did everyone a service by leaving a strong educational system behind them in their former colonies. For decades since independence, the nations of the Caribbean have maintained that tradition and invested a higher percentage of their GDP in education than have other nations, developing and developed alike.[10] Several nations are already making a determined effort to ensure full computer literacy among its young people. Barbados is well along in its policy to ensure that every child will learn by computer. Jamaica is investing heavily in domestic software and computer-processing companies in its micro–Silicon Harbor in Kingston. Internet and e-mail now connect the islands to one another and to the global information network in ways that were unthinkable only a decade ago.

Another major industry that can take advantage of the Caribbean's strategic position astride the sea-lanes to the United States is shipping. Expansion of the United States' east coast ports is not keeping up with the increasing volume of ocean trade. The Caribbean's natural harbors are ideal as redeployment hubs for global container traffic. New investment is taking advantage of their natural location. Freeport in the Bahamas, the Port Lises Industrial Park in Trinidad and Tobago, and new installations in Jamaica are rapidly improving port facilities, installing berths, cranes, and container storage ports.

In the long run, an integrated Caribbean market of 13 million people, linked by inexpensive sea routes and instantaneous telecommunications, has far more potential than it is generally given credit for. The region has come a long way in working together since union failed in 1972, and they signed an agreement establishing the Caribbean Common Market (Caricom). The move to a single passport and currency for the entire bloc, currently being considered by Caricom, will help considerably to unify political and macroeconomic policies.

It is noteworthy that these changes are taking place side by side with the reduction of U.S. Agency for International Development programs for the Caribbean, which were slashed from $226 million in 1985 to $22 million in 1995. This is unfortunate because building hospitals, roads, and airports costs just as much if not more to build in Barbados as they do in Baltimore. The tax base, however, is far too small for such infrastructure investment.

The contrast of priorities between Latin America and the Caribbean is stunning. In Latin America, democracy is weak so U.S. policies concentrate on achieving political democracy and focus less on economic and social issues. For the Caribbean countries, the reverse is true. They have achieved political stability and have a long, proud tradition of democratic values. The need in the Caribbean is for economic support to build an infrastructure for competing in the global economy. For a nominal cost, the United States can spur this effort by building a bulwark against illicit drug traffic and being a strong ally among the world's democracies.

11

The New Geopolitics of Latin America

IN MAY 1996, the price of copper crashed from $2,600 to $1,775 a ton. The Sumitomo Corporation of Japan acknowledged unprecedented losses of $2.6 billion from unauthorized trading by its chief copper trader, Yasuo Hamanaka. If the name is not familiar, it should be no surprise. He was but one of the thousands of faceless manipulators of the international commodities markets whose daily decisions of buying and selling affect all of us. Among the major banks caught in this modern variation of a Ponzi scheme were J. P. Morgan and the London Metal Exchange. Chile, whose economy still relied on income from the commodity, was quickly and painfully reminded that the highly leveraged markets on which it depended, even in the hands of the most reputable institutions, were fragile and subject to unexpected forces beyond its control. Copper prices began a downward spiral from which they have not yet recovered.

In 1998, the importance of natural resources to the Latin American economies again became apparent. The loss of demand for commodities resulting from the Asian financial crisis triggered the most severe recession in Latin America since the debt depression of the 1980s. Before that happened, the region had good cause to be optimistic. Economic reforms, privatization, and the opening of markets had led to infrastructure projects that were transforming the face of South America and promised to changed the region as much as did the opening of the United States' interior in the nineteenth century. The direct investment that accompanied the reforms helped blunt the impact of the global financial retrenchment.

Throughout history, access to natural resources has been one of the pillars of national power. Today, South America's natural resources are reshaping relations among the region's countries. The low-cost access to natural resources is attracting industries to the region. Suddenly, the ability to join natural resource wealth to value-added industry is positioning the region to become an important player in the global economy of the twenty-first century.

Intraregional trade is both the driving force and the benefactor of these changes. New roads being built across the Andes will link the Atlantic and Pacific Oceans for truck and rail traffic, opening land for agricultural production and opportunities for the poor to escape poverty. This transformation will affect the countries of the interior such as Bolivia and Paraguay, which will become the crossroads of hemispheric trade routes from Argentina and Brazil to Chile and Peru.

Large oil and natural gas reserves provide abundant, cheap energy. The mineral wealth of the Andes—gold, silver, iron, copper, zinc, tin, manganese, and other exotic metals—could fuel the global economy for centuries. The potential for growth is clear from the transportation and infrastructure projects already being planned. The Inter-American Development Bank is now studying fourteen possible passes over the Andes between Chile and Argentina. A new highway for high-speed truck traffic will link Buenos Aires to São Paulo. A master plan for transportation and energy for the Andean countries was recently completed by the Andean Development Corporation. Road and pipeline networks to handle intraregional trade among the Mercosur countries, crossing Paraguay and Bolivia, are almost complete. Newly privatized railroads are being modernized, providing intermodal transportation corridors from the Atlantic to the Pacific. Argentina's Ferrosur Roca now allows direct rail shipment to Asia with truck links to Valparaiso, Chile. Brazil is constructing one of the world's largest rail links, the 3,100-mile Ferronorte, to enable grain producers in the interior to reach global markets. Trains on the pampas, which only a few years ago took days to travel seventy miles to ports on the Parana River, now can carry their grain cargo there in hours. The new road from Santa Cruz, Bolivia, to Arica on the Pacific coast will reroute traffic, which now has to travel by barge out through the Amazon, thereby reducing the cost of shipping soybeans by $40 a ton and the time to reach Asian markets in half.

The controversial 2,200-mile waterway connecting the Paraguay and Parana Rivers with the Rio de la Plata will, when completed, extend inexpensive river transport from remote areas of Paraguay and Bolivia to the Atlantic Ocean. As a waterway, the impact of the *hydrovia* (literally, waterway) would be as important to the development of the region as the Mississippi River is to the United States. Its environmental impact, however, remains controversial, as it poses a threat to the

Pantanel, one of the world's most extensive wetlands. But even the partial implementation currently under way will alter the economic life of the region.

Opening the rich agricultural lands of the southern Mato Grosso, southeast Bolivia, and the Paraguay Chaco will create new sources of wealth as barge traffic reduces transportation costs for both fertilizer going in and grain coming out. Brazil's savannas—barren scrub only twenty years ago—with their new transportation routes, now produce 25 percent of Brazil's 80 million tons of grain, making Brazil the world's second-largest producer of soybeans after the United States. Bolivia's long-fallow Santa Cruz region, at the foothills of the Andes, has risen in only ten years to become the sixth-largest soybean producer in the world, attracting heavy investment from the world's principal agroindustrial companies, including U.S. multinationals Cargill, Continental Grain, and Archer-Daniels-Midland. More than a half-billion potentially productive acres in the Santa Cruz–Mato Grosso region still have not been cultivated. With reasonable transportation, the region's agricultural production could easily triple. Barges will also facilitate the development of some of the world's richest mineral deposits, such as the mammoth Matun iron ore deposits of southern Bolivia, providing market access for these and other bulk commodities like lumber, limestone, and petrochemicals. Imports and exports from Latin America climbed so rapidly in the 1990s that the region topped Europe as the number two destination for U.S. containerized shipments.[1]

The geopolitical impact of these changes will transform the continent in as yet unforeseen ways. For example, the high-speed road from Buenos Aires to São Paulo could wake up sleepy Montevideo, Uruguay, whose ports are deeper and feed more easily into southern Brazil and the rich lands of the interior. Buenos Aires, historically the preferred port because it served the extensive fertile lands of Argentina, will gradually cede part of its sea traffic to ports on the north side of the La Plata River, which will have cheaper and quicker land transportation routes to Brazil. According to Richard Klein of Transroll Navagação, one of the carriers active in the region, the flow of La Plata River depositing its silt on the southern Buenos Aires side gives Buenos Aires "an unresolvable draft problem" because the channel into its harbor is too shallow and dredging costs are too high. "Big ships with never be able to call there," he observed.[2] Montevideo, across the river, has a depth of 13 meters compared with 10.2 meters for Buenos Aires. A new port being explored in Uruguay at La Paloma on the Atlantic will take ships to a draft of 18 meters. Already, cargo handled in Uruguay ports has more than quadrupled in the last decade, growing from 985 thousand tons in 1990 to 3,507 thousand tons in 1998.[3] If it manages its infrastructure carefully, Uruguay could become the port of choice for the superfreighters and become vital to southern Brazil as new roads through Rio Grande do Sul and Curitiba to São Paulo make the ports among the region's most cost effective. Their considerably lower maintenance costs are projected to be less than $70 per container, compared with $120 in Buenos Aires and more than $250 per container in Brazilian ports.[4]

Even more impressive are the enormous deposits of natural gas being discovered on the east side of the Andes in Bolivia, Peru, Ecuador, and Argentina. Bolivia is particularly well endowed. The new $2 billion gas pipeline linking the remote gas fields of Bolivia to the markets of São Paulo and southern Brazil is providing much needed income for poverty-striken Bolivia and cheap, clean energy for Brazil, transforming the industrial potential of the entire southern part of the continent. These new pipelines have prompted further exploration of known but unproven gas fields in the east Andes, linking them to Brazil, Chile, and Uruguay. In hydroelectric power, the almost unlimited, untapped resources of the Bolivian lowlands, benefiting from their strategic position at the foothills of the Andes, could power half the southern hemisphere. Their development is already being studied.

Fifty years from now, southern Latin America will not look the same. New roads will penetrate a now isolated interior and stretch from coast to coast. The implications for the landlocked countries of Bolivia and Paraguay are immense. The historic trade routes of Latin America flowed from populations huddled along the coast outward to Europe and North America, making the interior countries marginal to Latin America's development. In the twenty-first century, as intraregional trade grows and trade routes cross the interior, not only will they unlock these countries' rich agricultural potential to produce for global markets, but the inland countries themselves also will occupy a far more strategic role in the economic development of the region. Instead of backwaters, countries such as Paraguay and Bolivia, as well as Brazil's southern Mato Grosso, will become new transportation and production hubs. Jobs, new living spaces, and new economic opportunities will be created throughout the region.

The Latin American continent's resources will become increasingly important in a world of depleting resources and political vulnerability. Its abundance of resources will enable the Latin American nations to prosper far more rapidly and cost effectively than other regions of the developing world.

RESOURCES IN THE GLOBAL ECONOMY

The backbone of the United States' power throughout its history was easy access to natural resources. The country's rivers enabled its settlers to tap its riches and to reach markets, opening thousands of miles of productive, fertile farmland from the Alleghenies to the Rockies, the bedrock of U.S. economic power.

An analogous development is about to take place in South America. The impact of the geopolitical revolution accompanying the opening of the South American interior will stimulate a wide range of collateral investment opportunities to use these resources to strengthen the institutions of democracy and deliver education and jobs to their people. The significance of access to resources in an energy-dependent industrial world is markedly different today from what it was in the past. Then it was primarily a source of hard currency from exports. Today, access to resources is an opportunity to build domestic value-added industries. While open markets and cheap transportation offer industries access to resources in all parts of the world in normal times, instability and religious and ethnic rivalries prevent many regions from transforming their mineral riches into value-added products. In the twenty-first century, the most important untapped reservoirs of resources are in South America, Russia, and Africa, and of the three, only South America is close to having an infrastructure that can access them.

The Western Hemisphere is the only relatively stable area in the world that has the potential for energy self-sufficiency. Venezuela alone has oil reserves, including the heavy oil of the Orinoco Basin, of more than a trillion barrels, more than three times those of the conflict-prone Middle East. The vast natural gas wealth of the eastern slope of the Andes alone could keep industry supplied with energy for more than a century. With energy security an increasingly important factor in investment decisions, capital from Europe and Asia is already turning to the Americas from more vulnerable areas of the world.

Most forecasts of the global economy in the twenty-first century, transfixed by the digital revolution, overlook the continuing importance of material resources. As development spreads throughout the world and billions of new consumers come onto the market, natural resources will remain in the forefront of the global economy. The Americas have one of the highest ratios of resources to population on the globe. Within Latin America, the population, projected to be 800 million by 2050, will drive up domestic demand and also affect global demand. The purchasing power of the emerging middle classes will inevitably be directed first to material goods, as it has everywhere else. The construction industry in Latin America will be among the first to feel the effects of the boom for infrastructure and housing.

Accelerating the development of Latin America's resources will ensure their supply in the face of possible instability in other areas of the world and will also consolidate economic growth within the hemisphere. Both Brazil and the United States depend heavily on imports of fossil fuels. For each, a secure supply of energy and resources is important to its national interests, and in no other area of the world are those supplies more secure than in the Americas.

ENERGY RESOURCES

The most significant potential of the Americas is its energy resources. The U.S. Department of Energy predicts that "the United States will rely on imports for 66 percent of its oil needs in 2020."[5] In contrast, the World Bank projects that Latin America will be the "major contributor to increases in [global] oil supplies."[6]

Of the world's total energy sources, Latin America and the Caribbean have the largest share of renewable energy, 35 percent, whereas the industrialized countries account for less than 2 percent. At present, 70 percent of the region's electric power stems from renewable sources. The Andean countries—Chile, Peru, Ecuador, Colombia, and Venezuela—will never lack electric power–generating capacity. Central America's hydro resources, which account for 65 percent of its energy consumption, will become more important with the completion of the integrated electric power grid being financed by the Inter-American Development Bank. Paraguay's main source of income is now the export of energy generated from the huge Itapu and Yacyreta hydroelectric projects, 90 percent of which is exported to Brazil and Argentina. Paraguay's current tiny internal demand compared with these projects' formidable generating capacity enable it to be one of the few countries in the world that can finance its government without collecting income taxes.

Nonetheless, the abundance of natural resources has drawbacks. Historically, resource-rich countries, especially landlocked countries, have lagged behind resource-scarce countries in economic development. The many reasons range from the narrow economic base of the mining economies to the concentration of wealth that enabled the elites to enjoy the good life without having to work to create a value-added industry. In addition, because of the debilitating tropical climates before the advent of air conditioning, almost no industrial capacity could have been created to produce value-added goods for global markets.

Venezuela's huge reserves of fossil fuels, often depicted as both a blessing and a curse, created an elite that skimmed the riches and adhered to a weak work ethic that undermined productivity and the innovative capacity of the middle classes. The country always had so much money from its petroleum exports that it rarely had to exercise the fiscal discipline required of other, less well endowed countries. Indeed, the people became so accustomed to cheap energy that riots broke out when the government tried to raise gasoline pries in 1989. In contrast, Mexico has better managed its vast energy potential because it was discovered more recently when its entrepreneurial class was more sophisticated.

As of 2002, most of South America's natural gas potential is still unexplored. Proven reserves are estimated at 300 trillion cubic feet, double that of the United States, and probable gas reserves are quadruple that amount. Most of the region's poorer countries, such as Bolivia and Peru, have lacked the financial resources to explore areas with promising geologic formations, many of which lie in the remote Amazon and Andean regions. Opening exploration to the private sector is changing that rapidly. Bolivia alone is now projected to have enough natural gas to supply all of the Southern Cone's needs well into the twenty-first century. At present Bolivia is starting to pump large quantities of natural gas to São Paulo and southern Brazil as the $2 billion Bolivia-Brazil pipeline is completed and is planning to build a new pipeline to the Pacific Ocean through Chile to manufacture liquefied natural gas (LNG) for export to California. Chile has tied its future to Argentine natural gas as new pipelines cross the Andes to supply pollution-plagued Santiago with clean natural gas. And Venezuela has long dreamed of using its natural gas resources to produce cheap aluminum from its abundant bauxite, which would require electric power.

Country by country, the prospects are almost uniformly promising:

Venezuela. While the new government led by President Hugo Chávez is reassessing its global oil production strategy and has embarked on a path of close cooperation with other oil-producing countries of OPEC to maintain balance in global markets, Venezuela's previous government succeeded in establishing higher quotas for the country. Indeed, the previous government projected reaching 6 million barrels a day by 2006, with an investment of approximately $40 billion, primarily from the private sector. The Chávez government temporarily reversed this as the glut of energy reduced prices to unprofitable levels. Venezuela's total energy reserves, including its heavy crude oil deposits in the Orinoco belt, called "Orimulsion," are estimated at 1.2 trillion barrels, triple that of the Middle East.[7] Six projects are currently under way to develop this heavy oil resource, led by the Hamaca $3.5 billion joint venture among Phillips Petroleum, Texaco, and the Petroleum Company of Venezuela, known by its acronym as PDVSA (Pedevesa), and another $2.5 billion joint venture of Mobil, Germany's Vela Oel, and Lagoven.

Enormous but isolated natural gas fields are being tapped, and liquified natural gas (LNG) plants costing more than $2 billion each are being constructed to bring gas to export markets.[8] The country's proven reserves are estimated at 145 trillion cubic feet (tcf) but could reach as high as 458 tcf (compared with domestic consumption of 0.7 tcf per year). PDVSA's ownership of the Citgo Service Stations now gives it control over fifteen thousand Venezuelan-owned gasoline stations in the United States. Production and marketing are being vertically integrated with distribution and consumer services abroad.

Peru. A remote rain forest on the eastern slope of the Andes holds the recently discovered Camisea oil-and-gas field with proven reserves of 11 trillion cubic feet of gas and 600 million barrels of oil. It is considered by geologists to be the first of many such fields in the unexplored area.

Ecuador. Ecuador is currently Latin America's fourth-largest oil exporter, shipping almost 400,000 barrels per day. Current investment in oil pipelines will lead to increased exploitation of the Amazon Basin, which is thought to be able to produce 1 million barrels a day.

Bolivia. Bolivia's natural gas potential was hardly realized by the impoverished former state petroleum monopoly, which could afford only $60 million in annual investment. As a result, only a fraction of Bolivia's potential has been explored. But this is now rapidly changing with the company's recent privatization, which brought the government of Bolivia $835 million for a 50 percent stake. Extensive new explorations with investment from international consortia led by Shell and Amoco have discovered enormous quantities of natural gas leading toward possible exports of LNG.

Colombia. The recent discoveries in the Cusiana and Cupiagua ranges in the northern Andes, being developed by Occidental and British Petroleum, have estimated reserves of 2 billion barrels. The discoveries now place Colombia in a position of potentially becoming a net exporter of oil, with production said to be able to reach a million barrels a day. Even more oil is expected in the nearby Piedemonte fields when the guerrilla violence is overcome. The potential of the region is estimated to rival that of neighboring Venezuela.[9]

Argentina. Argentina's gas reserves, second in the continent to Venezuela's, will now reach the market with major gas pipelines serving Chile, Uruguay, and Brazil. Offshore, the South Atlantic off the Malvinas–Falklands Islands has long been thought to harbor large oil and gas reserves. Indeed, the underlying cause of the conflict with Britain over the Malvinas-Falklands is widely believed to have been oil reserves that geologists estimate could be as large as those of the North Sea.[10] Recent agreements between the countries have begun the hunt for oil, led by Amerada Hess and Shell.

Trinidad and Tobago. Trinidad and Tobago, off the coast of Venezuela, has large offshore deposits of natural gas, which give the country one of the Caribbean's highest per capita incomes. New discoveries of natural gas have increased reserves from the current 18 trillion cubic feet. Trinidad and Tobago is using them for new domestic petrochemical industries

underwritten by investments by ExxonMobil and Amoco. Seven fertilizer plants now produce more than 5 million tons of fertilizer a year,
and cost-effective aluminum production will be increased with a new
$2.5 billion investment from Norsk Hydro.

Mexico. With proven reserves twice the size of those of the United
States, Mexico's production has long been hampered by rigid government policies and inefficiencies of monopoly government control.
These impediments became evident during the Asian financial crisis of
1998, when the government's first "savings" to balance the national
budget was to cut the allocation of money for oil exploration.

Guyana and Surinam. Disputes between the two countries of Guyana and
Surinam, bordering the same geologic formation that produced the
riches of Venezuela and Trinidad, have prevented exploration of an offshore area that are thought to contain oil reserves rivaling those of the
North Sea.

Brazil and Paraguay. Brazil and Paraguay are the only countries of South
America lacking adequate fossil-fuel resources. Abundant hydroelectric power remains the backbone of both countries' electric grids. Indeed, the revenue from the jointly owned Itapu and Yacyreta Dams on
the Parana River between the two countries is sufficient to enable
Paraguay to levy no income tax. With the growth of Brazil's domestic
market outrunning new discoveries, energy is a significant factor in
Brazil's geopolitical strategy. Wise investments in Bolivia's natural gas
pipeline and in the gas reserves of neighboring countries are helping secure supplies, and it is clear that Brazil's interests lie in developing the
energy potential of its neighbors.

In sum, Latin's America's actual and potential fossil-fuel reserves
means that the Middle East alone can no longer control oil prices.
"The center of gravity of world oil has shifted from the Middle East
to Venezuela and Canada," according to Joseph Tovey, a New York oil
consultant.[11] This was clear with the crash of oil prices in 1998. OPEC
tried to persuade Venezuela and Mexico to agree to cut oil production.
But Venezuela had ignored its OPEC quotas in the 1990s, raising its
production to 3.4 million barrels per day (bpd) from its 2 million bpd
OPEC quota, thereby giving notice that Latin America's role in oil

production would be based on its own national interests. Mexico signed an agreement with OPEC in 1998 but did not actually join it, giving new importance to Mexico in global oil politics. In March 2000, Saudi Arabia invited only Mexico and Venezuela to meet in London to discuss strategy before the OPEC conference. The ready agreement of Venezuela's President Chávez to cooperate in sharp production cutbacks halted the slide of oil prices in 1999 and boosted prices to new highs. OPEC's agreement to allow Venezuela to reduce production by only 200,000 bpd, however, was tantamount to legitimizing Venezuela's higher production levels set according to its own needs.

Despite its potential, Latin America's energy resources are still plagued with problems of lack of infrastructure, heavy-handed government regulation, and corruption. New investments are needed to get the resources out of the ground, and then the corruption surrounding the industry must be curtailed in order to apply these resources to overcome the region's pervasive poverty, the principal threat to sustainable democratic development.

BURIED TREASURE

Latin America's spectacular endowment of natural resources has dominated its history since the Spanish were first attracted to the region in the sixteenth and seventeenth centuries. Indeed, before air conditioning enabled extensive manufacturing in the hot, humid climate, natural resources were Latin America's only reliable source of hard currency.

The region's output was prodigious. In gold alone, South America accounted for between 61 percent and 80 percent of the world's production in that period, fueling the renaissance of heretofore poverty-stricken and fragmented Spain to become a major power of Europe.[12] The bureaucracies Spain established in its colonies served to direct the flow of wealth to Spain.

The lure of natural resources in Latin America continues and is now fueling a historic boom in mining investment. While the investment rush in the 1990s resulted in part from a period of catchup from the lack of investment in the 1980s, it also signaled an end to the decades-old hostility, caused by Spanish plundering, toward foreign investment in mineral wealth. For decades, strong nationalistic fervor advocated leaving the minerals in the ground until the country could marshal its own resources to exploit them rather than turn them over to foreign interests. The region's natural wealth can be better understood after a brief look at some of the more recent discoveries.

Gold. Spain's legendary El Dorado continues to spark the imagination of investors and adventurers alike. New discoveries in South America's "Gold Belt" promise to make it one of the world's largest gold producers outside China. The continent's production has almost quadrupled in the last decade, with Peru, Colombia, Venezuela, and Bolivia all increasing production. Indeed, recent investment in Peru has made it one of the fastest-growing gold producers in the world, placing it first in Latin America and among the top ten in the world. New finds raised annual production to 85 tons in 1998, overtaking Brazil's production of 67 tons. Yanacocha, a joint venture of the United States' Newmont Mining and Peru's Buenaventura, has become one of the most profitable mines in the world, with operating costs of $95 an ounce. Several new deposits under development in Peru's Sipan and Pierina areas are expected to have even lower operating costs, ranking them also among the richest in the world.[13] Bolivia's Inti Raymi mine and new explorations in the San Simeon tableland together have estimated reserves of close to 400 metric tons. Venezuela's Guyana provinces have attracted large investments from Australian mining companies. In Chile, Cerro Casale, being developed by Bema of Canada; the Tambo deposits; the famous El Indio managed by Barrick of Canada; and the El Refugio mines will increase production for the next several decades.

Silver. Long the staple of mining in South America and Mexico and another of the legends of old Spain, silver continues to be a major resource in many countries of the Americas. In Mexico, large quantities of silver are a by-product of its lead and zinc mines.[14] The most intriguing recent investment was made by George Soros, in the long dormant silver-mining area of Potosi, Bolivia, where a newly discovered vein is expected to revive production in one of the legendary mother lodes of South America.

Copper. The southern Andes is home to the richest veins of copper ore in the world. Production from Chile's west coast mines are capable of reaching 4 million tons a year, based on current investment projections, compared with 2.2 million tons in 1996. The east side of the Andes, in Argentina, is only now beginning to be explored. It has long been a mystery why until now only the west slope of the Andes had been actively explored. The Alumbrera mine being developed by MIM Holdings of Australia and International Musto of Canada will be one of the largest in Argentina's history, with an investment of more than $1 billion. Production is expected to reach almost 200,000 tons annually of copper and 730,000 troy ounces of gold, making it the world's fourteenth-largest gold mine. Agua Rica in northern Argentina, opened by BHP of Australia and Northern Orion of Canada, is alleged to be even larger. In Peru, a Canadian consortium is investing $2 billion to develop the huge mine at the Antomina polymetal deposit, also alleged to rival the world's richest copper-zinc resources. Production at this mine alone will increase Peruvian mineral output by 25 percent.[15]

Zinc. Most of the largest and richest deposits of zinc in the world outside Australia are in the Western Hemisphere, principally in Brazil, Peru, and Mexico, as well as in Canada and the United States. The Limpe Centro area of Peru, with ore grades of 21 percent, is one of the world's richest and lowest cost. Iscayacruz, being developed by Glencore of Switzerland, and exploration at Limpe Norte and Chupa, by Savage Zinc of Australia and Cominco of Canada, are even more promising, with ore grades expected up to 40 percent.[16]

Nickel. The United States, one of the major consumer countries of nickel, has virtually no reserves in this metal, which is needed to produce stainless steel. Our country must therefore rely on the output of the world's largest producers in the Western Hemisphere: Canada, Brazil, and the Dominican Republic, which have the world's richest ores outside Russia and Cuba.[17]

Alumina and bauxite. Jamaica, Venezuela, Guyana, and Surinam contain the largest reserves of alumina and bauxite outside Russia and Guinea. The enormous amount of energy required to convert bauxite to alumina and aluminum gives Venezuela, with its abundant bauxite deposits located close to its sources of cheap energy, a strong competitive advantage, a position that it has been unable, however, to exploit despite considerable state investment.

Iron and steel. Brazil accounts for 8.7 percent of the world's iron ore, with current estimates of reserves at 20 billion tons. Its Vale do Rio Doce

Company is one of the world's largest natural resource companies. Taking advantage of the cheap energy from Bolivian gas, Rio Tinto is investing $200 million to produce higher value-added briquetted iron for steel plants in Argentina. Canada and Venezuela rank among the world's other large producers, with Venezuela's CVG Ferrominera producing higher value-added products. In Mexico, the Grupo Acero del Norte and IMSA from Monterrey are expanding into global steel markets. The global demand for iron and steel emanating from the enormous demand from China has created new opportunities in the global markets that the Brazilians and Mexicans are beginning to exploit. Although China now has the world's third-largest steel industry, its iron ore reserves are of low quality, and the country is a major importer, which will increasingly influence global markets.

Tin. Tin reserves in Bolivia, Brazil, and China are among the world's largest of this relatively abundant, stable commodity. Its production is unique, since small individual "pick and shovel" producers called *garimpeiros* account for more than 50 percent of the production in the large Suracananus deposits and others in the remote Amazon regions of Brazil, near the Bolivian border. The reserves have hardly been tapped. Given the nature of the mining with small fortune hunters, the production is highly elastic and fluctuates with swings in the market.

Exotic and renewable resources. South America's list of exotic metal production is long. Brazil now ranks in the top five global producers of manganese, magnetite, kaolin, graphite, and fluoride. Argentina is a major producer of uranium and cadmium. Its large lithium deposits in Patagonia, now being tapped by the United States' FMI Lithoc and South Africa's Anglo-American, have led to a mining boom in that region.[18] Forestry, another of the continent's abundant resources, is a source of enormous wealth from the ever-producing tropical rain forests to the vast, untapped, heavily wooded, sparsely populated southern Andes of Chile and Argentina. When managed in an environmentally sensitive fashion by professional forestry experts, timber resources can boost the economic productivity of several of the poorer tropical countries, such as Guyana and Suriname. Timber can anchor the manufacture of nontimber products as well, such as resins, fibers, and oils that generate considerable value-added employment. A model of multiuse forestry management under an international trust fund was created with the Central Suriname Nature Reserve, covering almost 20,000 square kilometers. In fisheries, Chile, with a population of only 14 million, has a sea coast almost as long as that of the United States, as does the Caribbean, which has barely exploited its ocean resources. Finally, Peru is one of the world's largest producers of fish meal.

In 1996 in Brazil, foreign mining investments topped $2.5 billion, in contrast to the average annual investment of $40 million in the 1980s. In the past, with low local demand, opening remote areas to production meant exploiting resources for export. But inadequate transportation systems impeded the development of downstream enterprises, as did the lack of air conditioning.

Today, this scenario has changed. As new areas open, transportation networks expand into the interior on a scale far more extensive and efficient than ever before. With a more mobile population, opening remote locations to production often can have considerable collateral economic benefits. Owners of the new mines are making parallel investments in infrastructure, including transportation, power and water, which also serve a population base eager for new opportunities. For example, the Alumbrera development in Argentina is building a new port facility on the Parana River, a 150-megawatt power plant, a 30-meter dam for a water reservoir, and a 150-mile slurry pipeline from the mine to Tucuman Province. The Japanese consortium developing the $1.36 billion Los Pelambres copper project is financing even larger infrastructure in its base investment and still expects to bring the product to market economically. This new infrastructure has enabled small farmers and entrepreneurs to move into the regions, laying the foundations of new cities and more diversified wealth.

More significantly, Latin Americans themselves are beginning to accumulate sufficient capital to finance their own natural resource development, in contrast to previous generations when the capital necessary to penetrate the jungle for power, communications, and transportation was far out of their reach. As late as the 1960s, the land-rich but capital-poor Latin American oligarchy had insufficient private capital for the investments needed to exploit the minerals. This was one of the factors motivating state investment as the only source of domestic capital besides foreign investors. Today, however, the change in the region is evident in the activity of entrepreneurs such as Benjamin Steinbruch of Brazil, the Grupo Acero del Norte and the Garza Sada families of Monterrey, Mexico, as well as the many multinational corporations that understand the benefits of locating production close to the resource base. Latin American resources, which were once only for export, are beginning also to drive local industry and development.

Today, this is manifested in the cross-border investment among the Latin Americans themselves. Chile has been the leader as a result of the capital accumulation in privatized pension funds. Enersis of Chile purchased the electric power company of Rio de Janeiro; Chilgener now controls the 1,000-megawatt Chivor hydroelectric plant in Colombia; and Endesa is part of the consortium that won the 500-megawatt Colombian Betania plant. Endesa, joining with Spanish capital, now has the dominant position in the Buenos Aires market. Argentine investment was also moving into other countries before the currency collapse of 2001. The consortium led by Pérez Companc won rights to develop one of the Venezuelan oil fields. Cemex, the Mexican cement giant, has interests throughout the hemisphere, and Grupo México acquired the Southern Peru Copper Company.

AN AMERICAN ENERGY COMMUNITY

The lessons from the European Coal and Steel Community in the 1950s offer useful insights into the importance of small steps to realize greater goals. The architects of the European Common Market, Jean Monnet and Robert Schumann, set the basis for a regime by which Europe's coal and steel resources would be managed cooperatively in order to ensure access to all community nations. It was called the European Coal and Steel Community (ECSC). At that time, the convergence of European geopolitical interests in coal and steel had very different imperatives, but the concept is closely related to the mutual interests in the Americas today to develop the region's energy resources. In describing his goals for Europe, Monnet emphasized that it required a pragmatic approach. "Men's attitudes must be changed," he said. "Words are not enough. Only immediate action on an essential point can change the present static situation. This action must be radical, real, immediate, and dramatic; it must change things and make a reality of the hopes which people are on the verge of giving up." To him, the strategy was clear. "This proposal [for a coal and steel community] has an essential political objective: to make a breach in the ramparts of national sovereignty which will be narrow enough to secure consent, but deep enough to open the way toward the unity that is essential to peace [and we might add, for our purposes in the Americas, for development]."[19]

An American Energy Community patterned after the ECSC will provide a major impetus to the American nations to develop the hemisphere. In 1990, Norman Bailey and I proposed a pragmatic mechanism to finance energy development and serve as a magnet for both capital investment and greater inter-American cooperation.[20] The result would be similar to the European Coal and Steel Community and would ensure access to energy for every nation in the Western Hemisphere, structured to take into account the productive capacity and needs of each nation, with each one benefiting in areas in which it holds a competitive or comparative advantage.

The energy markets of the Western Hemisphere hold one of the keys to a new relationship among the nations of the Americas. Over the last several years they have begun to integrate. In NAFTA, a new North American Electric Reliability Council (NERC) is making long-term plans to integrate electric grids and protect against outages in the United States, Mexico, and Canada. It is a small step toward mobilizing the hemisphere's great natural wealth. To do this means adopting policies to harmonize legislation and the taxation of different types of energy sources and developing the economic and financial infrastructure for generation and transmission networks.

Besides the low investment in new facilities, Latin America has a high level of energy waste and diversion, reaching an average of 17 percent in some countries. Unreasonable bureaucratic delays in approving adequate rate structures also hurt investment. The result in some countries is that energy costs exceed global market averages, thus making industrial production more expensive. In others, rates charged to consumers are artificially maintained below long-term reproduction costs, discouraging new investment. Legal, economic, institutional, administrative, and financial barriers to competitive production and distribution are common. Anomalies in the system illustrate the problem:

- Public utilities have to get special authorization from their central government if they exceed their budget for imported fuel.
- No standard systems or procedures exist to set prices based on production and transmission costs.

- Cross-border sales are hampered by inadequate payment mechanisms that tie up intercompany exchanges. As a result, payments are often required in advance, resulting in overcharges because of uncertainty and delays in clearing through the bureaucratic environment.
- Taxes vary by country on different petroleum products as well as on different generating technologies, which distort the efficient operation of the regional pool through interconnections.

If the hemisphere is to grow into a Greater American community, the first challenge is creating a comprehensive framework for nondiscriminatory energy investment and integrated networks, similar to what the Europeans did in the 1950s. This means exchanging power based on reciprocal and nondiscriminatory treatment and market access, no matter where an energy facility is located. And it means reinforcing many of the region's power companies with better-trained, more sophisticated personnel.

In the early 1990s, Presidents César Gaviria of Colombia, Carlos Salinas of Mexico, and Carlos Andrés Pérez of Venezuela called on the nations of the Americas to endorse such a plan. They proposed an agreement

> to promote investment in exploration and in the oil, coal and energy industries in our continent through explicitly coordinated measures . . . through fiscal and de-regulatory incentives . . . a preferential tax regime for investments in the exploration of oil and coal and the production and distribution of energy. . . . We must liberalize inter-American energy trade and even create a preferential tariff regime for hemispheric producers and exporters of oil and coal.[21]

This was, in effect, a call for an American energy community. It is time to expand on this vision and adapt it to the global environment by creating in the Americas a mixed public-/private-sector authority to undertake energy-related projects.[22] Before such a community can be formed, however, the United States will have to confront the mythology of low-cost Middle East oil. As Bailey frequently points out, Middle East oil is the most expensive fuel the world has ever known and could become even more expensive, considering its penchant for extremism and that the region has yet to feel the impact of the information revolution and the pressures for democracy. When we calculate the cost of Middle East oil, we conveniently leave out all the indirect costs of security and intelligence purposes, including military and security assistance and other strategic commitments that are required to defend it. Right now, U.S. taxpayers foot that bill. A fraction of this investment in our hemisphere would yield considerable production and lead to economic development that would help reduce poverty, illegal migration, and narcotics traffic.

A long-term plan for the Americas to achieve energy security must integrate and interconnect the power grids and open them to private facilities. A model of the benefits can be found in a project sponsored by the Inter-American Development Bank to link the power grids of all Central American countries. The $200 million project is designed to facilitate cross-border transmission and harmonize the regulatory framework among the six participating countries. This will allow a power plant constructed in any of the Central American countries to supply all the countries. It also provides for private-sector management of the grid and a transnational entity to ensure compatible regulatory provisions. A similar project is now under way to integrate the grids in the Mercosur countries of South America.

International financial institutions have a limited capacity to make loans to reinforce private-sector initiatives without government guarantees. An American energy community authority would be dedicated to provide for the comprehensive, balanced development of the Americas' energy resources.

The goal of an American energy community would be to balance the distribution of energy supplies between the energy-rich and the energy-poor countries of the hemisphere, contribute to economic stability and job creation in the nations of the Americas, and invite inter-American cooperation. The community would encompass all forms of energy: fossil, hydroelectric, geothermal, solar, and renewable. It would expand its financing of the construction of dams and gas pipelines, integrate power grids, and expand distribution in rural electrification programs in both the public and private sectors by issuing bonds for specific projects secured by energy revenues. Financing also could be provided for countries lacking fossil fuels to develop alternative renewable sources out of the common energy fund as well as to promote energy diffusion and conservation initiatives. In addition, the community could

- Maintain a continuing energy inventory of the hemisphere, including geothermal, hydro, solar, wind, biomass, and other renewable energy sources.
- Issue bonds for specific projects with mechanisms to secure its obligations without requiring governmental guarantees.
- Provide funds to develop each nation's most economic sources of supply, such as hydroelectric, LNG, or nuclear plants, or to help finance energy conservation measures.
- Finance rural electrification and improve electric distribution by integrating standards, regulatory frameworks, and power distribution.
- Establish petroleum reserves not only in the United States but also in other oil-deficit countries such as Brazil or on a hemisphere-wide basis.
- Provide a consistent regulatory framework to ensure a level playing field for all types of energy generation and distribution.
- Eliminate barriers and subsidies that undermine cross-border trade and limit capacity to provide access to energy to all sectors, especially in rural areas.

In short, the rich endowment of natural resources in this hemisphere can provide energy to attract and supply industry and fuel development throughout the twenty-first century. The American nations working together on specific, solvable problems that are urgent national priorities for each country will offer practical experience. Most important, it will provide an impetus for developing the natural resource base of our hemisphere, altering our geopolitical interests in ways that help consolidate democracy, generate confidence among investors, and attract value-added industry to all the countries. Just as the European Coal and Steel Community was a catalyst for the European Union, so a new American energy community joining public and private sectors can fuel the building of Greater America and become the anchor of the proposed free-trade agreement of the Americas.

12

The Muse of the Markets

IN THE MID-1990S, an article in the *Journal of Commerce* on Latin America called it "one of the hottest markets in the world." Wall Street investors cheered the aggressive economic reforms undertaken by Argentina, Mexico, Chile, Brazil, and Peru, the region's main markets. "Across Latin America, you are seeing economic deregulation and industrialization; you're seeing foreign investment and internal investment; tariffs are being reduced and inflation is coming down. It is an economic renaissance fed by low labor costs, abundant natural resources and a very aggressive, hungry, dynamic population base," extolled Thomas Tull of Dallas's Gulfstream Global Investors.[1]

At that time, the top stock picks were Latin American companies going onto the United States stock exchanges: Telebras of Brazil; Telefónos of Chile; Mexico's cement company, Cemex; Vitro, in glass; BAESA, the Argentine Pepsi bottler; and Cifra, Mexico's retail store chain. Market makers were buying new Latin American issues the way they bought Internet stocks several years later. Stanley Lanzet, director of emerging market research at Bear Stearns, asserted that "investors are giving up a tremendous amount of potential if they are not invested in Latin America," and the *Journal of Commerce* touted that the region "offers a bonanza to exporters."[2]

Despite the later shocks from external sources, reverses, and rebounds, Latin America still has the potential to become one of the most promising consumer growth markets in the twenty-first century. The consumption patterns of its growing middle class parallel those of the United States, in contrast to Asia where the dominant pattern is saving instead of spending. The fact that Latin American consumers favor U.S. products means that the region's economic growth has a direct and immediate impact on the U.S. economy.

Years of painful economic reform amid a swing toward democracy have transformed Latin American markets. Decades of isolation from global markets under rigid protectionist policies are over. Recognition of the need for responsible fiscal management brought greater political and economic stability, luring back many major corporations that deserted the region in the 1980s. A free press, global satellite TV, and the Internet are stimulating consumer demand for new products.

These trends are important to the United States. On average, Latin Americans already spend in the United States 40 cents of every dollar earned from their exports, which is double the rate spent here by Europeans or Japanese. And Latin America's current GDP is only one-tenth that of Europe and Japan! It is clear that as Latin America's GDP approximates the levels of Europe, its impact on U.S. exports will be huge. Potential returns to the United States from building Latin American markets are up to twenty times higher than from other regions.

Over the five years before the 1998 Asian crisis, U.S. trade with Latin America grew at a rate of 12.4 percent, compared with 6.5 percent for Asia and less than 1 percent for Europe. In 1996, 39 percent of U.S. exports went to the Americas, compared with 30 percent to Asia and 23 percent to Europe. In 1997, an incredible two-thirds of U.S. export growth was derived from the Americas, with increases of 24 percent in both Brazil and Argentina. In 1995, U.S. cargo to South America surpassed that going across the Atlantic and has been growing, despite the recession of 2001.[3] Trade processed through Miami increased from $2.4 billion in 1971 to $40 billion in 1993. Even given the volatility of the markets early this century, the Americas could well outstrip Japan and western Europe combined as the export market for U.S. goods. That it will do so in the long run is inevitable.

The U.S. and Latin American markets complement each other, but U.S. products will really grow in Latin American markets only if Latin America can expand its trade with the United States. Access to the U.S. market, the largest in the world, is vital to the efforts of the American nations to modernize and overcome poverty. All the principal industrialized nations have targeted U.S. markets since the end of World War II. Only Latin America turned its back on them, preferring protectionism to competition. Then the collapse of their economies in the debt debacle of the 1980s changed that. Today Latin American leaders understand that they have the largest market in the world, the United States, in *their* backyard and that their path to development is to get a bigger slice of it.

Equally important, Latin America is good for U.S. business. Until the 1998 recession set back the timetable, Latin America's consumer markets were growing faster than those of any other area of the world. Retail sales in Brazil have consistently climbed more than 25 percent a year since 1995. Chile's and Mexico's sales were increasing at 15 percent, and Peru's, 12 percent. Argentina's sales were reaching 6 percent a year in the early 1990s before its currency became a problem. The average buying power of the top 10 percent of Argentine households had reached $17,000, and in Brazil, Chile, Mexico, and Venezuela it was more than $10,000. Several countries of the Caribbean, such as the Bahamas and Barbados, although their markets are small, have among the highest per capita incomes of the region. Although they differ in each country, new registrations of automobiles and sales of clothing and footwear, washing machines, refrigerators and household appliances, televisions, and cosmetics all pointed to the potential of the growing markets. As one investment adviser noted, the only thing growing faster than Latin America's human population in that period was its population of automobiles and washing machines.

The trend is clear. Private-sector producers now recognize that Latin America will be the next developing area to mature in the global economy. A look at some of the market components illustrates why.

AUTOMOBILES

In 1997, the number of new car registrations in Mercosur countries surpassed those in Britain and France, making Mercosur the fifth-largest automobile market in the world. A DRI/McGraw Hill study predicted that Latin Americans' demand for cars and trucks would rise by 65 percent to 4.1 million units by 2005, compared with the current consumption of 2.5 million units.[4] *The Economist* reported that between 1992 and 1997, Ford, Fiat, Volkswagen, and GM invested almost $15 billion to expand capacity in Latin America.[5]

Although production was sharply reduced in the recession of 1999, it quickly rebounded, only to be set back again after the financial collapse in Argentina. The explosion of automobile manufacturing in South America will continue over the long term, since it is rooted in several trends that quickly resume whenever economies rebound:

- Rapidly rising demand. Brazil, for example, has 1 car per 11 persons, compared with 1 for 1.3 persons in the United States.[6]

- Consolidation of production. The integration of global production patterns has favored the manufacture of specific components such as transmissions, motors, and drive shafts in one locale to service the plants of a particular company around the world. Latin America, close to energy sources and iron, steel, and aluminum supplies, has benefited from that trend.
- Low tariffs in intraregional trade agreements. Today, Latin America's tariff regime still imposes a 62 percent duty on firms with no local production, compared with half that on firms with local facilities. While the Mercosur market's sharing agreement has been criticized as blocking imports and reserving market share for companies that produce within Mercosur, the size of the Mercosur market makes it an important destination for specialized U.S. hi-tech components.

Latin America's growing importance to the automotive market also has attracted new production facilities:

- Fiat has been one of the most aggressive, producing in Brazil its new car, the Palio, for the global markets.
- Volkswagen and Fiat have taken a commanding lead in Brazil, where small cars account for 51 percent of the market.
- Ford, which broke up its Latin American joint venture with Volkswagen, allowing Volkswagen to take the subcompact end of the market, has begun to introduce new models that previously sold in Europe and has now taken the market lead in several Latin American countries.
- Mercedes-Benz dominates the truck and bus market, and Renault, which withdrew from the U.S. market, is now planning to reenter the South American market.
- Honda's new assembly plant in Brazil builds engines to supply the Civic sedan, produced locally as well as in the United States.

This surge of investment in Latin America's automotive industry is not the result of trade agreements. One of the largest investments made by a U.S. company was Ford's $500 million plant in Hermosillo, Mexico, in 1984, long before anyone ever dreamed of a NAFTA. The result of NAFTA on U.S.-Mexican-Canadian trade patterns, however, was a 17.6 percent increase in trade in automobile parts among the three countries in its first two years. Most important, the increased production in Mexico is substituting for automotive imports into the United States from other countries and has been counterbalanced by declines in U.S. imports from non-NAFTA countries. As a result of the NAFTA trade agreement, imports of vehicles from Mexico contain a far higher percentage of U.S. components than do vehicle imports from Asia.[7]

HOME PRODUCTS

The *Journal of Commerce* reported only a few years ago that "raging competition among makers of everything from soft drinks to shampoo" is sweeping Latin America. In many countries, such as Brazil, Chile, and Argentina, whose currencies are stabile, large-scale retailing has come into its own, compared with a decade ago when prices had to be changed several times a day to keep up with inflation. Wal-Mart, the U.S. retail giant known for its shrewd market analysis, made its first international forays into Latin America in the 1990s. Based on the company's favorable experience with its Tex-Mex customers, its ventures into Latin America were an indication that it had found something important in the region. Today Wal-Mart is a dominant market force in Mexico, Argentina, and Brazil. The company teamed up with Cifra stores in Mexico to blanket that country. In Argentina it has three supercenters and three Sam's Club discount warehouses in the Buenos Aires area and other provinces. The same "buy local" policy that worked so successfully in the United States now works in Latin America, only this time it is Latin American producers that are local.

The penetration of the Latin American markets by the world's leading corporations is shown in the sales figures of the top ten firms selling to the region as recently as 1999.

Table 12.1
Top Ten Firms Selling to Latin American Markets

Company	Sales (in millions $)
Unilever	$1,1417
Ericsson	822
Colgate-Palmolive	594
Coca-Cola	460
McDonalds	432
Whirlpool	432
Avon	401
Caterpillar	378
Best Foods	265
Goodyear	235
Kellogg	151

Source: *Latin Trade*, February 2000. Figures are for the nine months ending September 30, 1999.

The appliance sector—refrigerators, air conditioners, and stoves, known as "white goods"—is perhaps the best indicator of the robust potential of the Latin American consumer goods market. The emergence of a more stable middle class has created a market for these products. In Brazil alone, sales of these items tripled in the three years following the stabilization of the currency.[8] In 1997, the numbers of units sold were as follows:[9]

Refrigerators	3,720,164
Washing Machines	1,068,497
Ovens	3,922,296
Sound systems	2,888,845
Televisions	7,835,957
Microwave Ovens	1,497,048

While the numbers are mounting, what makes the market so attractive is that penetration is still very low. Ownership in Latin America of products such as VCRs is a meager 20 percent of households, compared with more than 75 percent in the United States.[10] General Electric's sales in Latin America of appliances, medical equipment, lamps, and plastics have more than doubled in the last four years. The sales patterns of Panama's Colon Free Zone, now the second-largest trade zone in the world, is typical of Latin American trade. Of the products shipped to Latin America, more than 70 percent are consumer goods, including electronic appliances, 21 percent; textiles and clothing, 17 percent; watches, 6 percent; and shoes, 5 percent.

The market for appliances is probably best exemplified by the growing competition in the Brazilian market. Brasmotor, SA, a joint venture of Whirlpool and Brazilian investors, now dominates 39 percent of the Brazilian market, with revenues of $2.5 billion in 1996.[11] New investments from Electrolux of Sweden, Bosch-Siemens of Germany, and the expansion of General Electric's production are now competing with them.

COMPUTERS AND THE INTERNET

The growth of computer usage is perhaps the prime example of the "buggy to jet age" phenomenon. While market penetration is still extremely low compared with that of countries with higher per capita incomes and education levels, it is useful to compare the short time of the growth and penetration of computers with the decades it took to build the transportation network of roads, ports, and railroads. Latin America has the potential to catch up to the state of the art in this technology in a short time, but many policy decisions regarding the legal and regulatory framework and the improvement of education are needed if the region is not to miss this opportunity.

The Inter-American Development Bank estimates that 20 million Latin Americans own personal computers. Brazil ranks eighth in the global computer industry, with 8.3 million computers in use and a $17 billion computer industry business. It is ahead of Russia and on a par with China. While ownership as a percentage of total population is extremely low,[12] for the top 20 percent of Brazilian households penetration is 39 percent, not that far below European figures. While overall use of the Internet is currently minute, at 6 per 1,000 in Brazil and Mexico and 14 per 1,000 in Chile, compared with 283 in the United States, 289 in Sweden, and 137 in the United Kingdom, the higher-income groups are not far below France, 47, and Germany, 86.[13]

Analyzing market growth patterns today in Latin America requires distinguishing the patterns among the upper-income groups from those of the total population. The upper-income groups approximate those of the more developed countries. In Brazil, the number of people with access to the Internet jumped from 5 million in 1997 to 12 million in 1999. A new U.S. company, Starmedia, from Riverside, Connecticut, began an AOL-type service in Spanish and Portuguese specifically aimed at Latin

America. Starmedia broke records in its largest initial public offering for Internet companies in October 1998, in the midst of the global financial crisis. But it faltered in the collapse of the Internet bubble in the early 2000s, mostly as a result of the fierce competition throughout Latin America. Brazil-based Universo Online (UOL), owned by two of Brazil's largest media conglomerates together with Reuters and Morgan Stanley, stole a march on America Online and is now establishing portals in Mexico, Argentina, and Venezuela. Telefónica of Spain is aggressively marketing its Terra Network, and Microsoft positioned itself in the market by entering into a joint venture with Telmex and Televisa in Mexico and acquiring a minority interest in Globo Cabo in Brazil. The Virginia-based Zonafinanciera.com was a pioneer in developing the financial information market and brokerage business in competition with AOL and the *Wall Street Journal*. Other Internet destinations such as Miami-based Patagon.com and Yupi.com are giving it competition.

Digitized information is now transmitted by seven Latin American–owned satellites: three Mexican (Morelos), two of Brazilsat, and two of Argentina's Nahuelsat. Panamsat from the United States covers the region with four of its own satellites. And Hewlett-Packard now gets 55 percent of its business from outside the United States, with a strong presence in Mexico, Argentina, and Brazil.

FOOD AND AGRICULTURE

In food production, one of the most exciting and rewarding developments for consumers in the Northern Hemisphere is the new ability to enjoy fresh produce year around, thanks to South America's food industry. The long overdue initiative by Chile and other countries of Latin America to dominate the global winter food market has been made possible by the reach and capacity of air freight. Chile is now one of the largest producers of winter fruits and vegetables, not to mention its wine that now rivals California in quality at half the price. Mexico is now the largest producer of lemons in the world, with an annual harvest of 300,000 tons, and Brazil has become one of the largest poultry producers, with strong exports to Asia. On the other side of the coin, for U.S. exports, Mexico has now become the third-largest market for U.S. feed grain after Japan and South Korea. Other agricultural exports such as eggs, poultry, peanuts, and rice have also substantially increased since NAFTA. Most interesting, however, is that salsa now outsells ketchup in U.S. supermarkets and the Mexican food producer, Corfuerte, now sells more of its salsa in the United States than in Mexico.

The most exciting developments in Latin American agriculture are in the interior of the continent, where Brazil and Bolivia together are the largest producers and exporters of soybeans in the world. Brazil's enormous herds of cattle make it one of the world's largest meat and leather producers. As new transportation routes open more land in the interior, the potential can remake global food markets, of which the Europeans and Japanese are painfully aware.

TELEPHONE

The magnitude of investment in the global telecommunications market was estimated by George Young of New York's Lehman Brothers at $1 trillion over the next decade, with Latin America accounting for 40 percent.[14] The impact, however, goes far beyond the investment, for it means the end of the isolation of Latin America—and other regions of the world—from global markets. As costs drop and new technology is created, the competitive framework is changing from monopoly to open competition. Undersea fiber-optic cables now reach throughout the Americas, providing access to broadband and next-generation installations. The latent demand makes Latin America's telephone market one of the most attractive in the world in the long term.

The average fixed-line telephone penetration in Latin America is nine units per hundred people. São Paulo, Brazil, which is one of the more advanced markets, has twelve per hundred. More than 2 million people who are able to afford and want phone service still have not received it.[15] This compares with the phone penetration of nearly seventy per hundred in the United States and Europe. Even Russia, which was touted as the most exciting telecom market in the world a few years ago, averages more phones than Latin America.

The lag in Latin American phone service is a classic example of government monopolies with little incentive to respond to consumer demand. Consumers often had to bribe company officials and workers to get phones installed. The horrendous service was directly attributable to government policies that based investment decisions regarding phone service on the government's budget, not on market demand.

When the budget needed to be balanced, cuts often came at the expense of government-owned private companies. Since privatizing its phone companies, however, new investment more than doubled throughout Latin America. The number of lines in Peru, for example, jumped from 665,000 lines in 1993 to almost 1,500,000 in 1997. In 1993, fewer than 100,000 new lines were installed annually, but in 1997, that number was more than 750,000.

Not only does Latin America lag behind the world in fixed-line telephone installations, but its cost is outrageously high compared with the cost in the developed countries. The Inter-American Development Bank reports that the cost of long distance service is the main reason that many Latin Americans are not connected to the Internet. Indeed, a single user's cost may be as high as $300 for twenty hours a month of Internet usage.[16] Cable and Wireless, the British phone company that had a monopoly in much of the Caribbean, charges the highest telephone rates in the world, which is thought to be the principal factor inhibiting the growth of the informatics industry in the English-speaking, highly educated Caribbean nations. Cable and Wireless's operating profit of $266 million on a turnover of approximately $750 million from the Caribbean region in 1996 is typical.[17]

The potential of the Latin American market is reflected in the prices being paid for privatized phone companies and new cell phone concessions. Brazil's privatization of its phone company in 1998 brought the government a record $19 billion in revenues when it was broken up into smaller companies known as the "baby bras." In addition, U.S. Bell-South paid $2.6 billion for the São Paulo cellular concession, and MCI acquired the prize Brazilian international carrier, Embratel. BellSouth has followed a strong corporate strategy to dominate the cellular phone market and now controls the main cellular phone companies in Argentina, Brazil, Chile, Ecuador, Peru, and Venezuela, besides having smaller interests in Colombia, Nicaragua, and Panama.[18] But Spain's Telefónica is the champion by far. It now holds the dominant position in the region, owning one in three telephones in South America. BellSouth of the United States, Alcatel of France, Stet of Italy, and Cable and Wireless of the United Kingdom all are distant seconds.

In Guatemala and El Salvador in 1999, more cell phones were sold than in all previous years combined. In El Salvador in 2002, the number of cell phones surpassed the number of fixed-line phones. The importance of the wireless revolution contrasts dramatically with that of the industrialized countries. Instead of supplementing the fixed-line system, wireless is rapidly becoming the core of Latin American telephone services. Projections are that the wireless market in Latin America will grow an average of 16 percent a year. The penetration of cell phones in 1996 was 0.9 percent, rising to 4.3 percent in 2000. In numbers of subscribers, this represented a jump from 3.9 million to 19.4 million in 2000.

One of the principal impediments to the growth of the telecommunications industry is the limited size of the market. The masses of people living in poverty are Latin America's potentially greatest asset as well as its greatest burden. Although ownership of telephones by the middle and upper classes is on a world-class level, overall penetration lags far behind that of Asia. New wireless services are one of the greatest hopes to accelerate development. *Business Week* recently described even poor entrepreneurs who are using modern electronic devices to open new businesses, like Alejandro Rios, a dog walker in Buenos Aires, who at the time earned $800 a month in his new trade, keeping in touch with his dog owner customers by cell phone.

The primary applications of the new generation of telecommunications service will be for business communications and the export industries. It will enable governments to change their relationship to the public, make it possible to bring government services into rural regions and help create transparency and minimize corruption. It is the instrument that offers Latin America the opportunity to change history.

ENTERTAINMENT

Satellite technology transformed the entertainment and media markets in the Americas in the 1990s. Favorable consumer patterns and attitudes toward entertainment have made its impact as great or greater than on any other area of the world. Global entertainment through cable, satellites, and microwaves now saturates the region. In 1997, Kay Koplovitz, CEO of the USA Network, described Latin American cable subscribers as "a more desirable demographic because they are younger, better educated and more affluent than their U.S. counterparts."[19] Fifteen channels programmed for Latin America now radiate out of the Miami area, including MTV Latino.[20] Started in 1993, MTV Latino now reaches more than 25 million households throughout Latin America and Brazil.

Today the media's global reach allows advertising to reach millions of Latin American households, stimulating demand for global brands. In a market in which $7.5 billion is spent annually on TV ads, the Brazilian market is one of the best, with sixty thousand new cable subscribers per month.[21] Advertisers drawn from the major multinational companies, ranging from Coca-Cola to Levi Strauss, sell everything from health foods to cell phones. Even basketball is finding eager new fans in the young Latin American audience, according to Rob Levine of the NBA, which now licenses its broadcasts around the world. The impact even reaches to government services. One health minister commented that the demand for the latest medical treatments, whether for diabetes or CAT scans, has generated enormous pressure for her limited budget because this is what everyone sees on the nightly news.

In the United States, the hungry Latin markets are helping Miami carve out a new place in the entertainment world. It is now the second most important city in the United States, rivaling Hollywood, for entertainment production specifically aimed at the Latin TV market. Latin America's Galaxy Group, which operates its own Direct TV satellite owned by a consortium of the Cisneros Group of Venezuela, Multivision of Mexico, and TV Abril of Brazil, with Hughes Communications in the United States, is beginning to produce many of its TV programs in Miami. Direct satellite and pay TV also are becoming popular. The U.S. cable giant TCI purchased 51 percent of Latin America's Cablevision for $750 million. Equally impressive, as literacy expands, so do the print media, magazines and newspapers.

The number of Latin American visitors to Disney World in Orlando, Florida, has been a key factor in exposing U.S. investors to the potential of the Latin market. "I'd rather have one Brazilian tourist than 10 Americans, because of the way they spend money," asserted Patrick Millay, president of Wet N' Wild International.[22] Entertainment theme parks are growing as "entertainment has graduated from a secondary theme into a central one in Latin America," according to Jorge Flom, a director of Maccarone, one of Argentina's cinema developers. A new theme park by Wet N'Wild is now opening outside São Paulo.

The huge growth in Latin America in the 1990s was partly dependent on its being largely overlooked in the explosion of entertainment over the previous two decades. Inflation and political instability, which deterred investors in every field, hit entertainment particularly hard. An Englishman, Charles Lewis, summed this up in his reasoning for acquiring the Hard Rock Café for Argentina and Planet Hollywood for all of Latin America. "I looked at a map of the world and South America was stunningly empty," he explained.[23] Theme park developers have learned from the enormous response to new Latin America festivals, such as the Rock In Rio festivals which regularly draw crowds of more than a million people.

FRANCHISING

As one of the most interesting and potentially influential trends in economic development for the last two decades, franchising has set the pace for small business growth in the United States and Europe for everything from fast-food chains to health products, clothing and shoes, dry cleaning, and recreation. It is spreading throughout Latin America for many of same reasons it has in the United States.

Franchising is given little credit for being an important agent for development. It provides sophisticated, albeit highly targeted, business training to people who have never been exposed to modern merchandising systems. The franchisee receives the equivalent of a postgraduate education in the elements of his or her product. Training and manuals cover management, quality control, accounting, and customer relations. McDonald's restaurant owners often joke about their Ph.D. from Hamburger University, attendance at which is a requirement for all McDonald's franchisees. Similar training in business systems and marketing is offered in every field, whether it is servicing automobiles, running a private post office, or opening a convenience store. This training has a far more important social and economic impact in Bolivia and Guatemala than it ever will in the United States. In Latin America and the Caribbean, the franchises' business practices are becoming one of the most important training grounds for the middle class, which has had little previous entrepreneurial experience.

Today, visitors to any city in the Americas will see Pizza Huts, Kentucky Fried Chickens, McDonald's, and Burger Kings. But they also will see new Latin American chains such as Campero, Pumperniks, O Boticáiro, Yázigi Language Schools, and Paschoal Automotive Services. While trademark protection remains a problem in some countries, the success of the ventures is building a new constituency for the protection of intellectual property and demonstrates the direction in which the economies are moving.

INFRASTRUCTURE

The largest growth market in terms of the amount of money involved is infrastructure. Power, telecommunications, water supply, sanitation, and transportation, including railways, urban transport, ports, airports, and waterways are what enable economic growth. In the past, the state assumed the dominant role in building infrastructure partly because the domestic private sector did not have enough capital and partly because nationalism had barred most foreign capital. The state's different priorities skewed resource allocations. Despite the tremendous demand for services, long-term capital investment in infrastructure was traditionally the first item to fall in the cuts required to balance budgets. The continued pressure for budgetary discipline today makes it essential for the state to attract private capital to meet the demands for infrastructure development, jobs, and services.

The infrastructure deficit in the region in the 1990s was painfully visible with all-too-frequent brownouts and blackouts in power systems, unhealthy water from municipal systems, long waiting periods for telephone service, and increasing traffic congestion. A comparison of Latin American infrastructure with that of the United States offers some idea of the magnitude of the task.

- The United States has 14,170 miles of roads per million of population; Latin America has 670 miles.[24] Eighty-five percent of U.S. roads are capable of truck traffic, but only 48 percent of Latin America's roads can handle truck traffic, and half of those are in bad condition.
- Latin America averages 69 telephone lines per 1,000 population, compared with 680 per 1,000 in the United States.
- Ports are in horrendous shape. Berths are inadequate for modern freighters; material-handling equipment is outdated; and warehousing is inadequate. It takes longer and costs more to ship from Caracas to New York than it does from Tokyo to New York. Brazil's major port, Santos, is now handling twice as much cargo

as it was built for, and costs are almost double those in Singapore or Baltimore.[25]

- Transportation routes among the Latin American countries, basic to serious integration efforts, are few. As of the beginning of the twenty-first century, Latin America had no direct Atlantic-to-Pacific highways or railroads.

- Power is underdeveloped everywhere, and brownouts for industry are common, interrupting production and forcing companies to make costly investments in supplementary private power plants. More than 100 gigawatts (billions of watts) of new generating capacity is the estimated need for the next decade.

- Safe drinking water is available to less than 70 percent of the population in almost every Latin American country except Chile, Venezuela, and Costa Rica. In rural areas, the deficit is far worse.

- Adequate sewerage and solid-waste disposal are available to less than 60 percent of the population.

In the 1980s, the investment in infrastructure in Latin America plunged to barely 3 percent of GDP, compared with 4.7 percent in East Asia and the Pacific. Minimal estimates for needed new infrastructure spending in the region are around $50 billion to $60 billion annually, or about 4.4 percent of GDP.[26] Even at that ratio, Latin America would be investing only 13 cents for every dollar invested in infrastructure in United States.

Inevitably, investment in infrastructure will rise in the coming decade. Without adequate infrastructure, trade treaties are just that: agreements on pieces of paper. It is one thing to sign trade agreements; it is quite another to actually trade, to move goods, which requires cost-competitive ports, transportation, power, and communications. The rapid changes in technology also require a motivated and flexible management to stay cost competitive.

During the 1990s, massive private capital inflows from institutional investors poured into Latin American countries. While lending dipped during the 1995 Mexican financial crisis and the 1998 Asian crisis, it quickly recovered. Several factors motivated investors, mainly the prospect of higher growth rates and far higher returns in the region. The key factors, however, were the region's commitment to economic stabilization and free-market reforms, paving the way for sustainable economic growth and development.

Infrastructure projects involve large sums of risk capital with long gestation periods. Low national savings rates and underdeveloped local capital markets for debt and equity finance mean reliance on external finance. If Latin Americans do not save for these investments, they must use the savings of others, called borrowing. No government in Latin America except Chile presently has the resources or the savings rates adequate for this task. Only private-sector finance can do the job. Attracting long-term capital from foreign sources requires better access to capital markets, a more transparent regulatory framework, new instruments to enhance the credit of the local borrowers, and integrity in the financial sector.

Two forces will drive this investment. First is international trade. A weak infrastructure adds enormously to the cost of doing business. Trucks on potholed roads wear out brakes, tires, and transmissions. Poor materials handling in ports, insecure warehouses, and corruption can, just by themselves, make production noncompetitive. The second force is that adequate infrastructure also is needed for social development. Poor people cannot escape from poverty unless they can produce value-added goods. They cannot produce value-added goods unless they can get them to market. And they cannot get them to market unless they have adequate roads and transportation. A few years ago a group of mayors from small communities in the highlands of Guatemala met with visiting "officials" of the Inter-American Development Bank. They wanted new roads. They told us that they had traveled for ten hours to come to see us, ten hours to cover 120 kilometers. That was an average speed of 12 kilometers, or 8 miles, an hour. They made their point. In those conditions, lettuce or melons cannot reach city markets while they still fresh.

The greatest risk for investors, domestic or foreign, in infrastructure investment is that politicians may change the rules relating to the project after the investment is locked in. One of the worst fallouts of the Argentine collapse in 2001 was that contractual obligations for privatized utilities set to provide a return on capital were blithely disregarded or broken. Risk is defined as dealing with the unknown, and infrastructure projects entail many unknowns. The crucial issue for those who bear the risk of these unknowns is determining a fair rate of return. If investors doubt that governments can be relied on to respect the obligations they undertake, costs will rise, and to the extent that the governments move to reduce risk, costs will come down. Indeed, most of the reasons for high rates are attributable to contractual uncertainty and corruption. All risk factors for private-sector investors who are unable to protect themselves in reliable judicial systems are reflected in cost. The vicious circle that Latin Americans often complain about—private investors' receiving high rates of return and wanting to get their capital out quickly—results principally from their lack of faith in governments' keeping their word or in a fair court system to protect them. Lawrence Summers, former U.S. secretary of the treasury, confirmed this when he noted that the market invariably recognizes and rewards fair, consistent, and transparent government regulation with lower interest rates. Countries thus must be able to assure investors that the rules will not change in midstream and that they will be administered fairly and transparently. If this fails, the penalty will be paid by the people who either will not get the infrastructure they need or will pay more than they would in the developed countries for the same product.

Almost all Latin American countries now allow private firms to invest in infrastructure. They are constructing generating plants and selling power to the national grid system. Investments in telecommunications are almost exclusively by the private sector. Private investors are underwriting leases and concessions for railways, port facilities, transmission and distribution of electricity, and toll roads. Concessions also include contracts to build and operate a plant for a specific number of years, after which it then reverts to the government. The international financial institutions, however, are frequently asked to supplement private-sector investment in areas where volume is insufficient to provide an adequate rate of return. Between 1971 and 1993, investments by the Inter-American Development Bank in roads, ports, power, water and sewerage, and telecommunications, including training, totaled approximately $35 billion. From 1990 to 1994, the bank provided sector loans totaling $6.12 billion to support and strengthen regulatory regimes to ensure more transparent and fair regulatory frameworks.

The capability of the private sector to meet this demand under the appropriate conditions is not in question, as the private sector has always played a pioneering role in areas neglected by the government. International submarine cable is a good example. Nearly all the world's submarine cable was laid by private companies. The first underseas cable was laid under the Atlantic in 1872 for telegraph traffic. Today, one of the longest submarine cables in the world, the 17,000-mile link from England to Japan, was constructed by a group that combined GE Capital of the United States with the Asian Investment Fund of Hong Kong and the Dallah Al-Baraka Group of Saudi Arabia. A new cable, Atlantis 2, financed by Embratel and Telefónica of Spain, was scheduled to bring high-speed transmission between Europe and Latin America by 2000. Advanced fiber-optic cables now linking Latin America to the rest of the world have capacity of 30 billion bits per second (30 gbps), more capacity than ever before in history.

The following short review of some of the infrastructure activities highlights the high-demand sectors:

Power. Worldwide capital needs for power generation until 2010, according to a recent study by the U.S. Department of Commerce, total more than $2.2 trillion for power generation, transmission, and distribution. That amounts to more than $200 billion a year. Of that, the estimate for Latin America is approximately 10 percent of the total, $202 billion, or $20 billion a year, of which Brazil accounts for more than half. Latin America is expected to be second only to China in hydroelectric capacity, but it will have to compete for dollars against enormous investments in the United States and Europe.

Rural electrification, greatly neglected throughout Latin America's history, will expand the demand enormously if the region is to alleviate poverty in the countryside. Costa Rica, one of the exceptions, has long emphasized rural electrification and is reaping the benefits of economic development that reaches more equitably throughout the country. Peru's former president, Alberto Fujimori, placed rural electrification at the top of his list of priorities, with an average annual increase of 20 percent in rural hookups since 1994. The Inter-American Development Bank lent almost $200 million to Central America and $450 million to Brazil in 1997 to integrate their electric grids and to accelerate the access of rural areas to electrical service. In Brazil, this is important to enable investments in generating capacity in southern Brazil, taking advantage of the new Bolivia-Brazil gas pipeline, to support power in the energy poor areas in the north of the country.

Telecommunications. Only Costa Rica and Uruguay, where consumer satisfaction with the service of state enterprises remains high, have resisted the drive to privatize their telecommunications sector. In all other countries, privatization is almost complete, and increasing competition is lowering costs.

Water and sewage treatment. The Pan American Health Organization estimates that barely half the population of rural Latin America has access to safe drinking water. Private capital, led by the French companies Lyonnaise des Eaux and Vivendi, is presently moving into the area. Several U.S. companies, including Enron and Ogden, decided to try to enter the field, but returns on investment remain weak and highly dependent on questionable government resolve regarding rates that will allow a fair return on investment over a period of time.

This is a difficult area because the provision of clean water is widely regarded as an obligation of government and poor people resist paying for it. To complicate the matter, most national governments have delegated their responsibilities to municipal governments. But municipal governments have weak tax bases and rarely can afford the heavy investment required, while their poor credit ratings make it almost impossible to obtain private finance at a reasonable cost. This has exacerbated the problem of financing the huge cost of constructing modern water and sewage treatment facilities. Poor communities cannot afford the tariffs required for an adequate return on private investment. The Inter-American Development Bank has made this one of its top priorities, investing more than $1 billion annually in water and sewer installations over the last several years.

In sum, in all areas relating to infrastructure, enormous investments, the lack of internal savings, weak tax bases, and high expectations all conspire to hinder the march to the future. As we proceed with plans for a free-trade area of the Americas, such investments will be essential to enable lesser developed countries to compete. Again, it is very much in the United States' interest that this happen because it is the only way it will be able to compete. A more competitive Latin America means more jobs, less poverty, and a less fertile breeding ground for international crime and narcotics. Indeed, the record shows conclusively that without a solid program similar to that which Europe enacted to help its weaker countries, the FTAA stands in great risk of being stillborn. That would be one of the major blunders of history.

13

Trade and Integration

COSTA RICA, a country of 3 million people, accounts for more trade with the United States than do all the countries of eastern Europe combined. U.S. exports to the Caribbean Basin countries in 1998 were greater than those to France or China.[1] The Caribbean countries, which President George W. Bush calls our "Third Border," are now our third-largest trading partner. In the year preceding the Asian financial meltdown in 1998, Latin America accounted for two-thirds of the growth in U.S. exports.[2] In September 1998, Mexico topped Japan as the number two U.S. trading partner for the first time, where it remains today. And Mexico has a GDP of less than one-tenth as large as Japan's.

The importance of trade and economic integration to Latin America cannot be overstated. Chile has shown what Latin America can do if it adopts and enforces adequate policies. Chile today describes itself to investors as a nation of 14 million and a market of 400 million. Its network of free-trade agreements has been central to attract investment enabling factories and service industries alike to reach broad markets without the penalty of tariffs. As a country emerging from divisive civil strains and dictatorship in the 1970s and 1980s, Chile is prospering as no other country in the Americas. The phenomenon of El Salvador, a country ravaged by civil war throughout the 1980s, is equally remarkable. Today, insurrectionist armed forces, now part of a democratic political framework, are working together with a conservative government toward the same strategy of opening the country to global competition and trade.

Today, Latin America is the only area in the world with which the United States maintains a trade surplus. Indeed, total U.S. trade with the hemisphere rose from $50 billion in 1990 to more than $140 billion in 1999. U.S. trade with individual Latin American and Caribbean countries shows exports to Mexico more than doubling, from $41 billion in 1993 to $87 billion in 1999, and exports to Brazil rising from $6 billion in 1993 to $13 billion in 1999.

Despite the global financial setbacks in the late 1990s, the United States' trade surplus with the region doubled in 1997 to an estimated $7.8 billion, up from $3.7 billion in 1996. In the first half of 1998, trade with Latin America showed a $6.8 billion surplus for the United States, up from $3.1 billion in the previous year. The surplus was $2.3 billion for Brazil and $1.8 billion for Argentina. All of this occurred despite tariffs in Latin America for U.S. products that, on average, were four times higher than U.S. tariffs.

For example, Caterpillar's 153 percent increase in sales in the five years after near bankruptcy a decade ago came largely as a result of its international sales. The rescue of Caterpillar is a tribute to CEO Don Fites's understanding of the global markets' opportunities. He forecast that in the next decade, 75 percent of Caterpillar's sales would come from foreign markets. He cited his concern about conversations with world leaders whom he considered hardheaded traders: "There is one message that America doesn't seem to get. If you don't come, others will. If it's not GE from the U.S., it will be GEC from Britain. If it's not Boeing, it will be Airbus. If it is not American banks, it will be European banks." Fites added that he is always waiting for his interlocutors to say, "If it's not Caterpillar, it's Komatsu."[3]

President Bill Clinton's analysis of the global economy centered on his question,

> How do we intend to continue [job growth] if we have 4 percent of the world's people and we already have 20 percent of the world's income? We have to sell to the other 96 percent of the world's people. And if we do it right, it will make the world a much better place because fifteen to twenty countries will move from the ranks of being very poor countries into being countries with sustainable incomes for their own people, making them better democratic partners more likely to be positive contributors to the world of tomorrow, less likely to be trouble spots that will command America's attention. . . . This is not a static situation. In order for us to continue to create jobs and opportunities for our own people and to maintain our world leadership, we have to continue to expand exports.[4]

This is precisely what is happening. U.S. prosperity has grown as trade has grown. As the value of our exports continues to rise in our economy, the number of jobs continues to grow. In 1970, two-way trade amounted to about 13 percent of the United States' GDP. By 1996, the role of trade in our economy more than doubled, to almost 25 percent of our economy, or about $2.3 trillion, and since 1992, U.S. manufactured exports grew an astounding 42 percent.

No magic is needed to sustain this trend. It is a two-way street. To continue the increase of U.S. product sales abroad, we must enable foreign countries to earn dollars to buy the goods. This means that the United States must let them sell to us as well. This is the heart of a sound strategy for U.S. foreign commercial policy.

THE CHALLENGE OF TRADE

U.S. trade policy is fundamentally about getting other countries to lower their tariffs on U.S. products; it is not about opening U.S. markets, as they are already among the world's most open. U.S. tariffs average about 3 percent. In regard to the impact of free-trade agreements on jobs in the United States and on the cost to U.S. consumers, the difference between tariffs of 3 percent and zero is hardly worth the fuss. Going to discount stores makes a greater difference! But there is a substantial difference, 20 percent, between the average tariffs that the other American nations pay among themselves and those imposed on U.S. products in the Americas. The real impact of trade agreements is the increase in U.S. exports to serve those larger markets. But this also troubles our prospective trading partners, as they have to be able to compete.

Global market advantages can change rapidly. Only a decade ago, an overindebted, noncompetitive United States was considered a basket case in the global economy, and Japan was touted as the model for the future. U.S. industry had enjoyed de facto protection from foreign competition for most of the twentieth century. But after World War II, with industry in Europe and Japan devastated, the United States was propelled toward global leadership in trade with more than 50 percent of global economic production. By the 1980s, however, the United States' share of the global economic pie had shrunk to 25 percent as European and Japanese companies gained market share. The key to their growth was their attention to export markets, particularly the U.S. markets. As late as early 1980, Europe and Japan were still small players. Only when the dollar soared in the 1980s because of the high interest rates in the Reagan years did European and Asian producers gain a price advantage in the U.S. markets. Up to then, U.S. producers had had a free ride. Americans bought American goods because they were the only choice they had, regardless of the quality. Then, in the 1980s, exchange rate fluctuation enabled foreign goods, which were improving in quality, to become far more price competitive, and imports surged.

The revolution in transportation and communications is changing more than consumers' options. It is changing the way corporations work. More than 40 percent of all international trade is estimated to be intrafirm trade, transactions between a parent corporation and its subsidiaries. In 1997, the *Journal of Commerce* reported that as much as 67 percent of all two-way trade "takes place *within* [italics in original] multinational companies."[5] This is up from 30 percent in the 1970s.[6] Furthermore, most of the production of U.S. firms located abroad goes to the markets abroad, with only about 11 percent returning to the U.S. market.

U.S. corporations will not grow if they do not participate in global trade. Accordingly, many corporations are reassessing their marketing strategies in regard to the Latin American markets as a result of the United States' lack of free-trade agreements with this region. Both Caterpillar and DaimlerChrysler announced recently that they will be forced to sell to Latin America from their Canadian and Mexican plants, because these countries are now party to more regional free-trade agreements. Congress's approval of trade promotion authority in 2002 is a step in the right direction, but the final agreement must still pass a contentious Congress. The failure to do so would mean a huge loss of jobs and opportunities for the United States.

PRODUCTIVITY AND PRODUCTION

The great fear that free trade would lead to unemployment in the United States in the "race to the bottom" as jobs gravitated to the countries with lowest wages never materialized. Ross Perot's "great sucking sound" turned out to be not factories relocating abroad but capital rushing into the United States to invest in new technologies that had the world's most productive and skilled labor force at its disposal. In most industries, the costs of low productivity and inadequate infrastructure today far outweigh cost savings from cheap labor.

The main concerns in Mexico during the debate over NAFTA mirrored the United States' concerns: that cheap U.S. imports would overwhelm high-cost Mexican enterprises and doom Mexico to continued low-end production and poverty. One of the presidential candidates in the 2000 elections, Manuel Bartlett, from the old conservative wing of the PRI, called for a complete review of Mexico's participation in NAFTA on the premise that free trade and globalization were depressing Mexican wages. He alleged that NAFTA was keeping rural farmers poor because they could not compete with the mass-produced, imported agricultural products. The political convergence of the far right and far left on this issue was demonstrated in the fallout from the insurgency in Chiapas. Indigenous advocates opposed NAFTA on the grounds that it was "a death certificate for the Indian people of Mexico." Complaints from the U.S. trucking industry to stop the implementation of NAFTA provisions opening U.S. roads to Mexican trucks were matched by the similar fears of the Mexican trucking industry that their domestic transportation companies would be unable to compete with U.S. firms and would rapidly be taken over by more efficient U.S. companies. The *Journal of Commerce* reported that Mexican clothing, shoe, and textile manufacturers were even alleging unfair trade, complaining that Asian competitors were dumping merchandise in Mexico, sometimes through the United States.[7] In a larger sense, the fears of the developing countries about being overwhelmed are far more real than the fears of the United States about losing jobs.

In investment to spur production, however, the Americas have a strong, untapped, advantage. The principal issues of corporate decision making are stability, productivity, and the cost to get goods to market. First is the issue of stability. Countries ruled by arbitrary governments that have yet to go through the transition to democracy are highly vulnerable to internal turmoil. Most of the countries of the Middle East, which control much of our energy supplies, are in this category. The United States cannot pretend that major disruptions in other parts of the globe will leave its commerce, production, and job markets unscathed. The situation is far worse for countries with few domestic resources. Japan, for example, imports almost all its natural resources. Consequently, its foreign policy will concentrate on tranquilizing events that might disrupt the commodities markets on which it depends.

This is why the Americas are important. The Latin American nations are attractive to companies seeking a stable access to resources. Many corporations are beginning to consider relocating their overseas operations from less stable areas of the world to more hospitable environments and so are moving from the Far East to Latin America. For example, in the two years after the signing of NAFTA agreement, Asian companies invested more than $5 billion in new plants in Mexico. The *Wall Street Journal* reports that Matsushita Electric, Mitsubishi Electric, Daewoo, and Sony "have erected massive assembly plants . . . transforming this region into a virtual Detroit of television manufacturing."[8] Other examples:

- Sinomex of Hong Kong moved its manufacture of computer toys to Hermosillo, Mexico.
- Devanshi, an Indian company, produced its blue jeans for export to India in San Luis Río Colorado, Mexico.
- Sana International, a Japanese-Mexican joint venture now exports *shabu-shabu*, a thinly sliced beef, to Tokyo from Mexico.
- Sanyo and Sony produce almost 10 million TV sets annually in Tijuana, Mexico. Sanyo is now Tijuana's largest employer, with 4,500 employees, and recently moved its U.S. headquarters from New York to San Diego to be closer to its production facilities.
- Samsung invested $2 billion in a Mexican plant to produce TV sets and cameras for the U.S. market.
- Hyundai manufactures its transportation containers for the U.S. market in Mexico.

None of this production was the result of a company's fleeing the United States, for the United States had already lost this production to Asian manufacturers. The point is that if Japanese companies find it more cost effective to produce for a U.S. market from Mexico, U.S. companies might, too. If the principal strategy of a U.S. corporation is to serve the U.S. market, this will be far easier from a base in Mexico or the Caribbean than thousands of miles away in South Korea or Thailand. Energy is abundant, transportation is easy, and the region's resources are less vulnerable to economic shocks from, for instance, volatile oil production in the Middle East. Not only will the looming labor-short condition of our own economy drive this, but the larger pool of U.S.-trained executive talent available in Latin America will more easily bridge the cultures.

The second factor influencing corporate decisions is productivity. As we have seen, low labor costs can quickly be blunted by other cost factors, which, in Latin America, are the following:

- Lack of skills.
- Lower productivity of workers.
- High power costs.
- Telecommunication costs averaging 300 percent higher than those in developed countries.
- Costly transportation with many delays.
- Corruption leading to unpredictable costs and other management problems.
- Weak rule of law for the fair settlement of commercial disputes.

The greatest factor, however, is productivity, which determines the true cost of labor regardless of wage levels. A McKinsey management study of Brazilian industry in 1994 reported that Brazilian productivity in the steel industry was 37 percent of that of the United States; in the food industry, it was 31 percent; and in the retail banking industry, 29 percent.[9] Professor Richard Freemont of Harvard University estimated that 80 percent of the gap in wages between Mexican and U.S. workers was related to differences in overall skill and productivity.[10] It does not take any special mathematical skills to determine that if labor costs are 70 percent lower than market, and the productivity is also 70 percent lower, there is no net gain.

The situation, however, is far worse for developing countries. A Brazilian entrepreneur I know was forced to close down his cacao (the bean from which chocolate is made)-processing plant in Bahia, Brazil, because of that country's environmental restrictions. Because of increasing competition from cacao produced in Africa, he decided to move the plant closer to his major market in the United States. To his surprise, he discovered that his labor costs were actually lower in his new New Jersey plant than in Brazil! Although the hourly wage paid to U.S. workers was triple that paid in Brazil, U.S. workers' greater skills produced the same product with far fewer workers. In Brazil, this entrepreneur required supervisors for his supervisors. Brazilian law also required full-time nurses and a part-time doctor at the plant to compensate for marginal municipal medical facilities. He also had to provide a free cafeteria and lunch. When he added in the numerous Brazilian governmental "assessments" for these same services (which it did not provide), the result was that the cost for labor was 15 percent lower in New Jersey than in Brazil. For him it was an unexpected gain and an illustration of the obstacles that entrepreneurs and businesses in Third World countries face.

The third factor in corporate decision making is logistics. Dell Computer recently moved part of its computer production from Asia to Mexico. The reason was proximity to markets, proximity to senior management, and proximity to easy transportation. Given a choice, companies prefer not to eat up management time, the scarcest of their resources, in traveling or to take weeks to transport goods to market when it can be done in days.

The Brazilians are acutely aware of the logistics of cost factors, describing their handicap in global competition as what they call *custos brasileiros*, or Brazilian costs. Brazilian costs come from lower productivity, obsolete technology, bad roads, slow transportation, high-cost ports, high depreciation of machinery due to incompetent handling, and wear and tear caused by the rough roads. Furthermore, goods that linger in warehouses are far more susceptible to pilferage and deterioration.

Several other factors are important. Trade agreements that lower tariffs often have unexpected effects. That is, instead of encouraging companies to transfer their production abroad, they enable many to service foreign markets more efficiently from their home factories. I recall talking to an executive of Philip Morris when the European Common Market began. Philip Morris had been considering opening a plant in Portugal as the best way to be price competitive in that market. After the advent of the European Common Market, it dropped the plan. With tariffs coming down, Philip Morris could now serve that market more efficiently by consolidating production in its plant in Spain. Productivity and transportation costs closely interact with each other.

In short, manufacturing moves to developing countries not because of lower wages but, often, in spite of them. It moves there primarily because of the economics of servicing the developing countries' markets. IBM now has located 40 percent of its workforce abroad, not to produce goods more cheaply to send back to the United States, but to sell more IBM products abroad. That eventually created more jobs for IBM employees in the United States who produce the components that can be made only in the United States. A large part of GM's expansion to build new plants in developing nations is to "woo new markets."[11] Today more than 60 percent of Gillette's and 50 percent of GM's profits come from abroad. GM has extensive operations in Brazil, lifting its production in the 1990s from 170,000 to more than 500,000 units a year and contributing 25 percent of its operating profit in 1996. This is why U.S. trade statistics are frequently misleading, as they do not include the exports from wholly owned subsidiaries of U.S. companies, a large source of income to the United States and a large producer of U.S. jobs.

In trade, reality also frequently gets lost in its own rhetoric. In considering the Americas, how many businesses could the small countries of the Caribbean or Central America, with small labor forces, absorb anyway? The answer is very few. When President Ronald Reagan initiated the Caribbean Basin Initiative in 1982, alarmist warnings that the United States would lose jobs to the Caribbean turned out to be wrong. Not many businesses can transfer operations to the Caribbean without immediately overheating the labor market. The average population of the Central American nations is less than that of Brooklyn, New York. When trade preferences are granted to small countries, as in the Caribbean, the potential loss of jobs can be made up in one week's new job creation in the U.S. market. In Barbados, 25,000 jobs can turn around its economy. In the Windward and Leeward Islands, 10,000 jobs make the difference between a prosperous and a collapsing economy. Nonetheless, the complaints about how trade agreements will mean the loss of U.S. jobs persist. It is astonishing that many labor leaders and lawmakers listen.

Generalizations about trade statistics also mask the real potential for growth in trade in the Americas. While the overall numbers for our hemispheric trade are impressive, if Mexico and Canada are excluded, trade with the rest of Latin America would amount to barely 10 percent of U.S. foreign trade. While in the aggregate the numbers are impressive and trade with the region is growing far more rapidly than with other regions of the world, trade with each individual country is small. Brazil accounts for barely 3 percent of U.S. trade, and few other countries come close to 1 percent. But for these countries, trade with the United States dominates their economic life. It averages more than 40 percent of their exports and imports, ranging from less than 20 percent in Brazil to more than 80 percent for Mexico and the Caribbean.

Opening trade not only with the United States but with Europe as well will have many collateral benefits in increased intraregional trade and integration. More opportunities for industrial development resulting from trade with the developed countries will diversify the Latin American economies even further. As trade with the developed world brings new types of production on line, they will have more to trade with one another. Regional integration will be the "third-party beneficiary" of increased U.S. trade, with a huge multiplier effect in the region's economic growth.

In the United States, the issues in the Americas will continue to press on U.S. policy makers and industry. The critical argument that inter-relates trade with domestic issues is not *whether* U.S. firms import from abroad, but *from where* they import. It is not whether we open our doors to trade but whether we adopt policies that induce business to invest in Latin America.

NAFTA, THE FUEL

The future of free trade in the Americas today is tied to the perceptions of the impact of NAFTA, which has been in operation since 1995. The most comprehensive trade agreement ever entered into by the United States, NAFTA opened the door to reductions of both tariff and nontariff barriers to trade in the United States, Canada, and Mexico. The real issue in evaluating NAFTA is not solely whether trade is up or down or whether it is creating more or fewer jobs. Rather, what is important is its success in bringing the nations of the Americas together to achieve economic and political stability and in addressing common problems such as drug trafficking, immigration, and demographic pressures, which are, demonstrably, not susceptible to unilateral policies or the exercise of raw power.

Despite the many discussions about the merits of NAFTA, the record shows considerable benefits for the first five years of its operation:

- Average Mexican tariffs have come down from more than 20 percent to 2 percent for imports from the United States.

- Overall trade between Mexico and the United States grew 78 percent, and merchandise trade grew 93 percent. The record was all the more impressive because the financial crisis of 1995 slashed Mexico's ability to import from anywhere. The same held true for Canada, our other NAFTA partner, which also benefited from the three-way trade. United States–Canada trade increased 51 percent in the same period.
- Regardless of who tries to tally jobs won or lost as a result of the open border, U.S. unemployment has plummeted to the lowest levels since World War II.
- Agriculture, hard hit in the global economy, has become one of the leading beneficiaries, with U.S. exports to Mexico increasing 45 percent and to Canada 29 percent since 1993.
- For the United States, its products now account for 76 percent of Canadian imports and 75 percent of Mexican imports.

For the U.S. labor market, tighter than it has been in decades, NAFTA has been good news. The U.S. Bureau of Labor Statistics predicts that job growth in the United States in the next decade will be the fastest in high-end jobs, following precisely the strategy articulated by President Clinton when he signed the agreement. The forecasts for job growth are 118 percent for database administrators, 109 percent for computer engineers, 103 percent for systems analysts, and more than 80 percent for health care workers.

For Mexico, after a stormy transition from the flawed economic policies of its past, the story is similar: NAFTA has been the driving force for the opening and modernization of its economy and its political system. The trends are clear that Mexico is today well on the way to the highest rates of economic growth in its history. The country has found the courage not only to embrace real democracy with the election of an opposition president for the first time in seventy years but has begun building its education system, remedying the injustices of its uneven development, and attacking the drug traffic.

When NAFTA entered into force in 1994, it brought the immediate elimination of tariffs on about 50 percent of U.S. exports to Mexico. Many Mexicans expected a flood of U.S. goods into the Mexican market that would overwhelm and bankrupt many local Mexican producers. Instead it encouraged investment in new industries that have a higher value added to their exports to the United States. The result has already changed the face of Mexican social and political life. Given the great economic and social disparities between the two countries, it has produced tensions but has helped the country open its political institutions.

The impetus for NAFTA was the free-trade agreement between the United States and Canada, signed in 1988, four years after it was proposed by Prime Minister Brian Mulroney of Canada. Shortly thereafter, President Carlos Salinas of Mexico proposed a similar agreement between his country and the United States. President Salinas's message was simple. "Let us send you goods or we will send you people." The proposal was soon accepted by President George H. W. Bush, who informed Congress of his intention to expand the Canadian agreement and negotiate NAFTA.

The financial crisis that battered the Mexican economy in 1995 was brought about by the confluence of circumstances of NAFTA's approval just as Mexico was entering a political transition with the elections of 1994. President Salinas knew he had to preserve the delicate balance in the Mexican economic structure leading up to NAFTA and the demands of the imminent election. This prevented him from making the adjustments needed in the economy, so he tried to erect a monetary dam to preserve the equilibrium. When the dam broke immediately after the election of 1994 was concluded and the new president, Ernesto Zedillo, took office, the resulting flood inundated all of his good preparatory work.

Remarkably, Mexico continued to reduce its tariffs in accordance with NAFTA even as it entered into a severe recession in 1995 and adopted one of the most rigorous economic adjustment packages that the International Monetary Fund (IMF) had ever offered, requiring tight fiscal and monetary policies and wage restraints. Unemployment ballooned, and many Mexican enterprises went bankrupt. But Mexico stuck by its agreement with the United States and Canada and also maintained its tariff walls on imports from non-NAFTA countries. The result was that the U.S. share of the Mexican market grew during the recession from 69 percent in 1993 to 76 percent in 1996. The free fall of the Mexican currency allowed Mexican exports to the United States to surge as many U.S. companies profited from importing suddenly very cheap Mexican goods. The contrast with the previous financial crisis in Mexico in 1982 is telling. In that downturn the Mexican government attempted to resolve its problems by cutting off imports from the United

States. Trade plunged by 50 percent in one year along with the highest surge in illegal immigration in U.S. history.[12]

Mexico's determination and steady course are beginning to pay off. Its economy today is one of the fastest growing in the region, and its investment ratings have risen at a time when those of the rest of Latin America have not. Moody's Investors Service upgraded Mexican bonds in 1999, thereby automatically reducing the rates of interest Mexico has to pay on its foreign debt and releasing money for social projects at home, money that would otherwise go abroad for interest payments. Mexico's reforms have also paid off in many other areas. In 1993, opponents of NAFTA objected to the virtual dictatorship of the PRI, Mexico's dominant political party, and the country's corrupt, centralized economy. Today the PRI no longer governs Mexico. Whether that would have happened without NAFTA is an open question. Illegal immigration has been reduced substantially, and diligent efforts are being made to curtail the drug traffic through the country. In addition, Mexico has

- Carried out a complicated political transition to multiparty political diversity with the election of an opposition party for the first time since its revolution.
- Accelerated economic reforms that have created a more transparent, market-driven economy that has pressed forward despite financial setbacks.
- Rebounded more rapidly from the 1994 financial crisis than from any previous financial recession.
- Fully repaid, in advance, the loans provided by the United States to tide it over its crisis.
- Increased wages in the growing manufacturing sector, which are now at an average of 60 percent higher than average Mexican wages.
- Established more constructive relations with the United States at all levels, despite extraordinarily complex domestic problems.

The opening between the countries has been complicated by the fact that Mexico is undergoing two transitions at once: an economic transition and a political transition, from closed economic and political systems to democracy and open markets. Without NAFTA, Mexico may well have been far less tolerant in confronting the insurrection of the indigenous people in Chiapas. NAFTA created considerable political space for those who advocated respect for human rights and transparency of government actions.

Finally, the integration of the Mexican and Canadian economies with the U.S. economy helped blunt the impact of the 1997 Asian financial crisis on the United States. In 1998, U.S. exports of manufactured goods to Asia fell 17 percent while exports to the NAFTA partners continued to grow, absorbing about 40 percent of the revenues lost in Asia.

Mexico now buys more from the United States than Japan does. While more than 20 percent of U.S. imports from Mexico are oil, nearly all U.S. exports to Mexico are manufactured or farm products, automobile parts, telecommunications equipment, electric machinery and distribution equipment, computers, aircraft, and the like. These are the exports that produce high-paying U.S. jobs. Equally significant is that almost half the products imported into the United States from Mexico contain U.S.-made components.

As the first major trade agreement between industrial countries and a developing nation, NAFTA is an indicator of what could happen as a result of a free-trade agreement with the rest of the Americas. The United States would gain far more jobs from trade with the Americas than we would from trade with almost any other group of countries. Increasing prosperity in the other nations of the Americas brings higher consumption levels and more shipments of high-technology goods such as computers, integrated circuits, aircraft, medical equipment, automobile parts, environmental products, and machine tools, as well as agricultural products. Jobs south of the border increase prosperity, stem migration, diminish the temptation of drug trafficking, and build stronger democracies that will be reliable allies in the struggle for economic and political freedom.

THE ROAD TO INTEGRATION

The dream of one single economic trade zone extending from the northernmost reaches of Canada to the southern tip of Chile and to the eastern Caribbean is not new. Commerce was the major topic when Simón Bolívar summoned the first inter-American congress in 1826. The Pan American Union established at the Washington Conference convened by U.S. President Grover Cleveland in 1888 had free trade as its principal goal. Meetings were held, pronouncements made, and agreements signed, but very little happened.

There were several reasons, mostly historic or geographic. First, the economies of Latin America and the Caribbean were competitive, not complementary. Until recently, the only products that the countries of the Americans successfully exported to one another were the tango and the samba. Industry was rudimentary. Indeed, before air conditioning was introduced into the region in the 1960s, it was impossible to consider building manufacturing plants in the region. Until the 1970s the countries produced the same things. Whether it was copper, coffee, or cacao, they had few goods that the others wanted to buy. Cross-border transportation networks were virtually nonexistent. Few roads led to frontiers, and those that did were incapable of carrying heavy traffic. Customs houses were corrupt, and the amount of paperwork required was sufficient to discourage everyone but the most determined. Except for traffic in drugs or clandestine arms, no competitive business could benefit.

Second, government controls and bureaucracy were so pervasive that no country could afford to trade with the others. I recall the Venezuelan businessman confessing his frustration when he wanted to set up a branch of his business in Ecuador under the recently signed Andean Pact. Ironically, the regulations the pact enacted to keep out foreign companies and encourage local production were so complex, he said, that only large multinational companies could afford to pay the lawyers necessary to manage the paperwork. Small Venezuelan and Ecuadorean companies would go bankrupt waiting for the bureaucracies—or paying the bribes—to get the papers moving.

Third, land transportation was so bad that a producer could ship only by sea. Impenetrable rain forests and the high Andes made it cheaper for Latin American exporters to ship their products to the United States or western Europe than to one another. Furthermore, for the few quality products that were competitive, it was far better to send them to the rich industrialized countries than to small, poor countries.

After World War II, false starts toward economic integration were numerous. Felipe Herrera, the first president of the Inter-American Development Bank in the 1960s, pressed the issue strongly. But the limits of intraregional trade would not go away without meaningful efforts to ensure intraregional transportation. Moreover, when trade liberalization affected industries that were not competitive, the governments generally succumbed to pressure. Most of the owners of the protected interests were part of the ruling oligarchies, and all fought to maintain their protection.

Despite these obstacles, however, intraregional integration made noteworthy progress in the early 1960s, encouraged by the motivation and policies of the Alliance for Progress. The Central American Common Market was formed and raised intraregional trade from 8.5 percent of total trade in 1961 to 23.5 percent in the mid-1970s before it collapsed in the debt debacle and civil wars in the 1980s. In the early 1960s, intraregional trade among South American nations averaged about 6 percent of their global trade. Today it approaches an average of 17 percent. Some countries, such as Bolivia, Paraguay, and Uruguay, depend almost totally on intraregional trade, which makes up more than 50 percent of their exports. As a result of the economic openings of the early 1990s, between 1990 and 1996 intraregional exports within the Americas quadrupled from $4.1 billion to $16.1 billion, growing from 8.9 percent of total exports to 21.5 percent.

Although the path to implementation is still arduous, leaders are conscious of the need to replace national policies with regional policies. Growing industrialization gives the Latin American nations an increasing number of products to ship to one another. The Andean Group's exports among themselves amount to 11 percent of their total trade. The Central American Common Market, undergoing major revisions, now accounts for 21 percent of the member countries' trade. The recent accord of the Central American countries to create an integrated electric grid linking all the countries and the proposal by President Vicente Fox of Mexico to build the Central American infrastructure as part of its "Plan Puebla-Panama" are constructive steps in this direction.

The development over the last several decades has enabled the Latin American countries to diversify their economies enormously. The manufacturing component of intraregional exports has grown from 18 percent in 1980 to more than 40 percent today. Brazil's, Mexico's, and Colombia's exports today are nearly 70 percent manufactured goods. Costa Rica has succeeded in attracting major hi-tech investments, with Intel building a chip-making plant there. As a result, Costa Rica has doubled its exports based on technology products alone. The percentage of manufactured goods in Latin America's exports to the United

States is even more impressive, having grown from 23 percent to 58 percent between 1980 and today. Only Cuba has been left behind, with a primitive economy dependent on commodities.

The promise of free trade with the United States will greatly accelerate this trend. As we noted, as each Latin American country produces more goods for the U.S. market, it will automatically have more goods to sell to others. Economies that were once competitive, all producing the same primary products, are now becoming complementary. While there is a considerable way to go, the trend is clear. Within a very short time the Latin American nations will be more prepared than ever to trade with one another.

MERCOSUR: BREAKING NEW GROUND

In July 1990, the momentum toward open markets in the Americas took a dramatic new turn when the new Argentine president, Carlos Menem, joined with the equally energetic new Brazilian president, Fernando Collor, to lay the groundwork for Mercosur, a new common market among the Southern Cone countries of Argentina, Brazil, Uruguay, and Paraguay. At the time, trade among Argentina, Brazil, and the Mercosur countries was only 8.9 percent of their total trade. Now Mercosur has become the world's third-largest trading block, after NAFTA and the European Union.

As a result of Mercosur, Argentina-Brazil trade has now surpassed each country's individual trade with the United States. This has created both benefits and problems. On the positive side, in the 1990s Mercosur became the number one destination for foreign investment in the developing world. On the negative side, currency imbalances became a problem for Argentina. The most promising development has been that in contrast to their exports to the rest of the world, which are predominantly commodities, 70 percent of the trade among the Mercosur countries is in manufactured goods, almost 60 percent of which comes from multinational corporations that have located production facilities in the region.

The agreement of Chile and Bolivia to associate with Mercosur (although they have stopped short of becoming full partners) made it by 2000 about a $1.3 trillion market with a population base of 225 million people, an average per capita income of about $4,000, and external capital flows that account for almost two-thirds of Latin America's capital flows.

Nonetheless, substantial problems still lie in the path to Mercosur's long-term success. The most glaring, the lack of a common fiscal policy, became apparent in the wake of the Asian financial crisis when Brazil decided to allow its currency to float freely in the market. The resulting devaluation gave Brazilian exports a huge advantage over their Argentine competitors, whose currency, rigidly tied to the dollar, did not allow the economy to adjust. Argentina's principal industries of timber, paper, pharmaceuticals, steel, and automobiles all suffered, and in 2001, the distortions caused an economic collapse. The crisis demonstrated the impossibility of two countries attempting to form a common market without a coordinated fiscal policy.

THE FTAA: THE BOLDEST STEP OF ALL

The American nations are now committed to achieving free trade for the entire hemisphere, a free-trade agreement of the Americas (FTAA), by the year 2005, and the adoption of trade promotion authority by the U.S. Congress in 2002 greatly enhances the possibility of its becoming a reality. Today the goal of a hemispheric free-trade area of 800 million people and a mammoth market of close to $12 trillion is a commitment of all of the nations of the Americas.

The implications for the United States were made clear in the testimony to Congress of Peter Algeier, deputy U.S. trade representative. U.S. exports to Latin America and the Caribbean, he reported, "have grown 37 percent faster than to countries outside of the hemisphere, reaching $59 billion in 2000." Further, he pointed out that "U.S. service exports to Latin America have also risen in recent years, to $26 billion in 1999. Our services trade surplus with Latin America stands at $16 billion, counting for 20 percent of the global United States trade surplus in services."[13]

With a specific timetable set at the presidential summit in Chile in 1998, the negotiations are now moving ahead. Nine working groups are addressing issues such as the rules defining the criteria for the origin of manufactured goods, market access, subsidies, competition policy, government procurement, investment, agriculture, services, and dispute resolution measures. The first draft of the free-trade treaty is now complete and was made public for comments by the private sector and civil society groups shortly after the presidential summit in Quebec in April 2001. For the first time, a trade negotiation process established a civil society committee to listen to citizens from throughout the hemisphere and to consider the accompanying social issues.

The FTAA's so-called business facilitation measures pertain to easy customs procedures for such matters as expediting express shipments, clearing customs, settling on a common customs terminology, facilitating business travel, and establishing uniform measures for certifying telecommunications equipment. In a major difference from the past, in which the nations embraced the rhetoric of integration but practiced protectionism, the negotiations for free trade in the Americas are firmly based on the acceptance of open markets.

The FTAA is one of the most prodigious, ambitious, multifaceted programs ever undertaken by a group of nations with such wide disparities of wealth and social conditions. The agreement will have an even more profound impact on a wide range of political, social, and economic issues between the United States and the other nations of the Americas. The FTAA is as much about investment, economic development, job creation, poverty alleviation, and environmental protection as it is about trade. The benefits from stimulating investment are probably the most important for continuing the economic and political reforms. Given the region's huge proportion of impoverished people, the markets are infinitesimal for efficient modern production. Without a free-trade agreement with the United States, growth will continue to be slow—far too slow to meet the expectations of democracy and to provide an escape from poverty for an increasingly aware body politic.

For the United States, the potential of hemispheric trade has, for too long, been the orphan of policymakers. Just as Latin America long ignored the United States' enormous markets right in its backyard, the United States is the only country in the developed world that has resisted looking at the natural markets in its backyard. Western Europe and Japan have had no such compunctions.

The major danger to free trade in the Americas is the attempt to make partners of nations with very disparate economic levels and capacities. The FTAA will be joining one of the world's most productive, efficient economies with some of the smallest, inefficient ones. Europe took this into account when it formed the European Union, by making special provisions for the weaker economies and offering special financial aid to help them develop, long before the market was to go into effect. This was in the interest of both the smaller economies and all of Europe, so as to achieve balanced growth in the process and not create an economic divide in which poverty would fester interminably. The resulting spectacular growth of Spain and Portugal and their increased contribution to the EU speaks for the wisdom of the policy. Today, thanks to the lessons learned by the Europeans:

- Wages have improved in all countries equally. In less than a decade, per capita wages in Spain rose from $4,800 to $15,000; in Portugal, from $2,250 to $5,600.
- The less developed countries are becoming larger markets for the more developed countries. Spain's and Portugal's economies grew at an average of more than 4.5 percent in the five years after it joined the EU, compared with an average of 1 percent in Portugal and 0.25 percent in Spain during the previous five years.[14]

The same will happen in the Americas if we have the wisdom and patience to pursue a farsighted policy, as our parents did in helping restore the productive capacity of Europe in the aftermath of World War II.

TOWARD A NEW INTER-AMERICAN DYNAMIC

The architecture of inter-American relations that will be needed to manage an FTAA as well as to strengthen democratic institutions will be vastly different from what exists today. A wide range of complex matters will have to be continually addressed in commercial, financial and taxation issues, customs standards, environment, labor migration, intellectual property issues, telecommunications, and transportation, to name but a few. These will require machinery that allows technical agencies of different nations to work directly with one another far more closely and effectively than is possible for the present inter-American political institutions guided by the Organization of American States.

The advances in global communication have facilitated direct contact among technical experts. Numerous "minisummit" meetings are now bringing together the officials responsible for commerce, energy, transportation, labor, health, the environment, and education. In securities regulation, the Inter-American Council of Securities Regulators (COSRA) is supported by the U.S. Securities and Exchange Commission. In tax administration, the Inter-American Council of Tax Administrators (CIAT) was initiated with the backing of the U.S. Internal Revenue Service. The U.S. Federal Aviation Administration has quietly expanded its technical cooperation to the airport authorities of the hemisphere in the wake of security concerns after September 11, 2001. In the battle against drugs, the Inter-American Drug Abuse Control Commission (CICAD) has established a collaborative inter-American mechanism, the multilateral evaluation mechanism, to monitor each country's efforts to combat drug traffic and thereby replace the United States' controversial unilateral decertification policy. In telecommunications, the OAS's Inter-American Telecommunication Commission (CITEL) is coordinating efforts to ensure rational harmonization of the legal framework to integrate telecommunications.

The new requirements of an FTAA will demand a new framework for hemispheric cooperation similar to that in Europe during the early years of the European Community. The issue is whether the OAS's current architecture, run exclusively by foreign ministers, is up to the task. The new framework must be able to engage many new forces, such as the private sector and civil society organizations. Legislators also must be involved in inter-American issues. An architecture that encourages technical experts to work directly with one another on their own technical issues is far more effective than channeling everything through foreign ministries, which have little technical expertise.

In short, the time for a move toward hemispheric integration, including the United States, could not be more propitious. It is clear that trade agreements have a direct correlation with progress in social and economic reform. For Latin America, a comprehensive agreement for free trade is the only way to build the economic base to create the jobs necessary to overcome poverty. It also is the only way to overcome the numerous nontariff barriers, quotas, voluntary restrictive agreements, and health barriers that still stand in Latin America's way to full access to the U.S. and European markets. The United States simply has too many agencies and interests to allow for a meaningful negotiation of individual issues on a bilateral basis. Even with NAFTA, Mexican exports to the United States have to comply with the rules and regulations of more than thirty different U.S. government agencies. At least Mexico now has a framework agreement to navigate the maze.

The question for U.S. policy in the twenty-first century is whether we will take advantage of our competitive and comparative advantages in world trade with wisdom and foresight. Do we have the political will to assist with the necessary economic reinforcement to poorer neighbors so that free trade will indeed be fair trade for all? The United States has long expressed confidence that trade will bring increasing prosperity in a world that provides a better market for everyone's goods. For decades, this was the basis of our foreign policy in Europe, Latin America, and Africa. It is needed again in the Americas. Indeed, it is the essential foundation for a strong long-term development effort in the Americas. It has nothing to do with idealism or altruism; it is about good business and smart politics.

14

Investment and Economic Growth

THE KEY TO DEVELOPMENT is access to capital. It is the lifeblood of economic growth. Everyone borrows. Businesses borrow, homeowners borrow, the U.S. government borrows, even Mr. Rockefeller borrows. Stable, consistent flows of credit are as necessary for an escape from poverty as they are for multinational corporations. Regardless of whether credits come from private capital, savings, governmental sources through taxation, or international markets, infrastructure will not be built, people trained, or services rendered without them.

The international community and financial institutions are still looking for a way to ensure the flow of capital on an international level without volatility. For governments, it means managing their budgets more realistically and establishing their creditworthiness. For the private sector it means more systematic approaches to expanding markets and productivity. There is little doubt, however, that the private sector of the Americas is fast becoming adept in the intricacies of global financial markets.

In the spring of 1997, Gustavo Cisneros of Venezuela stunned the commercial world by informing Pepsi Cola that he was abandoning his flourishing Pepsi bottling franchise and switching his bottling lines to Coca-Cola. In the old Latin America, such a decision would have been unthinkable. Pepsi was a family business started by his father as the outgrowth of their fledgling trucking company. The Pepsi franchise had given the Cisneros family its place in the world of multinational business and had been one of the most profitable in Venezuela. The move also stunned world markets. Never before had a major bottler jumped ship.

Cisneros then sold the entire Venezuelan Coca-Cola franchise to Panamerican Beverage, the Mexican soft drink giant, for more than $500 million, making Panamco the second-largest Coke bottler in the

255

world, with annual revenues of almost $3 billion.[1] The move comple-
mented Panamco's aggressive acquisitions of regional bottlers throughout Latin America and Brazil, adding capacity wherever it invested.

In another revealing transaction, in the midst of Mexico's financial
crisis in 1994, Cemex, the Mexican cement giant, made a historic decision. Instead of retrenching to protect itself in the volatile financial markets, it decided to take advantage of the depressed markets and prices
to expand its operations. So Cemex acquired Venezuela's largest cement
producer, Venezolana de Cementos, and several others in the Americas.
After doubling the company's cash flow through reorganization, the integration of operations, and new distribution systems, Cemex has now
become the world's third-largest cement producer, operating today in
twenty-two countries. Its CEO, Lorenzo Zambrano, a Stanford MBA
graduate, has built a major empire by understanding the dynamics of
the developing world.

A community of freely trading nations is not only about moving
goods and providing cross-border services but is also about making investments and building infrastructure. If capital cannot be mobilized
locally through savings or domestic capital markets, it has to come from
international markets. Surprisingly, a growing trend of cross-border investment among the Latin American and Caribbean nations themselves
is creating even closer relations. Argentina and Brazil alone formed 356
joint ventures following the creation of Mercosur.[2] Francisco Macri,
who leads one of the largest Argentine conglomerates with major holdings in the food industry, acquired Brazil's largest meat-packing company, Chapeco, which, with his other Brazilian holdings, gives him 20
percent of Brazil's market in food products. It positions his company,
SOCMA, as a dominant player in Mercosur's food markets. Argentinean and Venezuelan businessmen launched a joint venture communications satellite called IMPSAT. Techint, the Argentine engineering
giant, has taken control of the Mexican steel pipe–manufacturing company. Chile's Chilgener now controls Colombia's 1,000-megawatt
Chivor hydroelectric facility. Argentina's industrial giant, Pérez Companc, has a major interest in the petrochemical plant Companhia Petro-
quimica do Sul, in southern Brazil. Together with Brazil's major construction company, Odebrecht, they challenged Dow Chemical for control of the Bahia Blanca petrochemical plant in Argentina. Mexico's
Banamex acquired a major share in Argentina's Bansud.[3] Two of Mexico's leading bakery products companies, Bimbo and Maseca, are ex-

panding throughout Central and South America. Bimbo now controls more than 40 percent of the Peruvian market. In Central America, investments from Chile and Argentina have financed many new ventures in agriculture and fisheries. The TACA airlines group, led by the Salvadorean Federico Bloch, consolidated all of Central America's airlines into one large air carrier for the region. El Salvadorean banks now have outlets and branches throughout Central America. And Mexico recently proposed investment subsidies to build infrastructure in Central America as part of President Vicente Fox's Plan-Puebla-Panama.

Chile, as usual, is the best example of what may be the future of Latin America. From a meager $15 million in 1990, Chilean investments in neighboring countries rose to $10.7 billion in 1997. Of this, more than 60 percent of the investment, $6.8 billion, went to Argentina. Peru was second, for $2 billion,[4] making Chile one of the principal sources of foreign direct investment in Peru. Enersis, the Chilean power company owned by Endesa of Spain, which controls 54 percent of Chile's power generation capacity, has been the most aggressive of all, with plants in Argentina, Peru, Colombia, Venezuela, Brazil, and various Central American countries, where it controls both generating and distribution capacity.

New infrastructure is building new trading partners across the hemisphere's borders. A new paved road will soon link Brazil's Amazon free-trade zone in Manaus, its main electronics-producing area, to Venezuela's Ciudad Bolívar on the Orinoco River. This will form the first transportation link between two of the largest river basins in South America, the Amazon and the Orinoco. Venezuela is becoming one of the main suppliers of energy to Brazil's Amazonian north, with a new 400-mile transmission line linking the huge Guri power generation plant in Venezuela to the northern Brazilian state of Roraima. The Brazilian and Venezuelan petroleum companies, Petrobras and PDVSA, are aware of the region's oil potential and are considering an investment of $2 billion in a new 200,000-barrel per-day refinery for Venezuelan crude in northern Brazil, much closer to Venezuela than to Brazil's own industrial centers. Gas pipelines, as I noted, are proliferating in Bolivia, Brazil, Argentina, and Chile.

In the mid-1990s, Argentineans registered the Brazil Investment Fund on the Buenos Aires Stock Exchange. Venezuela issued bonds in Colombia's markets. Trinidad issued stocks in the markets of Barbados and Jamaica. Studies sponsored by the Inter-American Development

Bank are exploring the possibility of combining the thin capital markets of Central America and the Caribbean to provide more liquid domestic capital markets for the region. Panama is projecting its future as a center of intraregional trade as it converts its new ownership of the Panama Canal from a transportation route to a transportation hub. Astonishingly, under U.S. management, more than 700,000 tourists went through the Canal each year on cruise ships that never stopped, even for a day. But Panama is correcting that and is constructing new tourist facilities along the canal. Mexico's construction company, Tribasa, won the road concession for the Pan American Highway in Chile, and Mexico's ICA built the new highway to the airport in Panama. Most spectacular, however, is the invasion of the U.S. market by two Latin American construction companies, Odebrecht of Brazil and Dayco of Venezuela, both of which have won a considerable amount of public contracting in the United States. Odebrecht was an important partner in the consortium that won the bid to construct the high-speed rail system from Miami to Orlando and Tampa, Florida.

MONEY AND MARKETS

Capital flows depend on a huge number of factors, many of which are in the control of the developing nations. In the world's financial fabric, access is not a right but has to be earned, and it is earned largely by predictable rules, reliable management, and respect of obligations. Capital flows can be facilitated or discouraged but cannot be controlled by any government. Irresponsible economic policies by governments are reflected immediately in the cost and flow of global finance. Credit ratings, which govern the cost of money, affect investors' decisions and are deeply influenced by the fiscal behavior and responsibility of governments.

Most important, private capital is extremely sensitive to events that might cause losses. As demonstrated in the 1998 Asian financial crisis, it will abandon a country almost as quickly as it embraces it. In 1982 Latin America lost the confidence of the capital markets because of the failure of its leaders to understand the dynamics of the global markets. When a Mexican finance minister came to the United States in 1978, representing a country with less than 4 percent of the GDP of the United

States and with no capital markets of its own, announced restrictive investment rules, capital flows to Mexico stopped. Worse, Mexican investors, worried that the lack of new investment would undermine the local currency, started moving their capital out. In contrast, the capital flowed back at record speed after the 1994 Mexican crisis when Mexico announced, clearly and firmly, that it would continue to abide by the accepted norms of financial management. The competition for private capital is as fierce as the competition for commodities.

Net global private capital flows (new money minus repayments) into emerging markets reached a high of $329 billion in 1996 before plummeting to $137 billion after the Asian crisis in 1998. Significantly, as a result of Latin America's positive reputation in the global capital markets, capital flows remained relatively stable during this period at $100.6 billion in 1996, almost one-third of the total, and $87 billion in 1998, two-thirds of the total in that year. After the Brazilian devaluation in 1999, capital flows rebounded quickly to $92.2 billion in 2000. In contrast to Mexico's restrictive policies in the 1970s, investors in 1996 were so bullish on Mexico that they oversubscribed a $3 billion bond issue enabling the Mexican government to repay its emergency loan from the U.S. government years in advance. Significantly, the positive private capital flows during this period contrasted with net official flows to the region which were negative during most of this period, with repayments exceeding new official flows by $11 billion in 2000.

Many factors affecting the direction of capital flows, however, are far beyond the control of the developing nations, and international measures to mitigate the swings are still primitive. Research shows a close correlation of the rate of capital flows with interest rates and economic conditions in the developed countries. When interest rates in the developed economies fall, as they did in the mid-1990s, investors will accept higher risks in emerging country markets in order to get higher returns. When interest rates in the developed countries rise, the dollars flow back to them. Moreover, in times of growth and optimism in the developed countries, capital feels comfortable moving across borders. When turmoil affects the markets in the developed countries, capital quickly anticipates the reverberations in the emerging markets and seeks shelter from them. It quickly withdraws from riskier exposures, greatly accelerating the impact on the investment flows to the developing countries. The 1990s were particularly spectacular in this regard as low U.S. interest rates converged with the optimism generated by the huge gains from investing in privatizations in Latin America to produce record positive capital flows to the region.

The second consideration regarding capital markets is that they are hugely unbalanced. Some countries are more equal than others. In 2000, $91.5 billion of the $92.4 billion in total investment went to the seven largest countries, Brazil, Mexico, Argentina, Venezuela, Chile, Peru, and Colombia. Flows to the smaller countries are carefully targeted to their unique competitive advantages, such as tourism facilities or labor-intensive apparel assembly. Even in a small region like the Caribbean, 70 percent of the foreign investment goes to the larger countries, Jamaica and Trinidad and Tobago. More significantly, foreign investment has not been balanced so as to create jobs. In the 1990s, 80 percent of the investment in Latin America and the Caribbean went into telecommunications and mining or was transferred to governments in return for buying privatized state-owned companies.

Thus, the conditions in the larger countries set the tone for the entire region. When confidence surges or lags in their economies, it is reflected in the data for capital flows to the entire region. The smaller economies therefore remain doubly vulnerable, to the health of the global economy and to the economic health of their larger neighbors. Although Brazil's devaluation of its currency in 1999 made its own economy more competitive, it set off a chain reaction in Argentina and its neighbors from which they have yet to recover. And Argentina's financial collapse in 2001 effectively cut off all lending to the region. This will not change until the government policies after recovery begins are defined.

Small economies with illiquid capital markets have another disadvantage. Not only are they unattractive to outside investors, but thin local markets make it difficult for the companies that want to compete globally to raise sufficient capital locally. Reputable investors view thin, poorly regulated capital markets with skepticism, impeding the growth of small businesses and penalizing the middle class. Without sufficient domestic investment, the region will continue to be overly dependent on foreign capital.

American depositary receipts, known as ADRs, are negotiable instruments that qualify stock issuances by foreign companies for U.S. stock markets. They are increasingly becoming an accepted way for well-managed companies in Latin America to raise money. In 1997, trading in foreign stocks through ADRs in U.S. markets reached almost $600 billion.[5] Before the meltdown of the U.S. technology market, the NASDAQ was making strong overtures to integrate with South American markets. The Mexican Stock Exchange joined with the Chicago Options Exchange to open a new derivatives market that enabled companies investing in Mexico to hedge their currency risk. The new ability to mitigate those risks contributed substantially to increasing the liquidity of Mexican markets. When this is done on a broader scale, access to capital will be on its way to becoming universal in the Americas, and well-managed companies, from both small and large countries, will have better access to investors in the global capital markets.

The third consideration regarding capital markets is the need to distinguish between direct investment capital and portfolio investment capital. Direct investment capital is money going into long-term physical plant, and it reacts to long-term factors in global economics and domestic markets for goods and services. Portfolio investment capital refers to short-term investment in the stock or bond markets. It is a search for short-term gain and is extremely volatile, reacting almost instantly to suspected adverse developments. In the aftermath of the 1998 Asian financial crisis, U.S.-based mutual funds invested in Latin America dropped from $4.4 billion in 1997 to $1.4 billion in mid-1999.

The utility of sending portfolio capital to developing countries is widely debated. When conditions are good, the competition for the better investments greatly reduces the cost of capital to both industry and governments and thereby encourages development. During the financial competition of the 1990s, interest rate spreads in Latin America were reduced to below 1 percent. That is pretty cheap capital. But portfolio capital is fickle and can leave as quickly as it comes (and its ability to do so is relevant to whether it will come in the first place). In Argentina in 2001, the fears of devaluation caused lending rates to surge to more than 12 percent above U.S. Treasury rates, compared with less than 2 percent a few years earlier. For a loan of $10 billion, that amounts to an extra billion dollars a year in interest costs. The skyrocketing cost of money raised costs for both government and business alike, making the ultimate collapse almost inevitable. With Latin America's foreign debt reaching $700 billion in 2001 (compared with $400 billion in the debt crisis of the 1980s) and almost all of it in floating interest rates, it is necessary to pay attention to fundamentals in order to maintain manageable interest costs.

The fourth consideration is that reputable foreign banks help foster change. Domestically owned banks in Latin America are notorious for inside dealing, and unaccountable government-owned banks are shamelessly used for political ends and corrupt practices. Both have little regard for the security of depositors. Foreign banks often have far deeper pockets than do the cash-strapped domestic banks. And the foreign banks' adherence to globally accepted accounting practices and their capacity for risk assessment generate confidence in depositors and ensure far more transparency than is possible with domestic banks. They also provide an important safety net for national banking during difficult periods and, in good times, supplement local capital by recommending clients to their partner banks. The result in providing liquidity is as though the foreign bank had placed additional capital into the local markets.

More than one observer has noted that banking in Latin America has become more reliable in the hands of big global financial institutions. "The lender of last resort for these banks is no longer the central bank," commented Martin Redrado, executive director of Argentina's Capital Foundation, "but their new foreign patrons."[6]

For many years in the postwar period until the debt crisis of the 1980s, foreign banks played a major role in the region. During that period, U.S. banks reigned supreme. Citibank, Bank of America, and Bank of Boston were the leaders. In the 1980s, however, the top U.S. banks, stung by heavy debt exposures that made them unable to lend in the region, abandoned Latin America, and in the 1990s they were slow to react to the changing conditions. Accordingly, the European banks, led by the Spanish, moved in rapidly.[7] The Spanish banks Santander and Bilbao Vizcaya have now become dominant in Latin America. Japanese banks also channeled part of their excess liquidity into the region and became an important source of finance. Canadian banks, including the Bank of Nova Scotia and the Bank of Montreal, also moved to take strong positions in the hemisphere shortly after the approval of NAFTA.[8]

For these reasons, improving oversight of the banking system is paramount to improving capital flows for development. An enormous differential is paid in domestic markets of Latin America between interest rates paid for savings and interest rates charged for borrowing, in some cases up to 20 percent over the rate paid for savings. The differential is largely due to uncertainties from an unreasonable number of defaults as well as the extravagant expenses of the bank owners. Bank-holding companies are still inadequately supervised and weak. Regulations governing who can own a bank are poorly enforced, leaving many of the banks in the hands of people who use them for their own business purposes. Poor management of state and local banks is also the source of favoritism and corruption. In Argentina, for example, the internal debt of local provincial governments greatly exceeded the tax base of their small populations. Indeed, many of the local state-owned banks follow Ponzi schemes. The governments make deposits in the state banks; the state banks lend to favored businesses or the municipalities; the debtors do not pay; the state banks keep the loans open on their books and get new deposits from the government to paper over current obligations.

The importance of sound banking regulation was evident in the behavior of Argentine investors during the 1994 Mexican financial crisis, in contrast to that during the 1998 Asian crisis. In 1994, within weeks, $8 billion, or 18 percent of the country's bank deposits, fled the country.[9] During the ensuing years, prodigious efforts were made to clean up the banks, improve their capitalization, and impose new standards of disclosure and transparency. By the time the 1998 Asian crisis hit, even though it was exacerbated by fears of a run on the Brazilian currency, bank deposits in Argentina not only held steady, they increased. The intensifying competition began pushing down interest rate spreads to record lows in 1998. By 2001, however, the enormous debt load of the national government, compounded by the unpaid debt from the provinces and the stagnating export revenues caused by the Brazilian currency devaluation destroyed the Argentinean industries' principal market, causing them to default on loans and the banks to collapse.

Efforts are now under way, with the help of the Inter-American Development Bank and World Bank, to address the weak bank regulation in the Americas. In most countries, reserve requirements have been toughened; bank ownership criteria have been tightened; and accounting standards have been imposed. The lack of trained personnel remains a formidable obstacle. One finance minister told me that there was no way he could retain an adequate number of qualified people to manage bank examinations. Soon after finishing their training, they are hired away by the private sector at much higher salaries. The only way he could ensure strong banking practices was to invite in foreign banks and rely on their regulatory framework to maintain the integrity of the banking system in his own country.

Perhaps the most promising new development for the capital markets of the region is the privatization of pension funds. In many countries the new pension funds are bringing long-term capital to the local markets. Chile's pioneering role in privatizing its pension funds demonstrated early the positive effect of privatization on savings and the markets. Savings rates there reached 27 percent in 1997, a high for Latin America and significantly above those of the other major countries of the region. The amount of money in Chilean funds reached $36 billion in 1998, which amounted to 40 percent of the country's GDP.[10]

Not only do the new pension funds inject money directly into the capital markets, but they also stimulate changes in attitudes toward wealth and savings. In the 1980s, amid the inflation and currency devaluation, the performance of the state pension funds was a disaster. But under the new privatized and closely regulated systems, saving for a pension is becoming more meaningful. One worker proudly explained to me that he now considers his payment to his pension fund as part of his personal wealth, not just a tax paid to a corrupt government agency in money that was depreciating instead of appreciating.

Latin American pension funds now manage close to $200 billion, with projections rising to $900 billion before the financial setbacks of 2002.[11] In Mexico, twelve companies were approved to offer private pension funds, including such U.S. giants as Citicorp, Bank of Boston, AIG, and Aetna. In Chile, Chase Manhattan joined with the National Bank of Canada and a local financial group to become the largest fund manager in that country. While many problems remain to be ironed out in the administration of these funds, they are pumping more money into the region's capital markets than ever before. In Chile, the pension funds have already been responsible for helping municipalities expand infrastructure investment and domestic companies expand operations both at home and abroad. Most important, the new management has reinforced linkages with international capital markets.

CURRENCY STABILITY, TRADE, AND LABOR

One of the principal factors in calculating interest rates and potential returns on investment is the risk of currency devaluation. A devaluation of 25 percent has the same effect on a dollar loan as does an increase in interest charges of 25 percent for the remaining duration of the loan. If foreign investors fear devaluation, they will set their interest rates to cover that risk, greatly increasing the cost of capital to the developing country. The stability of Argentina's currency after it tied the peso in parity to the dollar in the early 1990s was a major element in eliminating that risk, thereby generating confidence and significantly reducing interest rates. The same thing holds true in Panama, which has been totally dollarized for decades, putting its interest rates and loan maturities on a par with the dollar. El Salvador, which recently made the dollar its legal tender, is experiencing the same phenomenon. Ecuador also decided that the only way out of its chaotic monetary policies was to fully dollarize, which it did in 1999. The small island nations of the Caribbean have a good record of managing their finances, having maintained stable currencies for decades without the need to formally tie them to the dollar.

Currency valuations also are one of the most formidable factors affecting trade. Devaluations have the same effect on exports and imports as does reducing or increasing tariffs. Indeed, exchange rates are the most underrated factor in trade discussions. Global corporations watched carefully when Asia collapsed in 1998 and foreign corporations rushed in to purchase goods for next to nothing. The fall of the Asian currencies against the dollar did more to open the door of the United States to Asian imports than could any trade agreement. Tariffs became irrelevant as prices sank to one-third of their precrisis levels. The competitive effect of the Asian devaluations was exactly the same as if the United States had reduced its tariffs to zero—or even negative—rates.

The value of currencies is thus at the heart of commercial relations among nations, affecting far more than just the balance of payments:

1. Labor. The real cost of labor also is highly dependent on the impact of exchange rates. A devaluation of a currency does more to reduce the comparative cost of labor than does an increase in productivity. For example, German wages were half U.S. wages in 1975 when the exchange rate was four deutsche marks to the dollar. That balance was turned around completely when the exchange rate fell below two deutsche marks to the dollar. That is, a German wage of 32,000 marks that was calculated at $8,000

suddenly became $16,000. The same repeatedly happens in re-
verse in Latin America as wages fall when currencies depreciate.

2. Assets. The values of companies in different countries are measured in proportion to one another's currencies. When currencies
are revalued, so are their assets in terms of credit capacity. That
is how Japanese banks, so small in 1971 when the yen was 350 to
a dollar, tripled in asset value when the yen rose to 120 to the dollar. There was no increase in deposits, no improvement in earnings. Their assets were simply revalued in relation to the dollar.

3. Per capita GNP. In the 1980s when the dollar fell to its lowest
postwar levels, many people criticized the United States because
of its falling per capita GDP. A major part of the issue, however,
was the fluctuation in exchange rates. Examples are legion:

   • Herman Kahn predicted in 1970 that Japan's per capita income would surge above that of the United States by 2000. It
   did, but not because the Japanese were earning more but primarily because of the devaluation of the dollar.

   • Mexico and Chile had the same per capita income in 1986.
   Today, Chile's is 80 percent higher, mainly because of Mexico's massive currency devaluations.

   • Russia had a per capita income of $3,200 in 1989, but today it
   is less than $1,000 because of the lower value of the ruble.

   • The little country of Surinam was considered to be making
   good progress with a respectable per capita income of $2,200.
   But it was reduced overnight to a level considered below international poverty levels of $800 per capita when its currency
   was devalued. Similar observations of the impact of currency
   devaluation on perceived per capita income can be made for
   every country, from Indonesia to Argentina.

4. National debt. Exchange rates have everything to do with the
sustainability of a country's national debt. When the value of
currency falls, more local currency is needed to service the dollar portion of the debt. This additional currency must be derived
from a national budget that has no such flexibility (and that is
generally required by the IMF to balance the budget and not to
raise expenses). An example was Uruguay in 2002 in which con-
tagion from the Argentinean collapse threatened a run on its
banking system and caused its peso to plummet. The peso cost
of the country's dollar debt, which had stood at a manageable 40

percent of the country's GDP a few months earlier, suddenly soared to an unmanageable 100 percent of the GDP.

5. Illusions of wealth. Overvalued currencies cause a country to live far beyond its real means. Not only do imports become unrealistically cheap, but they enable the elites to prance around the globe pretending they are rich while ignoring the real problems of their economies.

In short, rates of exchange have a greater effect on a nation's ability to manage its economy and trade than does its industriousness. This is the argument for creating a uniform currency in the Americas similar to the euro in Europe or through dollarization. The so-called common market between Argentina and Brazil in Mercosur is an example. Brazil's floating rates were able to adjust to the market, making Brazil's exports cheaper and imports from Argentina more expensive. With its rigid, fixed rate, Argentina had no such flexibility. With a fixed currency, the only way to remain competitive is to increase productivity, which requires investment which, in turn, is almost impossible to attract to a country whose economy appears fragile.

Another reason that fiscal responsibility is essential to developing nations is that weak currencies require a country to reduce its spending during economic downturns. The most visible reflection of this is in the IMF's traditional policy of restraining the economy, cutting budgets, and raising interest rates in times of financial crisis. The purpose is to reassure the markets that budgetary deficits will not rekindle inflation and cause further loss of a currency's value. The result, however, is that countries with weak currencies must follow policies opposite to what the United States and other developed economies do in times of economic stress. They follow Keynesian economic policies to lower interest rates and run budgetary deficits in order to *stimulate* their economies. The vicious circle in which weak economies are caught exaggerates the impact of financial downturns on the middle class and the poor. Only consistent sound fiscal policies controlling spending and restraining debt in favorable times to allow the economy room for stimulation in difficult times can cure this problem.

Increasingly, some economists are advocating dollarization as a solution to this dilemma. The argument, however, begs the real question. For successful dollarization, a government must maintain sound fiscal policies. It cannot run large fiscal deficits if it cannot print money to cover them. But if the government can maintain sound fiscal policies, its currency will be stable without the need for dollarization. A common currency for all of Latin America would be another solution, but even that means coordinated fiscal policies, which would require the same level of fiscal discipline. The one advantage for investment is that investors in a fully dollarized economy know that there is no risk of devaluation. In short, the most critical overlooked issue in expanding trade is not between free-trade advocates and opponents but between fiscal responsibility and recklessness.

Like the decisions made in Europe to create a unified currency to spur trade and investment, the nations of the Americas will, sooner or later, have to find the political will to stabilize their currencies and strengthen their capital markets if they are to gain maximum advantage from the prospect of a free-trade area. More than anything else, stable currencies encourage investment. A unified currency, fiscal policies, or dollarization of the economies must be on the table for discussion. While there are costs, they are minimal compared with the far higher costs of continued instability. For developing economies with a history of erratic fiscal policymaking, a stable currency opens the spigots of finance and investment. It benefits the middle class, which has never had reliable investment vehicles to enable them to participate in the economic growth of their countries. It spurs home building and long-term mortgages. It reduces interest rates and fosters small and medium enterprises, helping make the currency the engine of job creation as it is in the United States.

This is where U.S. policies can have the most direct and immediate impact. As was demonstrated in the 1990s and again in Mexico with NAFTA, a decision to open trade with the Americas will lead to investment and provide substantive and moral support for the advocates for reform, respect for the rule of law, and alleviation of poverty. At very small cost, U.S. policymakers have the power to help the nations of the Americas strengthen their capital markets and pave the way to fiscal responsibility.

I do not want to oversimplify the issues. The factors influencing the flows of capital, currency risks, the cost of labor, and the rate of economic growth are complex. No individual element can be addressed in isolation. Government regulation cannot be effective in countries prone to corruption. The private sector cannot play a constructive role if it has to spend considerable capital and energy to protect its assets. Socially deprived sectors cannot escape poverty unless productive, sustainable jobs are created. The great challenge for those in Latin America who are convinced that globalization and free trade are beneficial is to demonstrate that they are possible with transparency, fairness, and consideration of social realities.

15

Building a Greater America

AT THE BEGINNING of this book I explained why I considered Latin America and the Caribbean important to the United States and, vice-versa, why close relations with the United States were vital to the development of democratic societies in the Americas in the twenty-first century. I described the importance of a new American community by quoting Cormac McCarthy's observation about the world, in that nothing was insignificant, nothing too remote to be overlooked, that everything was part of the "joinery," the seams of our world that are hidden from view. The events of September 11, 2001, put to rest any doubts about the trend toward globalization. International crime and terror join the ranks of knowledge, capital, and disease as elements to which national borders are no longer relevant.

I would summarize my argument as follows: The importance of Latin America and the Caribbean to the United States relates largely to their impact on issues affecting our domestic economy and our negotiating position in global politics. A strong relationship with Latin America and the Caribbean will promote the growth of favorable markets and ensure secure supplies of vital resources. The region's predilection for building democracy and open markets was amply demonstrated in the 1990s. If it continues in this direction and is successful, it will open exciting new possibilities for economic growth and human development in this hemisphere.

These trends, however, remain extremely vulnerable to adverse external forces. The countries of the Americas cannot achieve the goals of development and democracy alone. The challenge of building representative and responsive democracies and respect for the rule of law and open markets amid the communications revolution and the pressures of globalization is unprecedented. And the danger of backsliding is substantial, as the financial crisis in Argentina, social divisions in

270

Venezuela, and the lawlessness in Colombia demonstrate. Without a strong and credible U.S. commitment to collaboration, progress will be slow and subject to great uncertainties. But because of the progress made in the last decade, such collaboration can have a relatively nominal cost and an enormous cost-benefit multiplier.

There are three reasons for the United States to take a more engaged role in Latin America: to expand the base of democracy and the rule of law, to build solid future markets, and to consolidate both by using our natural resource riches to encourage economic growth and overcome poverty. In short, it is strongly in the United States' interest to make such a commitment.

For Latin America and the Caribbean, the events of 2001 were devastating. The fallout from the terrorist attacks of September 11 diverted attention and exacerbated a series of adverse currents, including the prolonged recession in the United States and the implosion of the Argentine economy a few months later. These are a harbinger of what could happen on a broader scale if the United States abandons its support for democracy and takes a laissez-faire approach to open markets in the hemisphere.

The events in Argentina in 2001 are a good example. While dislocations from changing from a rigid currency to a floating one are unavoidable, I believe that the devastation caused by the collapse of Argentina's currency could have been avoided had the United States been more attentive. This was not a sudden event. For almost a year, the markets had been discounting the currency, capital was departing, and interest rates were soaring. There were many opportunities to act in ways similar to the active role that President Bill Clinton assumed in the Mexico rescue in 1995 and in Brazil's problems in 1998. U.S. action at that time not only prevented a collapse of those economies, it was a major factor in preserving the still fragile movements toward democracy and open markets. Similar preventive action was not taken for Argentina. However, President George W. Bush learned quickly, and when Brazil's economy was tottering a few months later, he offered a $30 billion rescue package. The real damage of financial instability in the Americas today is to democracy and confidence in open markets, which is clearly contrary to the long-term interests of the United States and all the Americas.

The attempted coup in Venezuela in April 2002 provided an instance of the damage caused by short-term policies. After almost two decades of unequivocal opposition to any interruption in the democratic process in several countries, including Ecuador, Paraguay, Haiti, and Peru, the United States hesitated in condemning the coup in Venezuela. Fortunately, the other democratically elected presidents of Latin America did not. They foresaw the damage that could result from tolerating a break in democratic legitimacy, and they acted immediately, in unison and without the United States, to issue a joint proclamation condemning the coup.

The problems of the region are complex, and after years of sacrifice and optimism, the current turmoil is dangerous. For Latin America and the Caribbean to regain confidence in democracy and to break the sway of narcotic traffic and corruption it engenders, farsighted policies will be needed on the part of everyone. The implications are seminal for the nations of the Americas where the indiscriminate violence and criminal activity now hold democracy under siege. In this dynamic, the most important element is the commitment of the United States to opening trade to the Americas. Simply put, there is no way to ensure the future of democracy without a massive effort to create productive and sustainable jobs. There is no way to create the jobs without investment. And there is no way to get the investment in the quantities needed without expanding the markets through a free-trade agreement. Indeed, it is in the interest of all the countries of the Americas that free-trade agreements for Latin America and the Caribbean be concluded with Europe also. Given the weakness of the region and the pressures under which they are trying to define and consolidate democracy, the deep engagement of both the United States and Europe is vital.

Looming large on the horizon are the Latin and Caribbean communities in the United States. Their ties to their families back home are as strong as those of any immigrant group. Remittances of U.S. dollars from immigrants from Central and South America and the Caribbean now constitute the largest source of foreign exchange for most of these countries, much larger than the foreign aid appropriated by Congress. Remittances from families in the United States to Latin America amount to more than $20 billion a year, according to estimates by the Inter-American Development Bank: $9 billion to Mexico, almost $2 billion each to El Salvador and the Dominican Republic, and smaller but equally significant sums to the other countries. As future generations become more conscious of their roots, their interests and concerns will have a profound influence on U.S. politics.

The consolidation of democracy in Latin America is of vital importance. It will help strengthen the capacity of the United States and western Europe to promote democracy around the world. To reinforce its role as a superpower in the face of rising turmoil in the Middle East and in Asia, the United States needs to make its primary sources of raw materials invulnerable and expand its markets. An alliance of Greater America would meet these criteria. An American alliance becomes even more important in the context of other world trends, including the following:

- Global productive networks. The ease of transportation and communications has reshaped markets and presented new opportunities for global production and marketing. Latin America and the Caribbean will have to move quickly to be competitive.
- Cross-border issues. It is not only the clusters of essentially stateless people who operate in criminal and terrorist networks that have no borders but also HIV-AIDS, arms traffic, and damage to the global environment. All must be dealt with on an international level or measures to contain them will not succeed. It is not in our interest to allow America to be a weak link in that chain.
- Poverty. If we fail to build economic opportunity and social mobility in the Americas, the most motivated and talented people will leave, and leave behind even more intractable problems of poverty and unskilled populations.
- Mass transportation. Cheap and accessible transportation makes it as easy and inexpensive to ship goods from Chile or China to New York as from California. This applies, however, not only to raw materials or manufactured goods but also to the movement of people and illicit goods such as narcotics.
- Aging populations. The aging of the population also means labor shortages that will increasingly plague the industrialized economies. Instead of enticing the educated and talented of the developing countries to emigrate, which will set back development, it is in the interest of the United States to adopt policies that facilitate the export of labor-intensive industries to create jobs and improve living conditions in the other American nations.

What should the United States do? We should embrace the long-term goal of building the community of Greater America in which the nations of the hemisphere are able to move toward democracy and respect for the rule of law in an environment of security and growing prosperity. This means building the infrastructure to enable people to overcome poverty through education, rural electrification, transportation to get goods to market, as well as to ensure transparent practices that generate confidence in democracy. For representative democracy to overcome the enormous hurdles in its path, the full collaboration of the United States is indispensable. Only in that way will we mobilize the human and financial resources essential to its success. We need to identify the following key issues and support incentives to bind the commitment of the real actors in each sector to democracy. In my view, ten basic policy decisions constitute the foundation for this objective.

1. First and foremost is the Free-Trade Agreement of the Americas, the FTAA. This is the essential building block of Greater America. It is more about investment than about trade. It is the only path that promises to attract sufficient investment to create the number of jobs required to overcome the onerous heritage of poverty. The private sector of Latin America has the principal responsibility of leading the way and investing its own money in the future of the region to increase productivity.

2. Initiate a comprehensive program of development assistance to the smaller and poorer nations. To achieve viable free trade in the Americas, we must come to terms with the profound dislocations that will result from merging the world's most developed economy with some of the least developed, low-productivity countries. These countries cannot succeed in open markets unless they reinforce their infrastructure and expand education, for which they have neither the capital nor human resources to do alone. The example set by Europe in establishing a support fund to help their weaker countries is relevant. The United States and Canada should commit themselves to a special fund of at least $100 billion over ten years to enable the poorer countries to build the infrastructure necessary to make them attractive for the level of investment needed to create jobs.

3. Implement a program of functional collaboration among the American nations in the field of energy. In the same way that the European Coal and Steel Community paved the way for the transformation of Europe, collaboration among the nations in specific sectors will set

the pattern for the Americas. Such measures are the practical building blocks to encourage business to invest in the Americas and to ensure that the poorer nations of the hemisphere are able to compete. Other areas suitable for more inter-American collaboration are combating drug traffic, dedicating satellite-based education systems to reinforce rural teaching, and monitoring the implementation of legislation to combat corruption and enforce core labor standards.

4. Address the source of poverty by expanding education and skills building. Without strengthening education, there can be no escape from poverty, no competitiveness, and no good governance. The revolution in information technologies has made it possible to reach all levels of the population and the remote communities of the Americas, communities long isolated from the mainstream of global ideas. The strengthening of ba:ic education should be accompanied by a vigorous program of education and cultural exchanges, and a hemispheric Fulbright-type program to build leaders for the future.

5. Obtain the commitment of all American nations to promote greater respect for the rule of law. An important step in this direction is strengthening the legislatures of the hemisphere's countries by ensuring that they are more directly responsible to their constituencies. Knowledgeable legislators with integrity are the core of successful democracy and essential to implementing legislation for trade agreements that will affect local interests in every country. Improved linkages between the United States and other American legislatures will increase understanding of one another's problems and promote shared efforts to improve respect for the rule of law.

6. Elevate labor standards throughout the hemisphere. No country will succeed in the twenty-first century on an economy built on cheap labor or drugs. Better-paid, safer, and healthier workers increase productivity and competitiveness and produce a direct, positive return on investment. In the Americas we need labor policies and practices to "raise the bottom," not "race to the bottom."

7. Create a NATO-like structure to combat international drug and criminal forces. Only multilateral collaboration along the lines of the NATO coalition can successfully combat the narcotics trade in the hemisphere. The implications of such a commitment go far beyond the battle against drugs. Lawlessness and violence threaten the personal life of almost every citizen of Latin America and are potentially a greater threat to the survival of democracy than is a stagnant economy. Given

its history, this is a delicate issue for the state in Latin America, which has had difficulty striking the right balance between protecting the security of citizens and respecting human rights. The discipline, dedication, and resources of a NATO-like coalition to professionalize security forces will not only defeat narcotics traffic and international crime but will also go a long way toward ensuring an environment of respect for democracy, human rights, and the rule of law.

8. Begin to explore the potential of a uniform currency for Latin America. This long, arduous path requires fiscal discipline and coordination. It can be done only in the context of a broader free-trade association and a vision of continuity. Its achievement is vital to the success of intraregional trade and to insulate the Americas from international financial volatility.

9. Expand the periodic presidential summits of the Americas by integrating them into a more systematic series of minisummits of ministers of different sectors, such as education, transportation, energy, and health. Collaboration in detailed technical areas is the key to practical progress. The new world of the Internet opens opportunities for rapid growth of sharing technical knowledge across borders and should be pursued in the context of decisive summit meetings.

10. Formulate a new and more comprehensive institutional basis for inter-American collaboration. The OAS's decision-making base must be broadened for the tasks that will be required under a new FTAA, or a new type of inter-American institution will have to be designed to address the new dynamics among the nations resulting from free trade. The OAS and IDB already have been delegated considerable responsibilities relating to policies to achieve the proper balance in the fight to reduce poverty. They should be expanded. This means involving representatives of national legislatures to precede what could evolve as a more relevant instrument, analogous to the Council of Europe, and for the goal of achieving a real community of Greater America.

For the nations of the Americas, the challenge is formidable. A great deal of trust has been shattered in the financial and governance crisis that engulfed Argentina, Venezuela, Colombia, and several other nations in 2002. The United States can be a strong partner, but it cannot save any nation from the consequences of failing to confront its own problems. The most important work has to be done within each country, which must strengthen the institutions that give substance to our shared goals: the rule of law, human rights, social opportunity, competition, functional open markets, and more balanced income distribution. A strong commitment is required of public and private sector alike. We must build infrastructure, schools, train teachers, create opportunities for the poor, advance civic responsibility, and enforce government accountability. The private sector must pay its legitimate taxes so that overall tax rates can be reduced and not be a disincentive to investment. Governments must take effective steps to deter and discourage corruption so that public funds can be used for the purposes for which they are collected.

In the long run, Latin America must also recognize the need to expand its domestic consumer markets. This can be achieved only by improving the conditions and productivity of labor. The Americas not only have the resources, but they also have more people on the brink of becoming active consumers of all the world's products. Latin America has one of the largest untapped, developing markets in the world, a market with more potential for the United States than any other except that of Asia—and it is a lot more accessible.

If we proceed along these lines, the systematic development of the Americas can be one of the brightest new engines to propel global prosperity. It is not foreordained that Latin America and the Caribbean will embrace open democracies. Storm clouds are everywhere on the horizon. When Washington turns a blind eye to the problems or applies shortsighted policies to the region, as recently occurred with the huge farm subsidy, protectionist steel tariffs, and the ill-timed contest against Europe's banana preferences, it severely exacerbates already difficult domestic problems for the countries of the Americas. It sends an unambiguous signal of self-centered diplomacy and says that Washington has not yet made the connection between the political issues that trouble its domestic agenda and the positive benefits that can come from a confident, prosperous America.

In sum, everything is converging to make this the time to build the foundations for the eventual emergence of a greater community of nations in the Americas, what I take the liberty of calling Greater America. The signs are everywhere that building a coherent vision of our future and setting in motion the policies to act upon it will be welcomed throughout the Americas. If we seek free trade alone, we will have missed the point, and probably miss the opportunity of trade as well.

In the Western Hemisphere the elements of economic power are most accessible and secure. Here are the markets that are among the most dynamic of the developing world. The nations of the Americas need U.S. markets today, and the United States will need the markets of the Americas tomorrow. If we can join the two halves of our hemisphere for our mutual objectives of democracy and open markets, we can create the largest, most dynamic markets in the global economy, the markets of Greater America.

In the long run, the emergence of Greater America is inevitable given the growth of the Hispanic and Caribbean populations in the United States. But given the stakes and the nature of the problems, it will be far less costly to undertake this challenge today than to leave it to our children. We can create prosperity; enhance our long-term goals to build democracy, respect for the rule of law, and economic opportunity; form a common sphere of prosperity in the Americas; facilitate access to knowledge and technology; and release the creative energies of the vibrant, motivated American people.

If we fail to act, our march to the future will be marred by new movements in which people take it into their own hands to create security for their families and to break the barriers of poverty. Such movements may not be so tolerant of democracy or respect for human rights. There is no doubt that it will be far easier to avoid this outcome with prosperous neighbors rather than with poor ones. It is, therefore, time for the United States to adopt a positive, proactive policy toward our neighboring nations of the Americas to form the next great economic and political force in the world, Greater America, and perhaps, one day, a Greater American Common Market. Together we can build one of history's greatest citadels of prosperity and democracy.

Notes

Most of my sources were IDB and OAS research papers, which do not require detailed notes, so I am not able to offer more specific information here. The source of the table in chapter 5 is cited as Jeffrey D. Sachs, "New Approaches to the Latin American Debt Crisis," unpublished paper presented to Harvard University symposium, Cambridge, Mass., September 1988. Although this information was probably published later, I am not sure where, but I do want to acknowledge Professor Sachs's contribution.

NOTES TO CHAPTER 1

1. Although the term *Latin America* clearly misrepresents the full scope of the Americas, including the English-speaking Caribbean nations and Canada, in this book, I sometimes use it to refer to the nations of all the Americas. Even though this term is not accurate, several of the issues discussed apply mainly to the Latin part of the Americas, in which case, the term is not only convenient but also more relevant to the problems in that part of the hemisphere.

2. One major exception was the brutal Chaco war between Bolivia and Paraguay in 1932/33.

3. Rudolfo O. De la Garza and Louis DeSipio, "Juntos pero no revueltos," unpublished paper, 1997.

4. *The News* (Mexico City), March 22, 1998, p. 6.

NOTES TO CHAPTER 2

1. Herbert Bolton, "The Epic of Greater America," *American Historical Review* 38, no. 3 (April 1933): 448.

2. The best chronicle of the "Western Hemisphere Idea" in the United States and in Latin America is by Arthur P. Whitaker, *The Western Hemisphere Idea: Its Rise and Decline* (Ithaca, N.Y.: Cornell University Press, 1954).

3. Arthur P. Whitaker, *The United States amd the Independence of Latin America* (Baltimore: Johns Hopkins University Press, 1941), p. 43.

4. Whitaker, *The Western Hemisphere Idea*, p. 28.

5. Samuel Eliot Morison and Henry Steele Commager, *The Growth of the American Republic*, 2 vols. (New York: Oxford University Press, 1955), vol. 1, p. 452.

6. Whitaker, *The Western Hemisphere Idea*, p. 29.

7. Ibid.

8. Ibid., p. 32.

9. Morison and Commager, *The Growth of the American Republic*, vol. 1, p. 453.

10. Ibid., p. 456.

11. Ibid., p. 460.

12. Ibid., p. 461.

13. Ibid., p. 39.

14. Whitaker, *The United States and the Independence of Latin America*, p. 465.

15. Whitaker, *The Western Hemisphere Idea*, pp. 48–49.

16. Morison and Commager, *The Growth of the American Republic*, vol. 2, p. 406.

17. Whitaker, *The Western Hemisphere Idea*, p. 100.

18. Senator Everett Dirksen listed seventy-four instances of unilateral interventions by the United States in the Western Hemisphere between 1806, when a squadron of troops under Captain E. M. Pike invaded Spanish territory at the headwaters of the Rio Grande, to the occupation of Nicaragua from August 1926 to January 1933. See *Congressional Record*, June 23, 1969, p. 16839. Most of these were minor police actions such as the suppression of piracy or the landing of marines for a few days to protect American interests during a revolution.

19. Harvey S. Perloff, *Alliance for Progress* (Baltimore: Johns Hopkins University Press, 1969), p. 20.

20. William Perry, "The Social Dimension of Economic Liberalization in Latin America," unpublished paper, March 1994.

NOTES TO CHAPTER 3

1. William Cohen, op-ed piece, *Washington Post*, July 6, 1999.

2. John Pomfret, *Washington Post*, August 8, 1999, p. A1.

3. John Kerry, *The Next War* (New York: Simon & Schuster, 1999), p. 87.

4. Ibid., p. 74.

5. Speech at the Inter-American Development Bank, April 1995 (my notes).

6. President William J. Clinton, *New York Times*, June 23, 1997.

7. Marta Lagos, "Political Attitudes in South America," *Latinobarometro Report* (Santiago, Chile), July 2001.

NOTES TO CHAPTER 5

1. Speech by Senator Mike DeWine to the Heritage Foundation, March 4, 1998.

2. Donaldson, Lufkin and Jenrette, *Research Bulletin*, December 1976, p. 1.

3. L. Ronald Scheman, ed., *The Alliance for Progress: A Retrospective* (New York: Praeger, 1988), p. 9.

4. Ibid., p. 129.

5. Roger D. Hansen, *Beyond the North-South Stalemate* (New York: McGraw Hill, 1979).

6. Secretary of State George Shultz, speech to the fifteenth OAS General Assembly, Washington, D.C., 1985.

7. Rudi Dornbush, "Argentina's Monetary Policy Lesson for Mexico," *Wall Street Journal*, February 28, 1997.

8. Norman A. Bailey, *The Post-World War II Economic Development of Sub-Caribbean South America*, Inter-American Security Educational Institute, April 1988).

9. Jeffrey D. Sachs, "New Approaches to the Latin American Debt Crisis," unpublished paper presented to Harvard University symposium, Cambridge, Mass., September 1988.

10. L. Ronald Scheman, "Alleviating Latin American Debt," in *The U.S. Approach to the Latin American Debt Crisis*, edited by FPI Policy Study Group, Foreign Policy Institute, Johns Hopkins University, February 1988.

11. The ratio at that time was $144 billion public and private debt with state guarantees, compared with $57 billion private debt without any state guarantees. See Organization of American States, *External Financing, Development and Inter-American Cooperation*, CIES/3789, August 26, 1983.

12. U.S. Department of Commerce, International Trade Administration, "The United States and Latin America in the Global Economic Environment of the 1990s," paper by the Council of the Americas for the Twenty-first Washington Conference for Corporate Executives at the U.S. Department of State, May 21, 1990.

13. Norman A. Bailey, "Life after Debt," paper presented to *Cercle*, Berlin, June 28, 1990.

14. President Miguel de la Madrid, address to a joint session of Congress, May 16, 1984.

15. Statement by Paul A. Volker, chairman, Board of Governors of the Federal Reserve System before the U.S. Senate Subcommittee on International Economic Policy of the Committee on Foreign Relations, June 15, 1984, *Federal Reserve Bulletin*, July 1984, p. 568.

16. Argentina, Brazil (which paid only if the banks lent it money to pay), Bolivia, Peru, Ecuador, Costa Rica, Dominican Republic, and Nicaragua.

NOTES TO CHAPTER 6

1. *New York Times*, September 10, 1997, p. D7.

2. Peter Drucker, *Fortune*, April 8, 1991.

3. Richard Ostling, "The Battle for Latin America's Soul," *Time*, January 21, 1991.

4. *Financial Times*, January 31, 1997.

5. *Wall Street Journal*, August 28, 1997, quoting Mark Schneider, assistant administrator of the U.S. Agency for International Development.

6. Senator Mike DeWine, Speech to the Heritage Foundation, March 4, 1998.

NOTES TO CHAPTER 7

1. The percentage of people living in poverty gradually fell between 1960 and 1980, when the estimate was under 80 million people. The number soared, however, during the high inflation of the late 1980s to more than 150 million. Except in Chile, little progress has been made since then.

2. Enrique Iglesias, speech to the International Conference on Population and Development, Cairo, September 6, 1994.

3. *CEPAL Monthly Report*, July 1996.

4. Inter-American Development Bank, *Integration and Trade in the Americas*, August 1998, p. 46.

5. Sidney Weintraub, *Los Angeles Times*, January 12, 1998.

6. *CEPAL Monthly Report*, July 1996.

7. UN Economic Commission for Latin America, *News Bulletin*, July 1996.

8. World Bank, *World Development Report* (Washington, D.C.: World Bank, 2000).

9. Inter-American Development Bank, *The Path out of Poverty* (Washington, D.C.: Inter-American Development Bank, 1998).

10. On a global basis, multinational corporations spent $25 billion on security measures in 1998.

11. Inter-American Development Bank, *Facing up to Inequality in Latin America* (Washington, D.C.: Inter-American Development Bank, 1998).

12. Albert O. Hirschman, *Latin American Issues* (New York: Twentieth Century Fund, 1961), pp. 194, 170.

13. UN Development Program, *Human Development Report, 1997* (New York: Oxford University Press, 1997).

14. In Malaysia, for example, economic reform and growth reduced poverty levels from 50 to 9 percent between 1960 and 1990.

15. *CEPAL Review*, no. 62 (August 1997).

16. See: Inter-American Development Bank, *Economic and Social Progress in Latin America* (Washington, D.C.: Inter-American Development Bank, 1996).

17. Ibid.

18. Sebastian Edwards, "The Disturbing Underperformance of the Latin American Economies," *Inter-American Dialogue*, January 1997, p. 4.

19. *Financial Times*, June 30, 1994.

20. Nancy Birdsall, *Social Development Is Economic Development* (Washington, D.C.: World Bank, 1993).

21. *Financial Times*, January 31, 1997.

NOTES TO CHAPTER 8

1. *Wall Street Journal,* December 14, 1995.

2. *Federalist Papers,* no. 18.

3. *Financial Times,* June 21, 2001, reporting that the ministers of finance and of communications both resigned over allegations of corruption.

4. *Financial Times,* December 3, 1997.

5. Bruce M. Bagley and William O. Walker III, eds., *Drug Trafficking in the Americas,* cited in "The Summit of the Americas and the Fight against Drugs," working paper of the University of Miami Dante B. Fascell North-South Center, 2000.

6. *Fortune,* September 4, 1995.

NOTES TO CHAPTER 9

1. Fareed Zakaria, *New York Times Magazine,* November 1, 1998. p. 44.

2. Paul Krugman, *New York Times Magazine,* September 29, 1996, p. 106.

3. *Wall Street Journal,* November 7, 1997.

4. Institute of Europe-Latin American Relations, briefing paper, April 20, 1998.

5. David Hirschmann, *Journal of Commerce,* October 9, 1996.

6. *Wall Street Journal,* September 18, 1997.

7. Inter-American Development Bank, "Integration and Trade in the Americas," October 1999, p. 71.

8. Inter-American Development Bank, "Integration and Trade in the Americas," August 1998, p. 8.

9. United Nation Economic Commission for Latin America and the Caribbean (ECLAC), *Foreign Investment,* 2000, p. 85.

10. *Financial Times,* November 17, 1997.°

11. United Nation Economic Commission for Latin America and the Caribbean (ECLAC), *Foreign Investment,* 2000, p. 62.

12. Ibid.

13. Comtex Newswire, February 13, 1998.

NOTES TO CHAPTER 10

1. *Wall Street Journal,* December 1, 1995.

2. Enrique Iglesias, speech to the annual meeting of the Board of Governors, March 15, 1999.

3. Shahid Javed Burki, internal report to OAS.

4. Enrique Iglesias, speech to the annual meeting of the Board of Governors, March 15, 1999.

5. *The Economist,* November 9, 1996.

6. *Financial Times*, May 14, 1997.

7. *Miami Herald*, October 20, 1996.

8. *Wall Street Journal*, September 25, 1997.

9. Mark Fineman, *Los Angeles Times*, December 9, 1997.

10. Barbados devotes 7.2 percent of its GDP to education; Jamaica, 7.5 percent; and St. Lucia, 9.8 percent, compared with a global average of 4.5 percent. See World Bank, *World Development Report*, 2000.

NOTES TO CHAPTER 11

1. *Journal of Commerce*, July 8, 1996.

2. Ibid.

3. Ministry of Transportation and Public Works of Uruguay, *Anuario estadístico de transporte*, 1998, p. 3/3.

4. *Journal of Commerce*, June 30, 1998.

5. *USA Today*, February 27, 1997.

6. World Bank, *Market Outlook for Major Primary Commodities*, report no. 814/94, February 1994.

7. *Financial Times*, October 29, 1997.

8. *Latin American Gas Newsletter*, March 1998.

9. *Financial Times*, November 8, 1996.

10. *Financial Times*, April 7, 1998.

11. *Los Angeles Times*, March 24, 1998.

12. Encyclopedia Britannica, *Macropaedia* (Chicago: Encyclopedia Britannica, 1995), vol. 5, p. 336.

13. *Financial Times*, July 29, 1998.

14. A significant portion of the world's silver production is obtained as a by-product of lead and zinc mining.

15. *Financial Times*, October 2, 1998.

16. *Financial Times*, September 6, 1996.

17. World Bank, *Market Outlook*, p. 99.

18. *Financial Times*, January 25, 1996.

19. Jean Monnet, *Memoirs* (London: William Collins Sons, 1978), pp. 291ff.

20. L. Ronald Scheman and Norman A. Bailey, "An Inter-American Energy Community," unpublished paper for University of Miami, North-South Center, 1991. See also Norman A. Bailey, "The Case for a Western Hemisphere Energy Community," unpublished paper for the Center for Strategic and International Studies, 1991.

21. Ibid.

22. The Latin American Energy Organization (OLADE) does not serve this purpose. First, it does not include all the countries of the hemisphere. Second, its primary role is to study, not to take action.

NOTES TO CHAPTER 12

1. *Journal of Commerce,* November 22, 1993.

2. Ibid.

3. *Journal of Commerce,* February 15, 1996.

4. *Financial Times,* July 12, 1996.

5. *The Economist,* December 13, 1997.

6. *Financial Times,* February 2, 1996.

7. *NAFTA Works Newsletter,* July 1996.

8. Bear Stearns, *Global Development,* July 15, 1996.

9. Comtex Wire, January 27, 1998, from Gazeta Mercantil, Brazil, January 27, 1998, p. C3.

10. *The Economist,* December 2, 1995.

11. *Wall Street Journal,* July 11, 1997.

12. Comparative numbers in 1998 per 1,000 in population were Brazil, 32; Chile, 55; and Mexico, 48. This compares with the United States, 499; United Kingdom, 323; and Germany, 268.

13. *Yahoo Internet Life,* September 1999, p. 120.

14. *Journal of Commerce,* June 28, 1996.

15. *Wall Street Journal,* July 10, 1997.

16. *IDB America,* November 1997, p. 9.

17. *Financial Times,* September 24, 1996.

18. *Wall Street Journal,* July 10, 1997.

19. *Miami Herald,* February 5, 1997.

20. *Miami Herald,* April 8, 1997.

21. Ibid.

22. *Wall Street Journal,* March 6, 1997.

23. *Wall Street Journal,* March 6, 1997.

24. *The Economist,* July 27, 1996.

25. *Journal of Commerce,* February 15, 1996.

26. See *The Economist,* July 27, 1996.

NOTES TO CHAPTER 13

1. In 1998, the United States exported goods worth $19 billion to the Caribbean Basin countries. U.S. exports to France were worth $16 billion and to China, $14 billion.

2. U.S. exports to Mexico grew by 25 percent; to the Mercosur countries, 24 percent; to the Andean countries, 22 percent; to Central America, 17 percent; and to the Caribbean, 15 percent. In contrast, U.S. exports to the rest of the world grew by 6 percent.

3. Donald V. Fites, "From Isolation to Engagement," CEO series 18

(November 1997): 5 (Center for Study of American Business, Washington University, St. Louis).

4. Comments at a White House press conference, September 11, 1997.

5. *Journal of Commerce*, November 6, 1997.

6. *UNCTAD World Investment Report*, 1996.

7. *Journal of Commerce*, June 25, 1998.

8. *Wall Street Journal*, September 6, 1996.

9. *Financial Times*, June 24, 1994.

10. See Samuel Britten, *Financial Times*, January 8, 1998.

11. *Wall Street Journal*, August 4, 1997.

12. Trade between Mexico and the United States fell from more than $26 billion in 1981 to $14 billion in 1985.

13. Statement to the House Subcommittee on the Western Hemisphere, July 12, 2001.

14. *U.S. News & World Report*, September 13, 1993, p. 65.

NOTES TO CHAPTER 14

1. *Wall Street Journal*, May 13, 1997.

2. *INTAL*, Monthly Newsletter no. 15, October 1997.

3. *Wall Street Journal*, May 28, 1997.

4. Carlos Sepulveda and Arturo Vera Aguirre, "Mercosur: Achievements and Challenges," Inter-American Development Bank, working paper no. 222, 1997.

5. *Wall Street Journal*, June 11, 1998.

6. *Wall Street Journal*, May 28, 1997.

7. *Journal of Commerce*, June 24, 1996.

8. In Mexico, the Bank of Montreal purchased a major interest in the second-largest bank in Mexico, Bancomer, and the Bank of Nova Scotia took a strong position in Mexico's Inverlat Financial Group.

9. *Wall Street Journal*, May 18, 1997.

10. Francisco Margozzini, "IDB Report on Pension Fund Conference" (internal paper), March 1999.

11. Pedro Corono Bozzo, "IDB Report on Pension Fund Conference" (internal paper), March 1999.

Index

About the Author

RON SCHEMAN has dedicated of his professional life to improving relations among the countries of the Americas, with a career in both the public and private sectors. He has held almost all the senior positions in the U.S. government dealing with Latin America and inter-American organizations. In his most recent position he was elected by the thirty-four nations of the Americas to lead the Inter-American Agency for Cooperation and Development, a new technical cooperation agency linked to the Organization of American States. In 1993, President Clinton appointed him, with Senate confirmation, as the U.S. executive director of the Inter-American Development Bank, in which he had a leading role in the $40 billion replenishment of IDB resources. Scheman was the founder of the Pan American Development Foundation in 1964, where he pioneered the concept of microenterprises. As the president of Porter International, a Washington, D.C., finance-consulting firm, from 1970 to 1975, he led in the creation of the first Latin American multinational computer company, InterComp. In 1998, he led the effort to build a new museum in Washington to celebrate the contribution of the Americas to global culture and development. The virtual Museum of the Americas was inaugurated at the Summit of the Americas in Quebec in 2001.

Ron lives in Washington, D.C., with his wife, Lucy Duncan Scheman. He is a professional vintner and manages the production of wine at his farm in Frederick, Maryland. He has four children by a prior marriage and six grandchildren.